BETWEEN THE HAMMER
AND THE SICKLE

BETWEEN
THE HAMMER
AND THE
SICKLE

ACROSS RUSSIA BY CYCLE

Simon Vickers

SINCLAIR-STEVENSON

First published in Great Britain by
Sinclair-Stevenson Limited
7/8 Kendrick Mews
London SW7 3HG England

Copyright © 1992 by Simon Vickers

British Library Cataloguing in Publication Data
A CIP catalogue record for this book is available from the
British Library.

ISBN: 1 85619 981 1

Designed by Beverley Waldron
Typeset by Phoenix Photosetting, Chatham, Kent

Printed and bound in Great Britain by
Clays Limited, Bungay, Suffolk

With great affection
I dedicate this book to my parents,
Philip and Katherine Vickers,
in token of a lifetime's
encouragement and inspiration.

ACKNOWLEDGEMENTS

IN A PERSONAL narrative of an independent journey, acknowledgements are inevitably few. The account of our six-month journey tries to portray faithfully our experience in the Soviet Union without elaboration or prejudice but the faults and shortcomings are those of the author alone. I would, however, like to thank my parents for their early encouragement to travel and their unceasing support whilst I was at home with them, writing this book. I would also like to thank Caroline Brandenburger, without whom the book might never have seen the light of day; my brother Paul and sister Myfanwy for their helpful comments on the manuscript; Howard Cooper and Gilles Mingasson, my unfailingly good-spirited and generous-hearted companions; Vitale, Sasha, Sergei and Maksim, with whom I always hope to share the closest bonds; and the Russian people who helped us so selflessly and generously on so many occasions.

It is a sad reflection on the limits to personal freedom in the USSR that I have still felt it necessary to change the names of a number of people we met so as to avoid possible complications for them.

CONTENTS

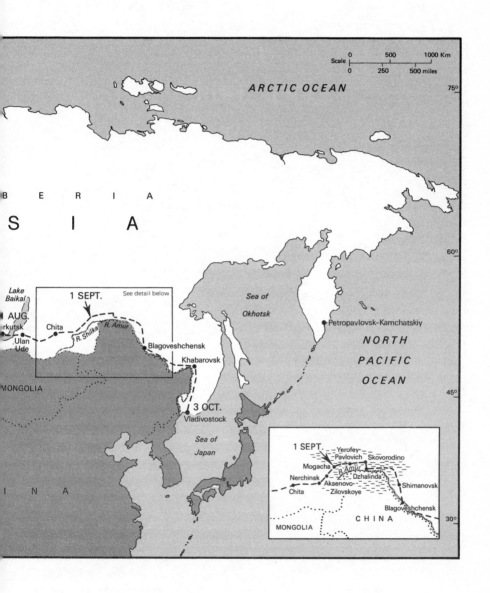

'I T WOULD SEEM an enormous waste of wealth, labour and even human life, but the strength of Russia and the secret of her destiny has always consisted to a great extent in the readiness and power to ignore the cost of obtaining a desired result.'

From Waliszewski's *Peter the Great*.

'T HERE CAN BE no doubt that diffidence and complete absence of personal initiative have always been regarded in our country as the chief and best sign of a practical man – and are so regarded still.'

Dostoyevsky. *The Idiot*, p. 339.

INTRODUCTION

W ET AND WINDY, it was a typical London evening in January. Dark by
4 pm, the rain fell steadily and red brakelights shone on the wet
tarmac. The 14 bus crept down Fulham Road, passing figures on the
pavement, their faces hidden by glistening umbrellas, that leant purposefully into the wind and rain. The telephone was ringing as I entered 6
Allestree Road, SW6.

'Simon, this is Howard Cooper, calling from Denver, Colorado. We
met in the Karakoram Mountains in Pakistan in 1986, remember?'

'Of course, Howard.'

'Simon, what would you say to being the first Englishman ever to cycle
across the Soviet Union?'

'Sounds great,' I said, 'but it's impossible to get permission. I investi-
gated that in 1986.'

'You guys haven't heard of *glasnost* over there yet? I've got permission
sitting right here in front of me.'

'Go on,' I said. 'Tell me more.'

'We're going to be a four-man team: American, French, Russian and
British. From Leningrad to Vladivostok there's about 7,000 miles and
much of it no one's seen since before the Bolshevik Revolution. Half our
route will be through Siberia. No one has been allowed to cross the
country like this before, period. We're going to be the first in. I reckon it'll
take us five months.'

'When's D-Day?'

'Oh, didn't I mention that? 30 April.' I looked at my watch.

'That's five weeks from today!'

'Jeez! It is? Maybe you're right. Time sure is passing fast. I'll fax you the package I've put together; it'll help you find sponsors. You'll need cameras, film, mosquito dope, visa photographs, medical shots . . . I've got the rest. That's all . . . oh yes! And 6,000 bucks, that's the cost of the package. We'll meet in Helsinki but bring some beers with you. There's nothing in the country, it's wiped clean.'

Howard rang off. Water that had fallen from my coat lay in a puddle on the carpet. The house seemed extraordinarily quiet. Muffled voices passed by outside. Only hastily scribbled notes and a telephone number in Colorado told me I had not been dreaming. I did not sleep that night. My mind ran fast, trying to conjure up 7,000 miles of the Soviet Union from the confines of a terraced house in Fulham. Was it all forest, steppe or freezing tundra? I hunted around in vain for books on Russia, but gazed at the double-spread map of the Soviet Union, a landmass that seemed to stretch half-way round the Northern Hemisphere from the Baltic to the Sea of Japan and Alaska. I paced around the house frustrated by a lack of information.

It is difficult to imagine a landscape more arresting than the Karakorams and Western Himalayas. Wherever one stands the eye is drawn across tier after tier of gold and dun-coloured rice paddies that rise in imperceptibly fine steps up a broad valley. The eye follows through to a lip where the land abruptly falls 200 feet to a wide and deep ravine in which the River Indus flows, metallic grey. Slowly, hesitantly, the eye picks out miniature figures, bent double, harvesting millet with a sickle or moving on the flat roofs of the mudhouses. But the eye is inevitably drawn higher still to the snow-covered flanks of Mount Rakaposhi. The rocky hillsides of scree that dwarf the villages on the lower slopes are themselves dwarfed by a massive expanse of snow of intense white, interspersed in the gullies by the reflective ice blue of broken glaciers. Above it all floats a peak of pure white, unbelievably smooth, brushed by a wisp of cloud. At 8,000 feet in the Himalayas the sky is cobalt blue and the peak of Rakaposhi seems both deceptively close and tantalisingly out of reach. At such moments it is easy to understand the call of the mountaineer.

Anyone standing high up on these slopes and gazing down into the broad valley of the Indus on 26 September 1986 might, with a sharp eye, have detected two minute specks toiling at snail's pace up the Karakoram Highway towards the Chinese border, and three further specks descending at an infinitely faster pace from the opposite direction. The latter consisted of three young Englishmen cycling from England to

Australia. Descending from 16,000 feet at speed on loose gravel we rounded a bend and saw two cyclists heading towards us. The gradient was steep, the air thin, the road broken and pot-holed, and the two cyclists were inching their way uphill. No one of an independent frame of mind and a love of the wild relishes coming across others in a place of exceptional remoteness. One cannot help but feel that they are intruding, even trespassing, on a place and time properly one's own, even though they have as much right to it as oneself. And the remoter the setting, the wilder the landscape, the more of an intrusion such an encounter seems to be. The magic that has been so artlessly woven is broken.

As we drew close each party stopped and surveyed the other, suspiciously, like stags on a narrow cliff ledge. Howard Cooper and his friend, Steve Reich, had just set out to cross the Himalayas into Tibet. They were desperately heavily laden with spare parts and camping equipment. Not a speck of dust or mud sullied their bikes, their clothes or their panniers. Everything was immaculate and new. In contrast my brother Paul, my friend Frank and I looked like a different species. After four months of cycling we were bearded and burnt black by the sun, our bikes were scratched, caked with mud and dust, and our clothes were faded by constant washing. And by progressively jettisoning equipment we had reduced our panniers from four to two. Howard traced for their route on the map, over the Khunjerab Pass, down to Kashgar, over the Kunlun Shan range, and across the Tibetan plateau to Lhasa and Nepal. We were astonished that anyone should be thinking of entering Tibet at such a time of year. It was late September and snow was expected to fall at any moment, heralding the arrival of winter, blocking the Khunjerab Pass and cutting Pakistan off from China until May of the following year. Howard's route lay above 16,000 feet and over passes as high as 19,500 feet. Even without snow, the Tibetan plateau would be freezing.

'Why are you going in now?' we asked, fascinated.

'There wasn't much information in the States on Tibetan weather,' Howard replied 'but we've got all the best cold-weather gear available.' It seemed folly but we wished them well and went our separate ways. That evening as we sat in front of a wood fire at 6,500 feet in Gilgit we chuckled at the thought of Howard and his friend pushing their way through waist-deep snow to Lhasa.

Three months later we ran across Howard and Steve by chance in Kathmandu. Notwithstanding their equipment, they had been compelled to prevail upon the Tibetans to make them yak-skin shoes and clothes to shield them against the biting winds that swept unfettered over the vast, open plateau. Arrested by the police and imprisoned for being in Tibet, after being forced to make a self-confession to a packed People's Court, they had evaded their police escort and disappeared onto the Tibetan plateau, cycling by night to avoid detection. The temperature at night had plummeted to $-20°$ but eventually they had made it to Lhasa and Kathmandu. Howard had looked jubilant but we were shocked when we saw his companion, Steve, who looked as if he had aged ten years in two and a half months.

Something nebulous had long fascinated me about Russia. It was, perhaps, a curiously different feel for life evoked by Russian novelists. In nineteenth-century Russian novels there seemed to be present a calm and tranquillity that conveyed an understanding of life quite different from our own. Even in the most chaotic writings of Dostoevsky, there always seemed to be something that resembled a still-life.

Apart from this, the unknown nature or Russia, its remoteness and vastness, could not help but excite my imagination. Cut off from the rest of Europe for nearly a century, the Soviet Union had been deliberately isolationist, presenting a hostile front to the world, while it conducted a vast social experiment behind closed doors. It seemed ironic that while the Soviet Union claimed to be in the vanguard of history, it had never felt confident enough of its assertions to allow Westerners to visit freely or Soviet citizens to leave and return as they liked.

Few foreigners had received permission to travel independently by train or in their own car. Such independent journeys as had been allowed were escorted by an Intourist guide and translator, or had to be arranged, down to the most minute detail, in advance. Not only did the exact route have to be specified and approved beforehand but every night's accommodation, whether in hotels or campsites, had to be booked well in advance – and once booked it was impossible to change. Innumerable areas, some larger than Britain, were officially closed to foreigners, while others which were theoretically open it was impossible to visit in practice because they did not have 'suitable tourist accommodation'. In effect, to organise and book an independent journey in the USSR was made so difficult and so expensive that the authorities succeeded in their unstated intention – of dissuading people altogether. Gorbachev's policy of *glasnost*, however, was creating a less hostile, less isolationist, attitude towards the West. If Howard had secured permission for us to cycle freely, without specifying where each night was to be spent, it was truly remarkable, and would enable us to explore the country and meet people in an astonishingly unrestricted way.

The prospect of cycling 7,000 miles on rough asphalt and dirt roads might appear somewhat daunting but I did not think twice about it, believing that success depended more on will power than physical strength. I felt there would be plenty of time to get fit for Siberia between Leningrad and Moscow. If Howard had suggested the same trip, but by car or train, I would most certainly have turned the offer down. I am far from being a fanatical cyclist and have little interest in cogs, sprockets and gear ratios. But as a method of travel the bicycle is, in my view, unsurpassed – for anyone prepared to put a little effort into their journey.

Travelling by bicycle facilitates contact with people along the route. The cyclist poses a threat to no one. He may be an object of curiosity, in which case a crowd may gather or, tired and hot, an object of pity, in which case he is likely to be offered something to assuage his heat and thirst. Either way the chances are that his arrival will lead to some sort of human contact. Nor is the cyclist ever viewed as rich or powerful, for otherwise he would be travelling in comfort and ease, and therefore people are less in awe or afraid than they might otherwise be. Everyone appreciates a stranger who makes an effort to get to know them. And to see someone straining himself physically when he could be sitting in a comfortable armchair back home with his feet up is the ultimate conundrum that rarely fails to amuse.

There is some truth in the theory that had I stayed at home and devoted myself to study, I would be more knowledgeable about the USSR than I am now after five months spent traversing it. But knowledge and understanding are rarely found in the same bottle, and given the choice between the two, I prefer the latter. I wanted to go to Russia for the same reason that Thoreau had gone to Walden Pond, 'because I wished to live deliberately, to front only the essential facts of life, and see if I could not learn what it had to teach and not, when I came to die, discover that I had not lived . . . I wanted to live deep and suck out all the marrow of life . . . to drive life into a corner and reduce it to its lowest terms, and, if it proved to be mean, why then to get the whole and genuine meanness of it, or if it were sublime, to know it by experience.'

It was not long since I had started working for Sotheran's, a well-known firm of antiquarian booksellers. Prospects were excellent and the Chairman was a pleasure to work with. A good part of the previous few years had been spent travelling and I felt it was perhaps time to settle. Besides there was a small technical hitch: I did not have $6,000. My last tangible asset had been a case of 1955 Quinta do Noval port that I had been given as a Christening present. I had sold it the year before to a wealthy stockbroker cousin and with the proceeds had bought three horses in South America. It had seemed a handsome exchange, both at the time and in retrospect, especially in view of the fact that whenever I showed up at my cousin's house there was always the guarantee of a massive glass of the very same port.

The 14 bus took me to Piccadilly as though nothing had happened. I peered out through the rain looking at London with a fresh eye: the little shops and restaurants of the Fulham Road, Pelham Crescent as white as snow, and bedraggled South Kensington Tube station. As the bus snaked left and right I caught glimpses of white stuccoed houses, the newly cleaned Victoria and Albert Museum covered once again with scaffolding and flapping plastic, and beyond Harrods a *mêlée* of black cabs and red double-deckers.

The bus ground its way jerkily round Hyde Park Corner past forgotten monuments, and inched its way down Piccadilly. Men and women enveloped in grey raincoats and clutching umbrellas emerged from Green Park Tube like a never-ending circus trick. Somehow it all seemed drearily familiar and depressing.

At work I began to feel penned in, constrained. Even the premises, which the week before had seemed quite normal, began to feel claustrophobic. Doubtless I appeared the same but in fact I felt restless, like a sailor keen to set sail to take advantage of favourable winds.

From that moment I had only one goal – to find the money I needed. Howard wanted to know soon if I was going to join him and I promised I would let him know if I was coming before seven days were up. Seven days to find $6,000. That meant fast spadework. From that moment I threw myself into raising the money, typing up proposals and letters, telephoning newspaper and magazine editors to secure commissions for articles, photocopying, preparing and sending faxes, drawing up maps, talking with film producers and editors, writing to potential sponsors. Soon the house was strewn with maps of Russia and piles of photocopies, letters, proposals, itineraries and screwed-up paper. Cast-off typewriter ribbons lay in the corner, and the table was littered with half-finished cups of coffee, lists and scribbled notes with names and telephone numbers. Long after the house had fallen silent I hammered away at a little portable typewriter, stapling and addressing envelopes. With less than a week at my disposal, even first-class post was too slow and in the early hours of the morning I jumped into the car and drove round the deserted streets of London to editors' offices in Gray's Inn Road, Fleet Street and the Isle of Dogs.

Meanwhile documents, equipment lists and faxes appeared from Howard in greater and greater numbers – including the 'International Soviet Trans-Cycle' presentation, a fourteen-page brochure immaculately printed in three colours and illustrated with photographs. It was a professional-looking document, complete with 'Mission Statements, Transit Maps, Resumés, Business Plans, Budgets, Time-tables and Sponsorship Details'. Howard was clearly thinking Big. From the 'presentation' I gathered that I was joining a 'goal-dedicated expedi-tion', the goals being 'motivational, educational, philanthropic, cultural and diplomatic', that we were a non-profit organisation and that 'Trans-Cycle officers and staff are experienced expeditioners and business people'. Assuming that I qualified as an officer rather than staff I learnt that I was 'well equipped to estimate, organise and manage both the time and financial requirements of preparing for and executing this event'. Considering that Howard had given me five weeks' notice, with just a week to find the money to pay for the expedition, I smiled wryly.

It came as something of a shock to learn in the 'General Operating Budget' that our 'Grand Total Costs' already stood at $100,000. Admin-istration costs stood at $14,500, 'Syndication writers and secretarial costs' at $9,800, expedition costs at a mere $21,350, Soviet Government costs at $18,000, against which $4,200 for office supplies and $7,200 miscellaneous expenses appeared mere trifles. Perhaps Howard wanted $60,000, not $6,000.

Three days later Howard phoned again in the middle of the night.
'How's funding, Simon?'
'No windfalls yet . . . By the way, it was $6,000, wasn't it?'
'Yeah, be prepared to wire it soon.' The following morning's fax read: 'Simon, some of the ideas I come up with in the faxes are bs [bloody silly] but sometimes they pan out. Blow off any of the ideas you think are bs and pursue the ones you think are viable. By the way, if you call and leave a message here be *very* specific; some of the receptionists are brain dead.'

Howard seemed to think that the Russian department of Lancaster University would like to give me a grant, an idea greeted with certain scepticism by the department's head. He also proposed that I arrange massive press coverage in the UK, sign up Prince Charles as the UK patron, follow up a list of twenty-five sponsors, locate the cycle club in Helsinki and arrange accommodation with them. The faxes flowed in, cryptic and to the point: 'Travellers cheques useless in the USSR. Bring $1 and $5 American bills for black-market exchange.' 'Bring condoms. You may fall in love with a 300-pound cross-Russian-Mongolian-Uzbek woman. The kind that kept Flemming, Shipton, Scott, Perry and Shackleton warm.'

After five days Howard phoned again. I had secured various commissions but not enough to cover the cost of the journey. 'Give me another forty-eight hours,' I said, 'and I'll let you know for certain one way or the other.' Two days later I phoned back. 'Count me in, Howard,' I said. 'I've got the money!'

One unpleasant duty that lay ahead was to resign. In the short time I had been at Sotheran's I had taken a great liking to the Chairman. He was one of that rare English species, an intellectual, an authority on contemporary English literature, a born raconteur with an open mind, a highly developed sense of humour and great personal charm. He was an ideal employer, giving a great deal of latitude in which to operate and always being receptive to new ideas. I had been with the company long enough to realise that working with him would be enormously rewarding and, as he had placed a certain confidence in me, I felt that I was letting him down badly. The only civilised way to handle the matter seemed to me to be to take him out for an extremely fine lunch. The following Tuesday we set off for Bentley's in Swallow Street.

We were ushered to a discreet table beside the window and, once an excellent Macon had been served, I began to tell my story. The Chairman continued with his lobster soup and then sat back, listening attentively. When I came to an end, I waited, braced for the Sword of Damocles to fall.

'Simon,' he said slowly, 'everyone gets these opportunities in life but most people don't recognise them for what they are. And of those that do, most are too afraid to take them up.'

I felt as though a cloak of lead had slipped from my shoulders. I was so relieved that I hardly heard what he said next. Rare for an employer, he viewed his staff first and foremost as individuals in their own right and only second as employees. Not only sympathetic to what I had to say, he seemed to understand intuitively the way I felt.

'As for when you want to leave, that I leave entirely up to you,' he added over a cognac. Three days later I was gone.

*

Howard's fax warned me that 'medical care in the USSR is free and terrible. Our medical kit will be very extensive.' When it arrived the list made depressing reading.

Keflex 500 mgm capsules (200)
Terramycin capsules (200)
Flagyl 250 mgm capsules (240) – for dysentery
Bactrim DS tabs (160)
Lomotil tabs (80) – for diarrhoea
Naprosyn 375 mgm tabs (200) – painkillers
Tylenol Number 3 with codeine (50)
Mycolog Cream (2 tubes 15 gm each)
Auralgam (10 ml)
Cortisone Cream (2 tubes 15 gm each)
Iodine pills
Diamox – for altitude sickness
Bactioban ointment (2 tubes 15 gm each)
Antibiotic eyedrops
Chloroquine tabs – for malaria
Bandages
Imodium tabs 80 – anti-diarrhoea
Presterilised needles and syringes (blood transfusions)
Throat lozenges
Antihistamines – snake and insect bites
Insect repellent
Sun block (23 strength for face and 15 for lips)
Needle and thread
Sterile knife to lance boils
Emergency stitches

Neither was the list of necessary vaccinations encouraging: yellow fever, rabies, meningitis, diphtheria, tetanus, hepatitis A and cholera.

'Are these really all necessary?' I asked a doctor at the Hospital of Tropical Medicine and Hygiene, after tracing our route on a wall map and tendering my list.

'Oh yes,' she said, 'and I'd recommend a TB booster and vaccinations against Japanese encephalitis and Lyme Disease.'

'What's Lyme Disease?' I asked suspiciously.

'It's a tick-borne spirochaste infection that occurs throughout deciduous forest areas in the north-west regions of Russia, including the

Leningrad, Kalinin and Moscow *oblast*s. It will be most prevalent at the time you are there. You will be camping, I suppose?'

'Yes,' I said.

'In that case, there's another type of encephalitis caught from ticks found on the edge of forests and in clearings, scrubland, pastures and long grass. You should be immunised against this too, but that's a course of three shots and you won't have time for all three and one is no use at all. You will just have to avoid those areas.'

'So where do we camp?'

'I'm not telling you where to camp, just how to avoid tick-borne encephalitis. If camping is unavoidable you must search the body every three to four hours for ticks which should then be detached with an application of nail varnish, petroleum jelly or alcohol.' The journey was fast losing its appeal. 'We'd better start with the vaccinations now unless you want them all on the same day. Please roll up your left sleeve. What blood group are you? You don't know? It's very unwise to travel abroad for months without knowing, so we'll take some blood at the same time, shall we? One last thing. Avoid eating vegetables and meat in the Baltic Republics and the Leningrad–Kalinin area. We believe the level of radiation is still high as a result of Chernobyl.'

'What can we eat then?'

She smiled.

'Pasta, rice, bread – anything but meat and vegetables. Gastrointestinal diseases are also very common throughout the USSR, so avoid under-cooked or raw meat, fish, shellfish, unpasteurised cow, sheep or goat's milk. Avoid raw vegetables and salad in restaurants and purify all the water you use. As far as injections are concerned you don't want Russian needles used on you at any time. Take your own syringes and needles. It would be best if you could take blood plasma with you because we think that not all their blood supplies are adequately screened yet for the Aids virus. The problem with blood plasma is that it has to be kept at an even temperature, something you won't be able to do. If you're in a bad enough state to need a blood transfusion, you'll just have to have it! There won't be time to have you flown home in any case. As for medicines, you must take all essential ones with you. As a result of an acute shortage of raw materials, pharmaceutical production has markedly decreased leading to a shortage of many drugs. Aspirin, antibiotics, anti-inflammatory, asthma medication and many other drugs are in short supply.' It seemed it would be a miracle if we emerged the other end alive. I rose to go and opened the door.

'Your greatest danger will be from trauma,' came the voice from behind me.

'Trauma?'

'Yes, being knocked down by a car or truck. Good luck!' She smiled for the first time and turned back to her computer.

I faxed Howard. 'Bringing 4 bottles of nail varnish (clear, 200 ml).' Howard faxed back. 'I like women too, Simon, but don't overload yourself with presents. We've only four small panniers each: I've got over 1,000 pounds of gear already and it's still coming in.'

A few days before departure Howard's final equipment list came through. It ran to three pages and listed 115 different items, including forty-eight spare tyres, twenty spare inner tubes and 168 pieces of clothing, not to mention $500-worth of vitamin tablets. Every conceivable spare part had been thought of. There seemed to be enough clothes for an entire mountaineering expedition but Howard asked me to report back if I thought he had overlooked anything.

It was an impressive list but I wondered how Howard expected us to take it all. My preference was for travelling light, as unencumbered as possible. Howard clearly had another philosophy. And then I remembered my first meeting with Howard and how astonished we had been by the quantity of gear he had had on his bike.

'What's the idea with all the equipment?' I asked him. 'We'd need a convoy of trucks to move it.'

'Yeah, I've got a *little* bit too much stuff,' Howard replied, 'but we'll have a two to three-week blowout period between Riga and Moscow and we can jettison what we don't need in Moscow.'

'But it'll cost a fortune to bring over.'

'Don't worry, Lufthansa is a great sponsor.'

The day before departure Howard was on the line again, checking last-minute details.

'The Soviets still haven't sent the visas they've been promising for six months. Now they say they'll arrive before my flight tomorrow. By the way, how are you thinking of getting home from Vladivostok?'

'On the Trans-Siberian, of course.'

'Why? Don't you realise it passes through exactly the same landscape that we will have biked?'

'Aren't we going to put our feet up and drink champagne and eat caviar for a week?'

'OK, you win. I guess we'll be due some champagne once we've finished the swamp.'

'Swamp, Howard? What swamp?'

'Didn't I tell you about the swamp, Simon?'

'First *I've* heard about it . . .'

'You've got a map there? Good. You see Chita, after Lake Baikal?'

'Yes.'

'You see the red line? That's the road. You see it stops at Chita? After that, there's 1,200 kilometres of swamp.'

I looked at the map. East of Chita the Soviet Union curved far to the North following the Amur River that served at that point as the Soviet-Chinese border. No road was marked until Svobodny.

'Looks interesting, Howard . . .'

'I knew you'd be game for it. See you in Helsinki. And Simon, don't forget those beers!'

1
HELSINKI

S IX WEEKS AFTER Howard's initial telephone call I was in the air to Helsinki. From high above, London resembled the vast ruins of an Inca kingdom, an intricate maze of rambling walls and fortifications, more complex and finely spun than any cobweb, before fading into an abstract patchwork of dun and pale green fields.

It was a bright, cloudless day, and the sky and sea, both a pale blue, merged disconcertingly into each other. Over Southern Finland lakes of blue lay scattered pell-mell over a smooth glacial landscape as far as the eye could see, homesteads and barns of a dried blood-red enlivening a bleak and lonely sculpted plateau. Snow still lay in drifts in north-facing gullies and lined the edge of the woods. There were no signs of spring: the beginning of the expedition was clearly going to be cold.

I had never met Gilles Mingasson, the French team member, who was a friend of Howard's. All I knew about him was that he was a ski instructor and a professional photographer. As we were to spend five months in each other's company I was naturally curious about him: a lot would depend on how well we would get on together.

Gilles was there to meet me: tall and thin, with a serious face and soft, rather reticent but humorous eyes. He greeted me in English with a strong Gallic accent and a smile. Dressed in the expedition jacket with the Tricolour, Stars and Stripes, Union Jack and Hammer and Sickle sewn on the back, matching trousers and running shoes, he looked professional and relaxed. After a season on the ski slope I guessed he must be very fit.

'I hope so!' he laughed. 'But the last few weeks I've been too busy to work out.' The verb 'work out' alarmed me; it was not part of my vocabulary. I'd have to find out discreetly what it meant. I'd hardly taken any exercise since the summer apart from the occasional leisurely weekend walk.

As soon as Howard spotted us, he gave a thumbs-up sign with both hands and a big grin.

'How's the team?' he asked, laughing. It was a little more than three years since I'd last seen him in Kathmandu. He was shorter than I remembered, well-built with a mass of wavy golden hair, a broad open face, clear blue eyes, one flecked with a tiny patch of green, and a direct, engaging smile. 'The good news is we've all arrived,' he told us as we sped towards the centre. 'The bad news is we don't have any visas.'

'What?' Gilles and I cried in unison.

'The Soviets have known about the trip for a year and a half, and they've had six months to prepare the visa. They said it would arrive a month before I left, then two weeks, then one, then three days, then the day before departure and then the morning of departure. So I guess we might have time to check out Helsinki.' None of us wanted to waste time in Helsinki, which we found a dull and expensive city, but we needed to make a few purchases, despite the vast consignment of equipment from the States – more insect repellent, mosquito nets, cooking pots.

'We have large thermal mugs already,' Howard told us. 'Do you think that we need to carry bowls as well?'

'I don't want to eat food for five months out of a coffee cup,' Gilles said firmly. Clearly the French contingent was not going to allow meals to be trifled with. I liked the sound of it. 'I need to eat,' Gilles told me, shaking his head appreciatively. 'I need to eat a lot.'

Anyone we met who had recently returned from Leningrad we quizzed about conditions.

'Be careful of the Goddamned mafia! They're entering the stores, lining people up and taking everything off them.'

'There's nothing in the country, period.' Howard told us. 'Thank God we're going in the summer, so we should be able to find food.'

'You're an optimist, Howard,' Gilles remarked drily, watching snowflakes fall gently outside the window.

Reports of the black-market exchange rate of roubles for dollars fluctuated wildly from person to person: fifty roubles to the dollar was the highest we'd heard. I asked Howard if he knew how safe it was to play the black market.

'At fifty roubles to the dollar,' he said, 'I think we only have to play it once.'

We were told categorically that there was only one restaurant where we could find good food in Leningrad – in a German place run jointly with the Russians – but no one could tell us where it was located.

'Food is non-existent and restaurants are really terrible,' Howard concluded. 'OK, so it tastes like shit for five months. But it should be alright in the countryside. Peasants don't starve. I've never been to a country where if you went to the farms the food wasn't good.'

'There's always a first time,' Gilles reminded Howard.

After two days we learnt that our bikes and equipment had arrived: all 1,150 pounds in fourteen boxes. Rather than sort through it in Helsinki and then have to repack it, we decided to send the whole lot to Leningrad and go through it there. I spent a day investigating the costs and logistics of transporting 1,150 pounds of gear to Leningrad. The cheapest was $70 by train. Howard was delighted.

'That's good news. Seventy bucks is something we can bite. Seventy bucks is a Goddamn beer down on the street corner here. How long do you reckon we need in Leningrad to put our stuff together?'

'Three days at least.'

'Yeah. I was pretty sick last time I was in Leningrad – bronchitis, alcohol poisoning and everything else.'

We looked out of the window. Leaden grey skies presaged a further fall of snow and a drunk tottered past searching vainly for a handrail.

'Considering that alcohol isn't on sale in Helsinki most hours of the day there seem to be an awful lot of drunks around,' Gilles reflected.

For us Helsinki was ruinously expensive. We had each brought $1,000 emergency money to cater for all possible eventualities over five months in the Soviet Union, but every day in Helsinki found us at the bank changing it. At the end of six days, when we boarded the train for Leningrad, over half had gone.

In the evening we gathered round a map of the USSR and Howard traced our proposed route over the vast semi-circle, one sixth of the world's land surface, across European Russia, the Urals, supposedly the frontier between Europe and Asia, the steppes of Central Asia and then Siberia, itself as large as the USA, stretching away to Mongolia and the Pacific.

'This trip is going to be different from any trip you can do,' Howard philosophised over a beer. 'When we cycled in Asia we met interesting people from all countries of the world but once we enter Russia we'll be alone. If we're lucky we may run into a few tourists in Intourist hotels at Irkutsk or Khabarovsk, but that's all . . . I just don't know what's going to happen out in Siberia.' We gazed, silenced for a moment, at the vast expanse of map. We had all been so busy with details over the last six weeks that none of us had quite had time to take in the enormity of the project. Spread out a map of the Soviet Union, stretching one third of the way round the world across eleven time zones, and Moscow seems on the edge of Europe while Leningrad, on the very Western fringe, hardly looks as if it belongs to the USSR at all.

'I've heard it's as isolated as hell,' Howard said.

'That's perfect,' Gilles said.

'I just think it's going to be different,' Howard continued, talking as much to himself as to us. 'I just have this feeling that it's going to be real different from any kind of travelling you can do.' Siberia alone stretched for 6,000 kilometres from the Altai Mountains to the Pacific. 'I want to get to the swamp. Of course, Simon didn't know about the swamp until a couple of days ago,' he added, laughing, 'but in the back of my mind this swamp is sitting there.'

'Yes, this swamp is exciting me too!' Gilles added. 'I want to be in that swamp right now.'

'I don't particularly want to *be* in the swamp,' Howard countered.

'I do! I do!' Gilles said.

'Well, it looks as though we're all agreed that we want to be in the wildest, remotest, most Godforsaken part, don't we?' I said.

'That's right,' Gilles replied.

'Up to your waist in water?'

'Yes, if possible, with mud in my eyes and mosquitoes. That's the way I see it . . .'

'We're going to be more dependent on each other on this journey than on any journey I've ever done,' I said. Howard agreed.

'Even in Tibet and Western China,' Howard said, 'we occasionally met travellers with backpacks but they haven't opened Russia up like that. The psychological aspect of being cut off from your own culture will be hard. Even in Africa it wasn't like that. But in Russia I think we're going to be asking ourselves what these people have been doing for the last seventy years.'

'Cutting wood and de-icing their front door,' Gilles remarked.

'Before, when I got fed up with Steve in Tibet,' Howard continued, 'I'd just blow him off and meet a bunch of Swedes in Lhasa and get drunk with them and forget about the bike ride.'

'I'm sure we can get drunk with Siberians.'

'Sure you can get drunk with them. I don't think that's a problem but it's always going to be Russians, day after day after day. As you said, we're going to have to rely on each other. And we're all from foreign countries, so a point will come when I'll say, "I'm tired of these foreigners. Get me an American!" And there won't be one. And if I meet some American in an Intourist hotel I'll stay up all night talking – probably with an idiot whom you'd hate if you were in your own country. But when you travel you speak to people you'd never look at back home.'

Howard disappeared to get some more beers.

'What's Howard's Russian like?' I asked Gilles.

'What did he tell you?' he asked, grinning.

'He said it was good enough to get by.'

Gilles guffawed. 'We'll get by, but it *won't* be because of Howard's Russian.'

Howard came back with beers, scrutinising his change. 'That was twenty bucks. Jeez, this *is* a tough town to enjoy a beer!'

We took a day to look round Helsinki. Modern, efficient and prosperous, it held few surprises. Curious leaden architecture co-existed with new plate glass. The cold climate eliminated any need for balconies and window-sills, giving the apartment blocks and houses a shorn, bald appearance. Tall and thin like their inhabitants, the old town houses stretched up like etiolated plants seeking the sun's rays. It was bitterly cold and we stamped our feet to keep warm. From time to time Howard drew a tin from his pocket and extracted a brown concoction which he stuck down behind his lower lip.

'Are those Peruvian coca leaves you're chewing?' I asked.

'No, this is tobacco, but right now I wish I had some *newzaf* from Pakistan – it just saved us on treks in the Karakoram. Did you chew that?'

The Finns struck us as purposeful and earnest. They have one of the highest living standards in the world but it didn't make them smile. Their long, glum faces provoked an irresistible desire to do something wild and shocking.

'At least they're not offended if you speak in English,' Howard remarked, glancing at Gilles, 'whereas in some countries they have a coronary.' We stopped outside a well-stocked *pâtisserie*, the window filled with mouth-watering flans, tarts and cakes, prohibitively expensive but exquisitely displayed.

'These people know how to enjoy themselves,' Gilles noted approvingly.

'How would you like to spend a year working in Finland, Gilles?' I asked.

'No way,' he said quickly. 'It's too cold! The girls are nice but there are nice girls everywhere. And the cold is useless because you cannot ski; the snow here is no good for skiing.' He looked around at the deserted streets. 'I think this place is a little boring. What I cannot understand is why the population is so small when they have to spend so much time inside.'

For three days Howard pursued our visas at the Soviet Embassy. On the fourth he returned, infuriated: he had been told to make an entirely new application! We couldn't believe it. And yet two days later we knew our luck was in when Howard walked into the Café Socis, our Finnish HQ, grinning from ear to ear, holding papers aloft.

'After one and a half years of negotiations I have the papers!' he announced triumphantly. We looked for somewhere to celebrate but in most bars people drank in a hushed silence. Eventually we found a Mexican restaurant which was lively by Finnish standards and we crowded round to scrutinise the visas. There were only three short lines for listing destination cities in the USSR, space for only nine cities. Curiously enough Helsinki was one of them. Perhaps in the haste to prepare the visas an overworked official in the Foreign Ministry in Moscow had overlooked the fact that Helsinki was the capital of a foreign country. However, we were delighted to see that Riga was included.

'That's great,' Howard said. 'So we can bike through Latvia.' We couldn't quite believe that we actually had the visas in our hands, giving us unparalleled access to the USSR from Riga to Nakhodka, the port for Japan. 'Well, now we can actually tell people we're going,' I said.

'And believe it when we tell them!' Gilles added.

'I've been pretty nervous about this thing,' Howard admitted. Suddenly we realised we were the only people laughing and making a noise. There was no music and at the other tables people were hardly talking above a whisper. Howard looked around him in amazement. 'Man, this is the quietest Mexican restaurant I've *ever* been in.'

We boarded the train and waited apprehensively for the Soviet immigration officers to request our visas.

'These visas are too good to be true,' Howard said. 'I don't think they're going to accept them.' He shook his head. 'I don't think they're going to let us in.' The immigration officer took them away with our passports and the customs officer no more than glanced round our cabin. Five minutes later the officer handed them back courteously and closed our cabin door. 'I don't believe it! I just don't believe it!' Howard exclaimed. 'You should have seen these same guys five years ago. They'd have made us empty every single thing and gone through it piece by piece. We're in!'

We were on a Soviet train, solid and comfortable. Traditional Russian songs, accompanied by a balalaika and somewhat mournful, were played softly over the loudspeakers. The train pulled across the border marked by wire fences, raked earth and armed guards on the Soviet side. As soon as we crossed the border everything looked old-fashioned and rather chaotic. Gone were the neat homes of the Finns, the smooth asphalt roads, the leather jackets. In their place were traditional Russian wooden houses, blue woodsmoke wafting from chimneys and dilapidated wooden fences leaning precariously. Small, old-fashioned cars lurched slowly down dirt roads weaving their way round large brown puddles. By comparison with the Finns, the Russians looked untidy and sombrely dressed.

2
LENINGRAD

NATURALLY WE WERE curious about the Russian who was to cycle with us. The one condition laid down by SovIntersport was that a Russian would accompany us. Even today, despite *glasnost*, the Soviet authorities cannot bear the prospect of allowing foreigners to travel completely freely in their country. Howard had therefore requested that the Russian be a 'cultural attaché'; what we feared most was that we would be assigned a professional cyclist obsessed with mileage and average speeds. Soviet bureaucracy, however, hardly aware that the technological age had long since dawned, viewed each fax sent as so much gold-dust blown to the wind and communicated with the greatest reluctance. So brief were SovIntersport's communications that all we knew about 'our' Russian on arrival was his age: thirty; his height: 172 cm; weight: 68 kg; shoe size: 270 mm; and name, Vitale Yakushkov. In Helsinki we had nicknamed him 'Boris'.

We were conscious that his function might be to prevent us from going where we wanted, and that he might be under an obligation to report our activities and political sympathies to the authorities. What we feared most was that he would prevent us from talking freely to whoever we wished or, by his mere presence, deter others from speaking to us. If the worst came to the worst we had decided we would have to throw him off! If at some intersection two of us peeled off to the left and one to the right, there would be precious little Boris could do about it. Howard, Gilles and I had been together a week, and we appeared to hit it off well. None of us doubted that there would be occasional friction between us but we felt that we were basically compatible. But what if, after a few weeks on the road, none of us could stick Boris? Howard had the answer.

'We'll tell him: "Boris. The good news is you don't have to bike any more. The bad news is you've got to strip and hand back all your clothes and equipment."'

At Leningrad we expected to be met by Boris and a representative of SovIntersport. As the train pulled through the suburbs of Leningrad the sky was transformed by the setting sun that cast a golden pink glow over new apartment blocks and old wood houses alike. The train stopped at the Finland Station. On the platform a short man held aloft an amateur sketch of a cyclist beneath the American flag. As we piled out of the train, a tall woman with an intelligent, open face and large brown eyes stepped forward to welcome us.

'Welcome!' she said. 'I am Olga. How was your journey? We are so glad to see you. We were worried for you. We have come to meet the train for three days now. Come please, let me introduce you.' To our surprise we found that the milling crowd around us on the platform were waiting for us too. They were a rough-looking group, their hair tousled and clothes slightly awry, like boys that had dressed in a hurry, late for school. 'Alexei, Ivan, Piotr, Sasha, Misha, Sergei, Nikolai and Valodiya.' We shook hands, forgetting the names instantly.

'And Boris? Er . . . Vitale . . . Vitale Yakushkov? Our cyclist, where is he?'

'He is not here. Sasha will cycle with you,' Olga told us by way of explanation. We looked at Sasha with renewed interest. He was short and pale, his shortness accentuated by an old blue anorak that was far too big for him, and his cropped black hair stood on end as though he had had some terrible shock. He was smoking furiously, his eyes darting from side to side. He laughed nervously.

'I cycle before. Come!' he told us, throwing his cigarette butt on the floor and grinding it into oblivion. His movements were abrupt and he seemed ill at ease. What had happened to Vitale?

'Vitale is in Moscow,' Olga told us as if that cleared up the matter once and for all. We groped around trying to work out who was who. Howard turned to Olga.

'And you're from SovIntersport?' he said hopefully.

'No, I'm a friend,' she said, as we moved off down the platform, our heavy duffel-bags borne by the mysterious gaggle of Russians who had melted into the crowd. Too late, we remembered the warning we had received in Helsinki about the mafia.

'A friend of whose?' Howard pressed on, bewildered.

'Of Misha's, Sasha's, Nikolai's and Ivan's!'

'Uh huh. And they work for SovIntersport?'

'No. Misha is a doctor, Sasha is an engineer, Nikolai works at the Leningrad Science Institute and Ivan is a scientist.'

By this time we had passed out of the station through a side entrance and our duffel-bags had been loaded into the back of a Lada van. Outside, a square crowded with people on the move was suffused by the red glow of the evening; people's breath hung in the cold air.

'You come with us,' Olga said. 'Misha will look after your things.' Olga, Sasha, Howard, Gilles and I climbed into a second, cramped Lada and watched the van with all our possessions melt into the Leningrad traffic.

'That's the last we see of it, I guess,' Howard said. 'What fools we are! We've been in the country ten minutes and we're stripped of everything. One and a half years to get it together and ten minutes to lose it.' We lapsed into silence, watching Leningrad rush-hour traffic bathed by the last rays of the red orb that had sunk low over the River Neva. We lurched over cobblestones and tramlines at half-destroyed intersections and crossed the Neva on Kirovsky Bridge. Downstream, façade after stuccoed façade of perfectly proportioned classical mansions and palaces lined the river banks, catching the last traces of the evening sun. Beyond the rooftops gilt spires touched the sky.

We appeared to leave the old city behind us and run along broad, tree-lined streets of residential blocks, big and squat, and then turned down others that looked identical. Shop façades were bleak and uninviting with their drapes of dusty white netting in the windows. Here and there little groups of Russians stood in knots, their coats drawn tightly round them. Most were making their way home purposefully in the cold air. We twisted and turned down backstreets, ran along beside a decrepit-looking factory and past a dilapidated church.

'So, *no one* here is from SovIntersport?' Howard said eventually, emerging from an anxious abstraction.

'No. You can meet them when you get to Moscow, if you like,' Olga replied. We gave up. We had no idea where we were going or whom we were with. We sat back, resigned to our fate. A short while later we swung into a large, scruffy courtyard surrounded on all four sides by sand-coloured apartment blocks. The large central courtyard was of beaten earth, worn smooth by constant use, from which rose tall and leafless trees. A few small patches of tired grass survived here and there. Small children, well wrapped up, were kicking a football around or playing on swings. Outside the communal staircases sat elderly women, *babushka*s, in woollen skirts, long wool socks, layers of thick cardigans and sweaters, lined boots and bright headscarves.

'Is this our hotel?' Howard asked, incredulously, looking around him in the twilight.

'This is Yuri's apartment. We go to hotel later.'

'OK, you win.'

We were almost surprised to see the second van turn up. Nikolai and Alexei locked the vans and removed the windscreen wipers, putting them carefully into their pockets.

'Windscreen wipers are impossible to find in our country,' Olga explained. 'If you leave them on the car they disappear. They are very precious.'

'In which case, I'm not leaving my gear in the car,' Gilles said, looking around the gaunt courtyard.

'Don't worry,' Olga said. 'It will be safe.'

'Maybe, but I'm taking mine with me.' We lugged our bags out, the mysterious crowd of Russians carrying them upstairs on their shoulders. We had no idea that Yuri lived on the sixth floor and that there was no lift. He opened the door to us, revealing a small entrance hall so crammed with objects that we could only enter two at a time. To the right was a living room, also full, papered with a heavy damask wallpaper, with glossy wooden cabinets stuffed randomly with papers, crockery and books. Hallway and living room were piled with odds and ends: clothes, pieces of metal, empty jars and bottles, empty tins of Brazilian coffee, bicycle parts, offcuts of wood, wire and metal, boxes, pieces of furniture stacked one upon another, a broken chair, lengths of flat rubber, scraps of plastic, wooden poles, fishing rods, the stuffed head of a wolf.

There was not the slightest sign that we were expected: no table prepared or laid. Everything was in a state of bachelor-like chaos. Chairs were extracted from the furniture mountain in the corner, a table with a broken leg was pulled into the middle of the room and precariously erected, and a pile of old newspapers pushed to one side. The Russians crowded in, quickly filling the small room, talking animatedly between themselves. Only Yuri and Olga appeared to speak any English. Yuri was an enthusiastic amateur photographer and started to pull out his albums, full of faded and greying snaps that looked as if they had been taken forty years before.

'I take colour slides in summer, and black and white prints in winter,' he explained, 'as colour films are available in our shops only in spring.'

Gradually the table was roughly laid and food began to appear from the kitchen – pickled gherkins, beans, smoked herring, sausage, potatoes, salads and roast chicken which was so tough that our forks crumpled. In England guests would have eaten it with a straight face pretending that it was normal, but the Russians pulled Yuri's leg mercilessly and fell about laughing.

'You see, even chickens have problems in our country,' Yuri grinned.

We had been warned to avoid tap water at all costs in Leningrad, which apparently was 'the ghardia capital of the USSR', ghardia being a particularly unpleasant gastric disorder caught from amoeba in unclean water. It was our intention to purify all water on the journey but to start filtering our own supply at the table on day one seemed a bit much.

The meal was otherwise dry – dry until there came a discreet though clearly expected knock at the door. Yuri excused himself for a minute, we heard whispering and then he came back gleefully carrying aloft a capacious black holdall. From this he extracted an unlabelled, three-litre glass jar of colourless liquid. A buzz of excitement filled the crowded room; this was clearly the moment they had all been waiting for. Small glasses appeared, a little liquid was poured onto a plate and lit with a match. A flame leapt up.

As we soon learnt, Russians seize any opportunity to celebrate and only one way is good enough – with vodka or, failing that, *samogon*, home-distilled alcohol. No other drink, not even champagne, is good enough, to toast someone's health. As the Soviet authorities had deliberately cut back on alcohol production in the latest of many bids to reduce alcoholism, the production of illegal, home-distilled *samogon* had accordingly been stepped up. *Samogon*'s virtue is that it can be made from anything that will ferment – fruit, wine, sugar, cereals, potatoes, yeast. We even heard of it being made from tomato paste and cockroach spray. According to *official* data one half of the hard liquor drunk in the Soviet Union is distilled by moonshiners, and Gorbachev's campaign against alcoholism was acknowledged to be a failure. The state had lost billions of roubles in revenue, while figures showed that people were not drinking any less. In the shops, vodka was virtually unavailable.

Hence the black holdall. Toast after toast followed, each glass being drunk by a backward toss of the head, the contents being downed in a single motion. Howard and I followed suit in the hope of seeing the Russians dash their glasses violently to the floor, one of the few traditions we all knew about before our arrival. To our dismay no one knew what we were talking about. Each toast was followed by a giant bite of gherkin or herring and bread, a kind of antidote that enables Russians to continue drinking well beyond the body's natural limits. First came a toast to our arrival, then to friendship, to the success of our journey, to beautiful women, to peace, to our families . . . The evening became noisier and noisier as the level on the three-litre jar steadily fell like a thermometer. Late in the evening when Yuri produced a large block of cheese there was a stir of interest.

'Where did you find that?' Nikolai asked him, while the others listened with interest.

'In the fridge,' he replied, enigmatically, before turning to us. 'Cheese in our country is a mystery product. One month there are seven varieties in the shop; the next month nothing. But recently there hasn't been any cheese for a long time.' So in our first evening we had come across four coveted items: windscreen wipers, colour film, vodka and cheese.

'Vodka is a unique drink,' Yuri assured us, with the air of a connoisseur. 'It is the only alcohol that never results in a hangover.' This is hardly true: one only has to see a Russian groping his way down a street trying to get home after a celebration to remember the forty-five per cent alcohol content, even though some Russians maintain that vodkas are now watered down in the distilleries, the purloined vodka being illegally sold on the side – *na levo*. It is just that the effect is immediate and debilitating rather than gradually intoxicating. So it was on our first evening in the Soviet Union that I felt absolutely fine until, at a certain moment, I was felled like an ox. I have a very vague recollection of my legs being lifted up onto a sofa and dropped like pipes of lead, of distant voices murmuring, and then of another inert body being deposited beside me like a sack of potatoes. A long time later I woke up feeling ghastly, to find Howard prostrate, fully clothed, on the sofa beside me. Yuri sat crumpled asleep in an armchair and Nikolai lay concertinaed on the floor. I picked my way over the bodies, strewn like corpses on the battlefield, and made my way gingerly to the bathroom, which was small and cramped, half taken up by an antediluvian water-heater, the bath filled with empty jars and distilling equipment. I filtered some water and groped my way back.

When I woke again it was broad daylight and Howard and I were alone in the apartment.

'Jeez, what was that stuff?' he asked in a pained voice before falling asleep again. A great theory of Yuri's! I thought, looking out the window. Television aerials sprouted from the tops of buildings; chimneys puffed black smoke into a grey, windy sky. It looked bleak and cold. I fell asleep. Later in the afternoon Olga, Gilles and Sasha returned.

'You two feeling good?' Gilles asked us, cruelly. Over strong Russian tea flavoured with blueberries we began to regain consciousness and focus on the conversation. Gilles hadn't touched a drop the night before.

'President Gorbachev is very popular in your countries, not popular here,' Yuri was saying. 'This I cannot understand. Look around you. Nothing has changed for the better. I do not trust Gorbachev. If nothing changes for the better in six years, how long is necessary? The *nomenklatura* will never accept change to a market economy because their privileges stem from the economic power they wield. They have their own system, they live well. They don't want change. They have too much to lose.'

'This is true,' Olga said, 'after six years of *perestroika* and *glasnost* nothing has changed except one thing – we now discuss them.'

'Surely,' I said, 'that's something – at least a beginning.'

'It is time for doing, not talking,' Olga replied, wearily, echoing a sentiment that we were to hear the length and breadth of the country. Yuri sat on a low stool, talking animatedly, waving his hands.

'The politicians talk and talk. It's all words. No one does anything. If we knew who the enemy was we could do something but we don't know who is in control. We never see these people. They are clever! They keep in the background and live a life apart. They have their own shops, schools, hospitals, everything. They are a self-perpetuating hereditary clique. Yes, they even intermarry to keep the system closed.' We were surprised to hear such frank and critical political discussion and were wary of making any political comment ourselves. We were not exactly sure who we were with or whether our political sympathies were being sounded out. 'The *nomenklatura* also wield economic power through what we call the "second rouble",' Andrei said, 'that is non-personal money that they control in industry. It can be passed around between them as favours and bribes.'

'As the *nomenklatura* monopolise all the best positions,' Olga continued, 'it is very difficult to reach the top in our country. We have many jokes about our strange life. For example, there is a general in the Soviet army who has a son who also goes into the army. He is young, he is very clever and he studies hard. He passes all his exams with good marks, he is liked by everybody and he graduates first from military college. So, even while he is still young, he becomes a general. But can he become a field-marshal? No, never. Because the field-marshal also has a son!'

We were to hear a great deal over the next five months about the *nomenklatura*, the Soviet élite, whose members are appointed by the Communist Party and which plays such an important role in Soviet life. The *nomenklatura* hold the most sensitive and important posts in the USSR – economic, political, military, scientific and academic. Membership of this élite overlapped until recently with membership of the Communist Party but was more exclusive, its members numbering approximately a million. At the heart of the *nomenklatura* system lay the Secretariat of the Communist Party Central Committee which was perhaps the most important body, after the Politburo, in determining Soviet life. It was responsible for appointing thousands of people to important positions the length and breadth of the country who, in turn, nominated others right the way down to village level.

A wide range of privileges is available to the *nomenklatura* that mark them off from the rest of Soviet society. Privileges at the top range from luxurious *dacha*s and chauffeur-driven Zils and Volgas to special closed and unmarked shops, access to which is only gained with the appropriate pass. Not only is the Soviet élite able, in this way, to buy goods that the ordinary Russian rarely sees, but it is thereby insulated from the chronic shortages, endless queues and abysmal service that are the norm for ordinary Soviet citizens. It was about the *nomenklatura* that Yuri was talking so exasperatedly.

'In your country, if you want to work, you can build a better life, better even than your President. But here that is not so, no matter what you do!'

Olga, a research physicist and professor at the prestigious Leningrad Academy of Sciences, agreed. Despite her profession and position she earned only 175 roubles a month ($30 at the official exchange rate of six roubles to the dollar, and only $11.60 at the widely available black-market rate of fifteen). She was married to a naval officer and both were about forty years old.

'For many years I have worked hard at the Institute, but I can't buy a car. I must work for more than ten years for that. I cannot go to a shop and buy one, not even if I have the money. There is no such shop. I can only buy through my institute and my name has been on the list there for many years now. There is a long waiting list for cars but some people have the right to go to the top – for instance, war veterans and people who lived in Leningrad at the time of the blockade.'

'Blockade?' I asked.

'In the Great Patriotic War, when the Fascists were attacking,' she replied. 'The only way to get a car is to buy one second-hand but they cost much more than new ones. A new car costs 10,000 roubles, but a second-hand one 20 or 30,000. There are four car salerooms in Leningrad for a population of five million, but if you go to the salerooms you will find no cars, only lists . . . My parents have a friend who waited twenty years for a car – he lived in the country where these things are even more difficult. Eventually it arrived but by that time he was too old and weak to drive any more!'

That evening we squeezed back into the Lada to go to our hotel. 'We're going to need the biggest room in the hotel to sort through our gear,' I said.

'The bridal suite!' said Howard. To our surprise we seemed to be heading further away from the centre, following boulevard after boulevard of sand-coloured apartment blocks.

'Where are we going, Sasha? Our hotel *is* in the centre, isn't it?'

'No, centre, no!' Sasha replied.

'But we requested a hotel in the centre of town, Sasha. We need to be in the centre to go to the post office, to send telegrams, to meet journalists, to make phonecalls to the US . . .'

'*Nomenklatura* hotel,' Sasha told us blandly, handing us each black and yellow pass cards on which were written Russian names. I was now 'Dmitri Chemezov', Howard was 'Mikhail Voronenko' and Gilles 'Nikolai Alexandrov'.

'What's the idea of the Russian names?' Gilles asked. 'Ours not good enough?' But Sasha was not listening. The van had stopped outside a forlorn, dilapidated building. There were no lights, no hotel sign, no hotel doorway, nothing. Sasha looked worried.

'Don't talk until in room,' he said quietly, although no one was within a hundred yards of us in the rain-swept road. We crossed the road, stuff-sacks on our shoulders, and the van drove off. At the corner were old wooden double doors with peeling blue paint. Sasha looked up and down the street, threw his cigarette butt on the ground and indicated with a quick sideways nod that we should enter. It was more as if we were a hand-picked group of commandos on a sabotage mission than foreign visitors arriving legitimately at a hotel.

Following Sasha we mounted a cold and bare concrete staircase in the unlit hallway to the first floor. Again indicating that we maintain total silence, Sasha opened an unmarked door and we filed through in front of a reception where a fat woman with piled-up blonde hair stared at us suspiciously. We flashed our passcards and Sasha motioned to us to keep moving down the corridor while he murmured something to the surly receptionist. The corridor was poorly lit and the walls and ceiling were plastered with a coat of cobalt blue reflective crystals giving the effect of a hallucinatory grotto. We climbed up another staircase past unnumbered rooms from which could be heard muffled voices. The keys fitted badly and, fumbling in the dark, we took it in turns to try and unlock the doors. Looking very unhappy, Sasha was forced to appeal for help to the receptionist who came back and glared interrogatively at us, while she unlocked the doors. Howard, Gilles and I, tight-lipped, tried to assume the air of men who thought it was entirely normal to be standing in a darkened crystal corridor of an unmarked building on the edge of Leningrad. When the doors opened we gave her a sickly grin and passed inside like deaf mutes.

Two single beds, a bare wooden table with two glasses, two hard chairs and a cupboard comprised the furniture. One naked light bulb illuminated the 1950s wallpaper, with its design of interlocking brown cubes, and the thin curtains, half-collapsed off the curtain rails. From the window we had a view of the rain-swept road outside and a cemetery beyond. Sasha wiped his brow, evidently relieved at the way things had gone, and addressed us in a hushed voice.

'Here your keys. Tomorrow for bikes. Now I go for food. Then back here.'

'Wa-i-i-it a moment, Sasha!' Howard stopped him, putting his hand on Sasha's shoulder. 'What is this?'

'Hotel,' Sasha answered simply.

'You're telling me this is a hotel?' Howard was incredulous. 'Why then do we have to sneak in like thieves?' But this was way beyond Sasha's English. He stared at Howard, blinking, uncomprehending, under the naked light bulb. 'Why can't we speak in English, Sasha?'

'In room, it's possible,' he replied, still in a hushed voice.

'Why, Sasha? Why?' Howard asked, exasperated.

'Better,' he said and he smiled nervously. 'Now I go for food. Keep door closed.' And he was gone.

We looked around us. It was dismal; where was that grand hotel, a stone's throw from the Winter Palace in the heart of old St Petersburg, that we had been expecting? 'God knows where we are!' Gilles said, peering over at the cemetery. Beyond, a factory sent smoke into the grey skies.

'This is absurd. We can't talk in normal voices! There's no restaurant, no bar, no telephone and we must be miles from the city centre,' I said. 'It took us nearly an hour to get here by car. What the hell is going on?'

'The whole idea is that we can work solidly on the bikes, go down for a quick meal in the hotel restaurant and get back to work fast. We won't be able to do that here.' Gilles looked angry.

'I know, Gilles, I know,' said Howard. 'I've got phonecalls to make to the States, telegrams to send and, besides, I'm going to need a beer. What are we meant to do here in the evening? Play snap?' He paused. 'Sorry about this, team. We'll sort it out tomorrow, OK?'

'OK.'

'OK.'

An hour passed before Sasha reappeared. From a threadbare bag he brought out our supper: four bottles of milk and four of yoghurt, a huge, deathly-grey sausage, bread, butter, and pickled tomatoes and gherkins in brine. The sausage was made from the worst possible meat and smelt revolting; the taste was worse. The tomatoes and gherkins, soaked in brine, tasted purely of vinegar. Sasha tucked in with gusto, cutting himself thick slices of sausage and crunching gherkins. Howard, Gilles and I ate the bread, butter and yoghurt. Howard shook his head.

We pressed Sasha again about the hotel. He insisted it was for the *nomenklatura*.

'For factory managers . . . and women friends,' he explained.

'So we're staying in a brothel,' Gilles said. '*Charmant.*'

'No, no!' Sasha protested, strongly, but he warned us to lock the communal showers from the inside. In any case the shower room was kept locked, the sole key being in the possession of the woman at reception. As speech was forbidden we evidently couldn't ask for the key – this was something Sasha had to do for us.

'Do you think every member of the *nomenklatura* has to trot down for the key every time he wants a shower?' I asked Gilles.

'Probably not if you're in the Politburo,' he replied.

We came to the conclusion that the *nomenklatura* brothel-hotel must have been a good deal cheaper for SovIntersport than the Intourist hotel.

'What food do you think we'll be able to buy on the journey?' I asked Sasha.

'Potatoes . . . cucumbers . . . onions,' he began confidently, before faltering, 'Bread . . . carrots,' he added, after a pause. 'Maybe cabbage.' He appeared to be casting round in his mind.

'Any fruit?' I asked, aware that Gilles and Howard had stopped what they were doing and were listening attentively.

'No, no fruit,' he laughed.

'Meat?' I suggested. He looked doubtful.

'Maybe.'

'Sausage?', I said, eyeing the venomous object on the table. 'No, I don't think so.' That just about covered it all. Howard and Gilles went back to their work in silence.

The following morning Sasha said we would go to a café for breakfast. Idly, foolishly, a French café sprang to mind. We set off at a brisk pace and walked for twenty minutes down a wide boulevard but there were few shops and no cafés. From time to time Sasha stopped a passer-by and asked directions. Some pointed further on, others back in the direction we had come from. Twenty minutes later we passed a viaduct where thirty or forty men were sitting on the ground or hanging expectantly around a small blue wooden kiosk clutching plastic containers.

'What's going on there?' we asked.

'They wait for beer,' Sasha replied. After thirty minutes of walking our patience wore thin, after forty minutes it snapped.

'Wait a moment, Sasha. Where *are* we going?'

'Café, 300 metres.' We walked on for 300 metres but there was nothing in sight.

'OK, we take a taxi, Sasha,' Howard said, launching out into the road, waving wildly at every passing car.

'No, no taxis here. Let's go,' said Sasha, looking very unhappy. And he was right; there were no taxis.

After walking for an hour we found a café with an extraordinarily tall ceiling quite out of proportion with the floorspace. Cheap formica tables and chairs, naked strip lights, and bare walls gave it a bleak, uninviting look. At the far end a queue of ten people, four in military uniform, waited for service at a metal counter. Sasha and I joined the queue. It inched forwards, stopped for minutes at a time, then inched forwards again.

Taller than the Russians, I peered ahead to see what was holding us up. On the far side of the counter was a single woman, obese and slow-moving. She listened to the orders with a bored, lifeless expression on her face, served food and drink with leisurely disdain, calculated the cost on a wooden abacus, slowly flicking wooden beads to and fro, and searched around in a little saucer for change. Each stage seemed to demand a Herculean effort. She breathed heavily. I looked at the faces in the queue to see if they were worried about her condition. They had vacant, bored expressions but looked neither impatient nor concerned. I glanced at my watch, exasperated. It had taken us an hour to get to the café and we had queued for over twenty minutes. Allowing only fifteen minutes for breakfast and another hour to get back, I calculated it would be quarter to twelve before we returned to the hotel from breakfast. If we were going to repeat the process every mealtime, three-quarters of the day would be spent pursuing food. When Sasha and I arrived at the table with our fare, I noticed that Howard and Gilles were looking angry and frustrated, but as it was only day two we tried to keep our cool.

First meals in a foreign country are significant; they give the visitor a feel for a country's priorities and its approach to life. Our breakfast consisted of warm risotto, over-cooked and drenched in oil, half a kilo of plain biscuits, dryish pastries filled with unbelievably sweet cream, glasses of *smetana* or sour cream and a hot drink, midway between tea and coffee. We pushed our risotto to one side and ate the pastries. A tiny old woman beside us was eating one small pastry with her tea. She spoke intermittently, mostly to herself and occasionally to us but without appearing to expect an answer. After a while Sasha said something to her and she drew one of the untouched plates of risotto to her and began to eat it.

'What did she say?' Gilles asked.

'She complains of her hard life,' Sasha replied.

We explained to Sasha and Alexei why we needed to move to a decent central hotel. It was no good being stranded on the edge of Leningrad, without transport, far from the main post office and with nowhere close by to eat. Quite apart from everything that we needed to do, we wanted to be able to saunter out of the hotel in the evening to explore the old city. But what appeared to us a simple and straightforward request seemed to cause a great deal of consternation to Sasha and Alexei, who spent the rest of the day making endless telephone calls to Moscow. In the evening they told us it was impossible, every room in the city being booked. 'Bullshit!' Howard exploded.

The following day we were dismayed to find that we had been lined up with a tour of the St Peter and Paul fortress and cathedral, the burial place of the Russian tsars. In principle there was nothing we would have liked more but, exasperated by the apparent inability of Alexei and Sasha to find us decent accommodation, we were not in any mood for sightseeing. While the guide reeled off the dimensions of the golden spire we made for the nearby Leningrad Hotel, Sasha trailing along behind us. It took a minute to establish that there were rooms available, provided we were prepared to pay $129 per room in US dollars.

It was the same story at the Moskovskaya. Clearly SovIntersport preferred not to spend the dollars we had paid them. Seventy years of Communism hadn't quite killed off the commercial instinct.

The following day Howard insisted on speaking to Mr Vyshnikov, the director of SovIntersport, with whom he had arranged the expedition. He came back into the room, exasperated. 'Vyshnikov hung up on me. It wasn't a great conversation: he is being unreasonable. He says we can't cycle through Latvia because it's too dangerous. That's not correct; he just doesn't want us to go. But he clearly doesn't know we have Riga on our visas. So we just didn't understand, OK? He didn't know anything about the hotel we've been put in either; he thought we were in the Sport Hotel, so we can move.'

On the fourth day Howard went to check out the Sport Hotel; like everything we had done so far it took almost an entire day and when he came back he was in a foul mood.

'We're staying here!' he said. 'The Sport's isolated, the people are as unhelpful as hell and it's full of black-market mafia types. One of us would have to be there to guard our gear twenty-four hours a day. We're ten times better off where we are.'

Naturally we expected to sit down and have a meeting with SovInter-sport to discuss the route, the budget, how we were to pay for food and hotels along our route, whether we were to be supplied with roubles or vouchers, whether any hotels in major cities along the route would be reserved, how bicycle spares could be got to us in case of an emergency and so on, but it soon became clear that no meeting was planned. Such information as we received we gathered piecemeal from Sasha, Alexei or their friends.

At this point Vitale, the Soviet cyclist we had originally expected, turned up in Leningrad. His father had been ill but had recovered enough for him to join us after all. He was the same age as us, athletic and rather boyish, with fairish hair, and blue, slightly hooded eyes. He spoke English tolerably well and he was enthusiastic about the journey, having given up his work in the Moscow Sports Centre to join us.

With Vitale's help we began to piece the jigsaw together. From him we learnt that SovIntersport had delegated the organisation of the expedition to one of the new private cooperative firms called 'Este', something no one had thought of telling us. Alexei worked for Este and it was Este that had invited Vitale to cycle with us.

Alexei was something of a puzzle. He was in his middle fifties and had a long oval face, a short, almost monastic haircut and an absorbed expression. With his outgrown trousers, his top shirt-button always done up and the way he stood, motionless, hands hanging beside his body, he looked like a schoolboy waiting for morning inspection. And yet there was something of the philosopher about him too, with his dream-like and faraway expression. Out in the streets, wearing a brown felt hat that seemed to perch on his head like a bird and an old raincoat, he looked like the classic detective from a black-and-white movie.

He was a curious choice to have been delegated to oversee and help organise the beginning of our expedition, as he spoke virtually no English. Communication from day one was therefore fraught with difficulties. Alexei would follow our conversation or questions with intense concentration and furrowed forehead, looking up words in a pocket Russian-English dictionary that was never out of his hand. When he had something to say he held up a finger and cocked an eyebrow, his eyes half-closed. He spoke rarely but when he did it was slowly, quietly and with great deliberation, and his replies to questions were short and enigmatic. Once Alexei had spoken, Gilles, Howard and I tried to work out the meaning of his words as though unscrambling a secret code. Even the simplest question or proposal that we put to Alexei, Vitale and Sasha always seemed to result in lengthy, animated conversation between them and endless, inconclusive telephone calls to and from Moscow. So much time was wasted with each question or idea that the three of us agreed to keep them to the minimum.

A number of simple differences soon became apparent between the way we and the Russians were used to doing things. Not only would we find that pre-arranged plans had been abruptly dropped or forgotten but rarely was any explanation forthcoming. We made a very clear arrangement with Alexei that he would collect us at 8.30 am so that we could go and collect our equipment. After waiting outside the hotel for an hour, we asked Sasha to telephone and find out what had happened. At 10.00 am Sasha was back with the news that Alexei would come at 2.00 pm instead. Over the next few months we realised that attempts to get explanations in the Soviet Union were usually fruitless and that Russians accepted there was little point in trying to get them.

Relying on Alexei to be there at an agreed time to do a specific task seemed to be an alien concept. We wished to start early so that we could spend a full day sorting equipment but, dependent as we were on Russian organisation, we rarely arrived at the warehouse where our equipment was stored before 3 pm. This gave too little time and would necessitate yet another journey on another day; thus mornings and afternoons repeatedly trickled away. It all seemed such a disastrous waste of time. But these delays, which we found so maddening, appeared to be of little concern to the Russians. Whether it took one day or four to rearrange a hotel or sort through and collect our equipment was really of no great consequence. Eventually it would be done.

Howard was very keen to start the expedition from Latvia, so that our journey would lie between the furthest extremities of the Soviet Union.

This had been agreed to by the Soviet authorities until shortly before our departure when they requested us to start from Leningrad instead. It was the increasing political volatility of the Baltic Republics that lay behind this change of attitude.

'Vyshnikov made it pretty clear he didn't want us to go to Riga,' Howard said ruefully. 'But he didn't say so explicitly.'

'I don't see why we can't just buy tickets to Riga,' Gilles said, 'hop on a train and start cycling from there. There's no reason why SovIntersport should know – unless Vitale tells them.'

'We can definitely get to Riga and probably through Latvia as well – we've got it on our visa.'

'For us it may be alright,' I agreed, 'but what about Vitale? After all he's coming too and this could land him in real trouble.' We consulted Vitale, Alexei and Sasha, all three of whom were strongly opposed to the idea.

'Maybe you will be stopped by the military – and then many problems, I think,' Alexei told us. We looked at him expectantly. 'I think if you go to Riga' – he shut the dictionary and sat back with his eyes closed – 'your journey will finish very soon.'

'You mean, we will be thrown out of the country?'

'Maybe,' he nodded slowly, pulling a long Pierrot-like face. We were silent for a while. We hadn't thought of that; and we did not want to find ourselves back in Helsinki in a week's time.

'I guess it's just not worth the risk,' Howard concluded. Sadly, we agreed.

That evening we were invited to the birthday party of one of Olga's friends, Misha. The table was spread with dozens of dishes of *zakuski*, Russian *hors d'oeuvres*: marinated mushrooms, salted herring, red caviar, gherkins, half a dozen different salads, followed by delicious homemade cakes and pastries. Vodka, champagne and Hungarian Tokai wine covered the table. We were to find the excessively sweet Russian champagne available at some of the big hotels at an official price of 12p a bottle.

The conversation turned to the new, privately owned cooperatives that had been set up in Leningrad following the liberalisation of the law on small businesses under Gorbachev.

'The new cooperatives are not serious,' Andrei told us. 'They are mostly set up by black-marketeers. They don't make their money through the cooperatives but through buying and selling on the black market. The cooperatives are only used to launder money.'

'But who are these black-marketeers?' Howard asked.

'They are a mafia,' Andrei said, 'with connections, with contacts in the *nomenklatura*, because it is the *nomenklatura* who have the power to give or refuse permission to set up these cooperatives. And unless the *nomenklatura* receive the *baksheesh* they demand they don't give their permission. It's as simple as that.'

'Is it possible for people to open their own restaurant now?' I asked Andrei.

'In theory, everything is possible in our country. But the law is one thing and reality is another. Laws are passed but they mean nothing. Yes, there are now a few cooperative restaurants in Leningrad but the only people there are black-marketeers, mafia and Finnish tourists. No one else can afford to go!'

'But doesn't Gorbachev want these private businesses to succeed?'

'Of course he knows about these problems,' Andrei said. 'But how could he throw away his neighbours? His friends? He is a product of the system.'

'Don't you think Gorbachev genuinely wants reform?' I asked.

'Some change is inevitable, but we do not trust him in the Soviet Union like you do in the West! We say he is two-faced; he says one thing and does another. The Communist leaders, Gorbachev included, made a lot of noise about giving up their luxurious *dacha*s, saying they will be turned into schools and hospitals, but they are building new ones! Yes, I have seen this with my own eyes – beautiful houses. And you are not allowed to get close to them. They spend millions of roubles on them. I know one part of the coast not far from the city very well because I used to go there often when I was a child. At that time the beach was bad: it was rough, with stones and pebbles only. Now luxurious *dacha*s have been built there, the beach has been transformed with sand and the area has been closed off. Our country is too big and our problems are too big to solve. Our system is much slower than yours. People demonstrate in the streets and what happens? Nothing. Nothing changes in Leningrad. In Moscow some homeless families occupied the empty houses of the *nomenklatura*, it's true; nowadays it's hard for the government to fight with these people because of *glasnost* and *perestroika*.'

'Maybe in five years' time,' I said, 'these things will be possible.' Andrei laughed.

'Changes will happen but slowly, very slowly. Maybe my grand-children will see some difference from today, but not me. Maybe in fifty years, maybe a hundred.'

'What does the mafia deal in?' I asked Olga.

'Everything!' she said. 'Before, when there were a few shortages, we had a small mafia but now that we have a shortage of everything they are everywhere. As long as shortages last, so too will our mafia.'

'For instance,' Andrei continued, 'we have the Arbat, a pedestrianised street in Leningrad where artists sell their paintings. But to exhibit their paintings the artists have to pay 500 roubles a month – to the mafia.'

'And if they refuse to pay?' Howard asked.

'Their paintings are slashed with a knife,' Andrei replied.

'It is impossible for the *nomenklatura* to exist with an open market,' Misha said. 'That is why they resist it. But at present whatever changes are introduced, the *nomenklatura* benefit – they are, of course, best placed to take advantage of them. But the production of the cooperatives is not a real market. I don't see many people buying cooperative clothes, the cooperative is only a front.'

'But the private food markets are legitimate, aren't they?' I asked Olga.

'Yes, they're legal now and country people can bring their food to sell it in the towns. But I only buy food from state shops: I cannot afford the private market. My salary is 175 roubles per month and tomatoes cost ten roubles a kilo in the private market. Good fruit and vegetables are difficult to find in the state shops but, at the moment, for milk, eggs and potatoes, there is no problem.'

One of Misha's friends at the birthday dinner had said nothing but had been watching intently. He seemed to listen to everything that was said with a sense of wonder. At the end of the meal I turned to him and smiled.

'English?' he said.

'Yes, from London,' I replied.

'Ah!' he smiled, his face radiating joy. 'Jerome K. Jerome?'

'Yes,' I replied.

'Three men in the boat and nothing of the dog?' he continued. 'Oh, wonderful book.' His eyes sparkled. 'Sherlock Holmes?' he asked.

'Elementary, my dear Watson!' I replied. He shook his head as if it was too good to be true.

'"The case of the Red Headed League?"' he continued, watching my face intently.

'"The Boscombe Valley Mystery",' I countered. He was overjoyed.

'Robert Louis Stevenson?' he whispered.

'"Travels with a Donkey".'

'Dr Jekyll and Mr Hyde?' He blew a kiss, enraptured. At the end of the evening he tugged at my arm and said earnestly, quietly, 'This is the first time I see Englishman, American, Frenchman. I thought you would be so different, bad maybe. We heard that you were bad for so long. But now I see that you are the same as us.' He shook his head in disbelief. 'Let us live in peace!' he said, giving me an enormous hug, his eyes full of tears. Out in the street we waited forty minutes for a taxi, shaking hands again and again, until he was reluctantly borne away.

The following day we sorted through our gear, all 1,150 pounds of it. The boxes were opened by a Soviet customs officer who was intrigued by our Swiss Army penknives. He studied them carefully, opening the blades one by one, and peered at the scissors and magnifying glass.

'You may use!' he told us regally, handing them back with a generous gesture. Quite why the penknives should have so interested him was a mystery. Alexei had an identical one in his pocket. We spread out all our gear: vast stacks of brilliantly coloured Helly Hansen clothing, hundreds of spare pieces of bicycle equipment, box after box of medical supplies and vitamins, and enough vacuum-packed dried mountaineering food to feed us for two weeks. Olga walked about looking increasingly worried as box after box was opened up. She stooped to pick up a spare pair of dayglo orange laces.

'This alone is worth ten roubles on the black market!' she said. 'I am afraid for you. You should not have brought these bright-coloured clothes. Maybe it is alright for your countries but not here. Every day we read now in the papers of people leaving Leningrad by car who are stopped on the road and forced to hand over their possessions. You could be hit on the head. It is not good.'

Eventually all the clothes were sorted into piles. Howard's clothing list catered for every possible eventuality. It included:

Four Rain Jackets
Five Rain Pants
Four Winter Full Body Jackets
Four Gortex Down Vests
Five Midweight Full Body Jackets
Four Insulated Pants
Eight Stretch Bike Shorts
Eight Pro Seats (bike short liners)
Eight Briefs
Eight Stretch Lycra Tights
Four Thermal Tights
Four Pile Pants
Four Pile Jackets
Eight Turtleneck Long Shirts with zippers

Eight Crewneck T-Shirts
Four All Purpose Shorts
Four T-Shirts
Eight Pants
Eight Poly Pro Hats
Four Balaclavas
Twelve Pair Socks
Four Pair Wool Socks
Four Pair Winter Gloves
Four Pair Summer Bike Gloves
Eight Pair Poly Pro Glove Liners
Four Gortex Mitten Shells
Four Pair Bike Shoes
Four Shoe Covers
Four Helmets

After all the clothes had been split up into piles, Howard called us over.

'OK, I'll tell you how the clothing works. It's based on a layering system which worked well for Steve and me in the Himalayas. You start off in the morning, say, with your stretch bike shorts, your thermal tights, your stretch lycra tights and, if it's raining, your rain pants. If it's snowing you'll want your snow pants too. By the time you're warm you can dispense with your thermal tights. On your top half I suggest the crewneck T-shirt followed by the crewneck or turtleneck long shirt – that's up to you, with the pile jacket or midweight full-body jacket on top. If it's raining you'll need the rain jacket or the lined winter full-body jacket. If it's real cold you'll need Gortex down vests. They saved our lives in Tibet. For the hands you'll need the Poly Pro glove-liners, the summer bike gloves and the winter gloves. The liners keep you warm, the summer bike gloves give you protection when you fall, the winter gloves you'll need when it's real cold. I leave the Gortex mitten shells up to you. Any questions?'

He had brought over 1,150 pounds of equipment, clothes and spare parts. As we could carry no more than sixty pounds each, at least 800 pounds would have to be left behind. Howard seated himself, Buddha-like, in the middle of vast stacks of gear, while Gilles and I experimented with these layering systems. Eventually the stuff was sorted, the excess being sent ahead to Moscow where we would review our equipment again before being setting off East.

*

In the hotel we finished assembling our Raleigh mountain bikes. Vitale had brought his own equipment but decided to use what Howard had brought for him. Nevertheless, from his home-made bicycle panniers he pulled out a few pieces of equipment that he said we should take with us. Everything was worn and wrapped in old dusty plastic bags, making the contrast with our immaculate gear all the more striking. The first item was a piece of chain attached to long lengths of stretchable cord. We looked at it, puzzled.

'Chain for cooking on camp fires,' he said, 'to tie between trees . . . an axe . .'

'An axe!' Gilles and I gasped in unison, weighing it in the palm of our hands; it must have been two kilos.

'For cutting trees,' he added, looking at us surprised. 'Dry food,' he continued, pulling out worn silver packets, so old that no printing remained visible on them any more. 'A sheet of plastic.'

'What's that for?' I asked.

'To put our food on at mealtimes.'

'A tablecloth!' I'd never thought of taking a tablecloth on an expedition before. Judging by their grins, neither had Howard or Gilles.

'Sugar,' Vitale continued, bringing out three kilos of sugar in cardboard boxes.

'Surely we're not taking all of this?' Gilles asked, amazed.

'Later we will not find. Sugar is rationed,' Vitale continued. 'Salt . . .'

'We don't need *quite* so much salt, do we?' I said. There must have been half a kilo of the stuff.

'A water bottle,' he continued, pulling out a collapsible four-litre plastic bottle. 'These are for you,' he said, handing us each a thin piece of rectangular rubber twelve inches by eight with two short elastic straps and a buckle.

'What's this?' Gilles asked, bemused.

'To sit on when we stop for lunch in the countryside. You attach it so,' he said, fixing it round his waist. 'And then when you sit down you stay dry; when you get up it goes with you.' Ironically this ugly but practical invention was to fascinate Russians more than anything else we had with us. 'Two oven gloves . .' They were made of asbestos.

'Banned in the States,' Howard said, looking at them with curiosity. 'We'll jettison this stuff in Moscow.' As it happened, however, most of Vitale's eccentric items proved invaluable.

Olga was genuinely worried for our health and safety. She warned us to take utmost care of ourselves and our possessions through European Russia – 'the most dangerous part'.

'When people leave prison they are not allowed to live in big cities. They have to live in the country, and between Moscow and the Urals there are many regions where such people live. But it is not only that. There are a lot of people living in the European part of our country and there is very little food for them. We call these regions "the hungry regions" because there is nothing in the shops. In Siberia there are less people and they are different in character somehow. A lot of people went there before the Revolution and they are masters of their own life. In that part you will have fewer problems. Everyone in this country knows that European Russia is the dangerous part.' She shook her head with maternal concern. 'Poor, poor boys, to come to all our problems!'

The day before we left, we went with Olga to the Arbat and walked down Nevsky Prospect, the main thoroughfare of Leningrad. Warning us to be careful and to stick close together, she took us to the black market which was tightly packed with people furtively selling stolen goods, half-hidden under their coats.

'These shoes are 120 roubles,' Olga said, showing us a pair of ordinary women's shoes. 'That's three weeks' salary for me.' Extricating ourselves from the seething, shoving mass of humanity, we looked for a café. We were surprised that Olga had to ask people for directions.

'We never go to cafés,' she said. 'Once you have worked all day and queued for food, clothes and everyday things, you don't have the energy to queue for coffee or tea as well.'

After what seemed an age in Leningrad we were ready for departure. We tried cycling the fully laden bikes down the crystal corridors of the 'hotel' and found them wobbly and difficult to control. We shared out our communal equipment, dividing it up equally by weight: every conceivable spare bicycle part, pumps, tents, medical kit, water-filters, cooking pots and pans, primus, fuel bottles, tool kit and axe. Each of us carried a total of twenty-five to thirty kilos of equipment.

On the morning of 21 April we took our bikes outside into the street. It was cold and foggy with a hint of pale sunlight. Close to us a long queue of women had formed outside a shop waiting for it to open. In our brilliant cycling clothes we made a dazzling splash of colour on the foggy street: bright red, pink, black, white and navy blue. Our expedition jackets were adorned on the back with the four expedition flags, red, white and blue, with the red Hammer and Sickle diplomatically positioned in the middle. The mountain bikes with their hi-tech webbed back wheels were sky blue and silver, the panniers black, the reflective Bolle glasses dayglo green, pink and red. Everything was bright, colourful and immaculate, and yet in the queue twenty yards off hardly a head turned to glance in our direction.

We set off for the old Winter Palace of the tsars, the Hermitage, in the cold air. Crossing the cobbled intersections was a feat. They were half-destroyed and cobblestones were strewn around in the road, the tram-lines somehow precariously surviving in the middle despite the devastation. At each intersection cars and lorries wove their own way through as though crossing a minefield, trying to avoid the gaping holes or grounding on the tramlines to be left high and dry like driftwood at high tide. Although causing total chaos to the traffic flow, there was no sign of anything being done to repair the holes, even though plenty of people could be seen engaged in quite inessential tasks, like repainting wire railings and sweeping up leaves. Such manual work as was being done was done almost exclusively by middle-aged women. 'I don't see how the trams can still operate on such bent and loose rails,' I said to Gilles.

'That's the amazing thing. It works,' Gilles remarked as we arrived, unscathed, on the other side of an intersection.

Cycling through the streets of Leningrad, we expected a cheery wave, a few smiles, a few shouted greetings. Not only were there no welcoming smiles but there was no interest in us at all. The only real reaction came from a little old lady who lunged suddenly at Howard shouting and waving an empty bottle over her head. None of us caught her words but it seemed unlikely they were words of welcome. If anybody's eyes met ours they looked away quickly, as if they'd been caught peeping. No one seemed the least bit surprised or curious, or even amused, to see us ride by. Lady Godiva would have had no problems here.

We stopped in front of the Hermitage for a couple of hours. Although quite a few people came up to talk, curious to know what we were doing, with one exception they were all foreign tourists. The fog had cleared and Rastrelli's palace stood out crisply against a light blue sky, it's long Rococo façade, turquoise and white, bright in the thin spring sun. The classical and baroque palaces and mansions of pale pastel hues seemed too perfect to be real, resembling an enormous stage set that had not yet been dismantled. The trees were leafless but the air was exceptionally clear and invigorating. The sun sparkled on golden cupolas and spires, the roofs of the palaces and the Neva. Despite the sobering impressions, it felt good to be alive.

Who could say if we would return? Busy with our preparations we had seen little of the Leningrad the average tourist sees. One day, I felt, I would come back to this muffled, ethereal city, known as the northern Venice.

Alexei's parting words were enigmatic.

'Simon,' he said, 'don't hurry the romantic.' His meaning was open to interpretation but I took it as 'Don't expect too much too quickly. Don't have too high expectations.' In this sense, I remembered his words and, as months went by, found them valuable and instructive.

We set off. As we cycled away from the centre we passed abruptly from one historical zone to the next. Beyond the elegant eighteenth- and nineteenth-century classical buildings lay the heavy, squat Stalinist blocks and streets of the 1930–50s, solid and substantial, and beyond them hundreds of massive apartment blocks that stretched away, grey and monotonous, into the distance.

After a while we cleared an area of grimy ramshackle factories, their entrance gates topped by a rusty hammer and sickle, and made it into the countryside. The roads were rough but not as pot-holed as in the city and at last we had left behind the endless forest of apartment blocks. We breathed a sigh of relief. We were on our way to Vladivostok.

3
NOVGOROD

WE HAD CYCLED thirty kilometres and had left Leningrad behind us when a shout from Howard brought us to a halt. We found him bent over his back wheel.

'I don't believe it!' The screws have fallen out and the wheel's wrecked. Damn it!' He stood up, spun round and kicked the dust in fury. His wheel was so warped that it touched the rack and made further cycling impossible. Instead of a conventional back wheel we were using a new hi-tech one made of artificial fibre 'kevlar', stretched over a plastic disc, which was exceptionally light and strong. To our disbelief, Gilles, Vitale and I found that our wheels too had lost half their screws and the threads were stripped. At first it appeared that thirty kilometres of Soviet roads had sufficed to shake them out but this hardly seemed possible. In fact there was a very simple explanation for this apparent catastrophe: the cycle shop in Denver, Colorado, which had supposedly checked the wheels thoroughly, had forgotten to tighten the screws. 'Those sons of a bitch!' Howard said.

The wheels were beyond repair. We looked round despairingly; the suburbs of Leningrad were just visible on the horizon. It was 3.00 pm, we had cycled thirty kilometres and destroyed four new wheels. It was not an auspicious beginning. However, we had spare wheels in Leningrad and reckoned that we could hitch back to the city, collect them and be back to the stranded bikes before it was dark. Howard and Vitale flagged down a passing truck, while Gilles and I carried the bikes out of sight of the road. Olga's parting words of warning still rang in our ears.

We looked around. The land was mostly a rich, dark, loamy earth, recently ploughed, but close by there was a large area of rough long grass, unfenced and unused to which we ferried the bikes. Not far off there was an elegant classical rotunda that must have once been part of a large estate, now in ruins and overgrown.

Surrounded by dismembered bikes and broken wheels, we found our primus and prepared tea. The sunshine was warm, the sky a thin, pale blue and birch trees were just beginning to burst into bud. A few hazy clouds passed overhead in the still afternoon. Only at dusk did Howard and Vitale reappear, and shortly afterwards Alexei turned up in an old buff-coloured Lada. Vitale and Alexei were clearly not impressed by American hi-technology.

'With Russian wheels many thousands of kilometres and no problems,' Alexei said, shaking his head.

As it was too dark to continue, we pitched camp, Howard and Vitale preparing a stew, while Gilles and I put up the tents. We decided we would share the tent with someone different each week so no one would run the risk of being cooped up every night for months on end with the same person. But as everyone seemed happy enough at the end of the first week, no one saw a necessity to change and so it was for six months.

The tents had not been up for long before a woman appeared and belaboured us angrily for having set them up. That we had been forced to stop, that the land was rough, unenclosed and clearly unused, made no difference. Red in the face, she shouted at us apoplectically. Seventy years after the Revolution the spirit of private property, it appeared, had not been entirely eliminated.

The following morning we set off again, on new wheels, along the Leningrad–Moscow road. Considering that we were leaving a city of five million there was remarkably little traffic. Trucks predominated with no more than a sprinkling of old-fashioned cars, overladen with passengers.

There were shortages of vegetables and fruit in Leningrad, partly because the transportation system was breaking down. In most parts of the world large cities are surrounded by intensively farmed market gardens that provide fresh fruit and vegetables daily to the shops and markets of the city. We saw no market gardens and glasshouses on the outskirts of Leningrad. Good arable land which could have been used to feed a city desperate for vegetables stretched to the horizon with winter wheat.

We stopped at Tosno for lunch. Old rickety wooden houses along the road gave way to apartment blocks of grey concrete. On the ground floor were grimy plate-glass windows, some with posters baldly announcing 'Milk', 'Sausage' and 'Fish'. Apart from the posters, there was nothing in the windows to indicate they were shops. Nor was there anything to tell us that we were in the centre of the town: no market square, no church, no cluster of old houses. We followed Vitale into a *stolovaya*, leaving our bikes outside where we could keep an eye on them. '*Stolovaya*' translates literally as 'dining room' but it is also the name given to the basic cafeterias where most Russians eat at least one meal a day. As the word 'cafeteria' gives a misleadingly favourable impression of these establishments, I prefer to use the Russian word. Over 12,000 kilometres in six months we never saw a man cooking or serving in a *stolovaya*; it is entirely women's work. The interior was spartan, with little decoration, plastic chairs, and a meagre collection of sad-looking pot plants. Spoons and forks of thin, flimsy metal were available; knives, curiously, never. The cooks wore a surly and defiant expression as if anticipating complaints about the food.

Before leaving Britain friends had assured me, with what I detected was a certain hidden relish, that Russian food was comparable to English school food. I doubt that such schools still exist, except perhaps in Dickensian fiction. As time went by I found this association increasingly ironic as it appeared that the enduring image in Russia of life in Britain is derived more than anything from the reading of Dickens at school where, through a clever sleight-of-hand, children are left with the impression of *Nicholas Nickleby*, *Bleak House* and *Little Dorrit* representing more the current conditions of life in Britain, unchanged since Dickens's day, than as the masterpieces of England's greatest social novelist 150 years ago.

We queued up for lunch: *shchi*, a thin, watery cabbage soup, boiled meat and rice, bread and tea. The cashier wore the same uniform as everyone else – a white coat, to symbolise the concept of hygiene. She flicked beads to and fro on a wooden abacus before ringing the individual items into her cash register. It is easy to imagine monks in pre-Reformation England working out tithes and manorial duties on a wooden abacus, but to find them in use in a superpower not long before the year 2000 was a continual shock. The total cost of our meal for four came to four roubles, eighty kopecks – eighty US cents at the official exchange rate and forty at the real. Ten cents per person. At least if we starved it wouldn't be due to lack of money.

It appears that it is only in those parts of the world that have suffered from a surfeit of tourism that the foreigner is taken advantage of. It was only in Moscow that any individual in the Soviet Union tried to over-charge us, and even there only in large hotels that catered for foreigners. In the hundreds of other cities, towns and villages that we passed through over six months, no individual ever tried to overcharge or shortchange us. I choose my words carefully when I say 'no individual', because the Soviet state itself consistently overcharges foreigners for everything as a matter of policy. The official attitude would appear to be based on the principle that if foreigners have hard currency, why not relieve them of it? For a country that officially despises capitalist values there is an astonishing official rapaciousness for hard currency.

Over the next few days we began to cover the ground between Leningrad and Novgorod. The nights were still very cold, the temperature falling well below freezing, and we awoke to find ice covering the tents. Little pockets of snow still lay on the north-facing edge of forests, and in drifts and gullies. We got up as the sun rose, quickly built a wood fire to warm us, and breakfasted on coffee and porridge spiced with dried apricots while the tents dried in the sun.

Cycling through Russian villages we were struck by their uniformity of layout and style of building. Little wood cabins were strung out along the highway facing an identical row on the opposite side, both set back a little distance from the road, with a wooden fence in front, woodstack at the side and vegetable plot behind. Almost without exception they were of a single floor, unpainted and black with age. Many were genuine log cabins made from tree trunks with layers of moss or strips of rag blocking out the draught between one tree trunk and the next. Some of the older ones had sunk a little, with the constant thawing and freezing of the land, so that they listed drunkenly. Virtually every cabin had three windows that faced the road, set within decorative, ornately carved window surrounds and lintels, and rare was the cabin with no red flowering geranium in the window. One specifically Russian feature of these windows was the 'window within a window', a tiny aperture the size of a single pane of glass in a casement which could be opened in winter to allow in a modest current of fresh air. On the newer houses the roofs were of corrugated iron or asbestos but poorer houses were covered by strips of old roofing-felt over wooden tiles and looked far from waterproof.

As log cabins were rarely more than one deep on either side, Russian villages were extraordinarily drawn out, sometimes as long as two kilometres whilst only a hundred metres wide. As a result, there was no feeling of a nucleus, no visible historical or communal focus where the villagers could gather together. Compared to Europe, these Russian villages seemed sadly dispersed. If they had ever had a communal meeting place it looked as if they didn't have one any more.

The Leningrad–Moscow highway was marked with thick double lines on the Soviet road map and we expected it to be one of the most important highways in the country. But it was mostly a single lane in each direction, no wider that a provincial English road. On either side dark forests of dripping pine trees alternated with flat and open agricultural land. By European standards the fields were vast and day after day passed without our seeing anyone at work on the state farms. In contrast the private vegetable plots behind the houses were a hive of activity. All the able-bodied men of normal working age were busy at work on their own plots, planting and sowing to ensure that they had vegetables for the following winter, and buckets of onions and potatoes stood for sale beside the road. We stopped one evening to buy vegetables for our meal from a *babushka* in a bright, floral-patterned dress and orange headscarf. During the war her home had been burnt down four times, she told us, and her husband and one of her sons had been killed.

'But we must be cheerful!' she said with a smile.

Prices were astronomical compared to the state shops. Garlic which cost ten roubles a kilo at the roadside cost two roubles in a state shop. Russians bought privately produced vegetables at high prices either because such vegetables were simply not available in the state shops or because those that were were of such inferior quality.

Prices in Soviet shops, we learnt, are determined without regard to supply or demand and bear no relation to the cost of production. They are set centrally in Moscow by government ministries and apply uniformly throughout the Soviet Union. Also, because of massive subsidies to keep food prices low, when supplies do arrive they are very cheap. Nikolai Ryzhkov, the Prime Minister in 1990, confirmed that part of the Soviet Union's economic problems stemmed from the fact that prices for many goods and services had not altered since the 1930s. Inevitably when deliveries arrive everyone tries to buy as much as they possibly can to take advantage of the cheap supply while it lasts. Who knows when garlic, toothpaste, shirts, writing paper or fur-lined boots will next be seen again? Stampedes and struggles ensue as everyone tries to lay their hands on precious goods. Woe betide anyone who gets in the way! As for the old and frail, they don't stand much of a chance, except with rationed goods; and relations who have to buy on their behalf, as well as for themselves, are naturally doubly determined. The scene is appalling, with adult, even aged, men and women pushing and shoving as if life itself was dependent on their success. Food supplies had deteriorated to such an extent that the latest Soviet joke envisaged customers asking not for a kilo of sausage or sugar but merely for 'a kilo of food'.

Vitale issued us with a small string bag called an *avoshka* (a just-in-case bag) in case we came upon a delivery unexpectedly. He also urged us to join a queue, even if we did not know what it was for.

'Even if you don't want what you buy, we can swap it for something you do.'

One one occasion I saw a woman of seventy carrying away what must have been well over a hundred packets of cigarettes in a plastic bag; on another, a man had just bought two fifty-kilo sacks of onions – enough to last his family for a year; on a third, a man was having difficulty carrying frozen chickens – he had bought more than he could physically cart away. The queues and the stampedes last for a few minutes or a few hours and then, just as suddenly, the supply runs out and the shortage, or 'deficit' as the Russians call it, begins all over again.

For water we were dependent much of the time on village wells ranged along the edge of the road. Only a hundred kilometres from Leningrad, the second biggest city in the USSR, we were lowering buckets for water. To draw water from a well was at first a novelty, but it was completely normal in the villages we passed through. Many houses also had their own wells in a back garden operated by a massive wooden beam fixed on a fulcrum, similar in appearance to a 'nodding donkey'. Villagers collected their water in a metal churn pulled on wheels or in buckets hung at either end of a wooden yoke, such as are portrayed in Regency aquatints of English dairymaids. In many villages wells had been replaced with cast-iron pumps which were still widely used in towns and even such big cities as Irkutsk.

After cycling through wide areas of open ploughed fields, it was incongruous to come across apartment blocks, five floors high, suddenly, in the middle of nowhere. These were the newest villages, their sites determined by bureaucrats in offices 1,000 kilometres away, rather than by any specific local, historical or geographical factors. Shabby and grey, they rose starkly from wasteland sprouting television aerials and washing, their concrete pockmarked and streaked, innumerable cracks pasted over with cement. In such villages and towns there were no public gardens and no flowerbeds. Rusty metal pipes snaked between the blocks raised two feet above the ground on concrete plinths. Where they came to a road they snaked vertically into the air and descended to the ground again. Steam puffed and hissed as it escaped under pressure at the joints. The lagging was punctured and torn and sagged in droops from the pipes or lay fallen on the ground. The loss of heat over one or two kilometres must have been phenomenal.

We arrived at Novgorod mid-afternoon, catching glimpses of red Kremlin walls clinging to a green hillside that sloped steeply to a broad river. Above red crenellations rose the whitewashed walls of the Kremlin churches and their golden domes, radiant and sparkling in the sharp air. Here perhaps, we thought, we might find something of beauty.

Novgorod, one of the oldest Russian towns, sits on a hill above the River Volkhov and low-lying floodplains, and was once known by the title of Lord Novgorod the Great. Situated on an important trading route between the Baltic and the Black Seas, an entrepôt for silks, spices, gold, silver and furs, it thrived from the tenth to the end of the fifteenth centuries, rivalling in power and magnificence the principalities of Suzdal and Moscow. Its power and prestige began to erode after its defeat in 1471 by the combined armies of Ivan III of Moscow and the Tatars and was dealt a final blow in 1570 when Ivan the Terrible is said to have butchered 60,000 Novgorodian citizens to preempt a plan to kill him. By the middle of the seventeenth century the population had fallen from an all-time high of 400,000 to about 2,000, and by the end of the Swedish war of 1627 only 850 people survived.

For the first time since leaving Leningrad we planned to stay in a hotel. There is an Intourist hotel at Novgorod, but we intended to stay in one that catered for Russians.

Our request for rooms at the Volkhov Hotel spelt confusion. The administrator denied categorically that rooms were available and tried to direct us to the Intourist hotel. Vitale patiently explained that we were a special case, telling her about our journey and that we only had roubles which would not be accepted at the Intourist hotel. As she wavered, Vitale played his trump card, pulling out the official document entrusted to him by SovIntersport that authorised our expedition. It was on official headed paper, impressively stamped and signed. It had the desired effect, but as they had never had foreign tourists before the director had to be consulted. By special dispensation we were allowed into the restaurant where we were served with the greatest possible reluctance by another bored and unsmiling waitress. Nothing, no amount of politeness, friendly conversation or smiles on our part could produce a reaction. As there had obviously been unoccupied rooms all along we asked Vitale why we had been told 'no' so categorically at first.

'No one can say "Yes" in this country,' he commented philosophically. '"No" is an automatic reaction. There is a Soviet saying: "Initiative must be punished." This is true, initiative in our country only leads to trouble. But there is another problem; they do not know how much to charge you for the rooms.'

'How about charging us the normal price?'

'There is a normal price, of course, but that is for Russians. They know foreigners must pay more but they do not know how much more. They have to ask.' In the end Vitale paid three roubles while Gilles, Howard and I each paid twenty-one.

'Our introduction to the Communist notion of equality, I guess,' I remarked as Vitale handed over sixty-six roubles, the equivalent of an average week's salary.

'Bandits!' Gilles said. 'If we did the same for Russian visitors to Paris, they would be paying 5,000 francs a night.'

We crossed a deep moat and passed through the thick red-brick walls of the Kremlin. Square brick towers, bull's-blood red, with wooden-tile roofs, punctured the walls at intervals, but within there was a feeling of space and light. The notes of a piano and flute from a music school floated clearly across the grass.

Due to its fabulous wealth and power Novgorod once had a greater concentration of churches than any city in Russia. In the twelfth century there were more than 200 but by the beginning of the twentieth century less than half remained. Today forty remain, but in a poor state. Most have been gutted of their interiors and turned over to other uses.

St Sophia's Cathedral, dating from 1050, was open as a museum, with gaping holes where icons with their frames of chastened gold and silver had been torn from the iconostasis. Upstairs was a gloomy museum of roughly rendered concrete where the icons removed from the church below were exhibited in anodynely, glass cases. The treasure of the cathedral lay outside in two massive sculpted doors reminiscent of Ghiberti's doors of the Baptistery in Florence. They were once the town gates of the ancient Scandinavian capital of Sigtuna and were brought to Novgorod after Sigtuna had been captured in 1187. Made of oak and overlaid with forty-eight plates of sculpted bronze, they depict scenes from the Old and New Testaments, and allegorical and mythological subjects. Of the two other churches within the Kremlin walls, the tiny Church of Andrei Stratilat was locked with a rusty padlock and the Pokrov Church had been gutted and turned into a restaurant.

From the Kremlin there was a view across the River Volkhov to a group of small medieval churches so closely crammed together that they appeared to touch, their delicate gilded and painted domes rising above whitewashed walls. St Nicholas's Cathedral, for many years after the Revolution the only church in Novgorod allowed to conduct services, was open as a museum. The Church of St Michael was open for the sale of postcards, guidebooks and trinkets; the Church of the Assumption had been turned into a warehouse; the Church of St Prokopii had been gutted inside and crudely rendered with concrete; the Church of Zhon Mironosits was securely locked. The Vechevaya Tower, where the popular assembly used to meet to decide town matters, was in a pitiful state. Outside three workers lay dozing in the sunshine against a pile of wooden scaffolding.

Looking upstream, on the banks of the River Volkhov the eye is arrested by the silhouette of a huge Orthodox church that appears to lean out over the river in which it is reflected, imposing and isolated. The Yuriev Monastery is one of the few remaining of the twenty that existed in Novgorod's heyday. The principal church of the monastery is the Cathedral of St George which, externally, is as beautiful as St Sophia's which it was intended to surpass in grandeur but inside it is irredeemably ugly, the original frescoes having been removed in the 1840s and replaced by lifeless murals. The massive bell tower, under which we entered the monastery, was in a state of advanced dilapidation, the stucco long having fallen away to reveal crumbling brickwork. Within the walls were the ruins of the monastery gardens, overgrown and uncared for. Sheep nibbled at the long grass and empty cattle pens were ranged against the monastery wall. Depressed by the atmosphere of neglect and abandonment, we returned to the hotel.

The restaurant of the Volkhov Hotel was virtually full when we descended to eat in the evening. Like most Soviet hotels the doors leading directly from the rooms to the restaurant were kept permanently locked and we went outside to gain access from the street. These doors were also locked from the inside and were guarded by a woman of no mean dimensions, the *dezhurnaya* or duty woman. Relishing her position of authority she discriminated between those waiting outside in the cold, unlocking the doors to let one or two in, shouting vociferously at the others, and slamming and locking the restaurant doors again as soon as the chosen ones had entered. She stood guard, jailer-like, with her large bunch of keys and grim expression.

Vitale tried to get her to unlock the doors so that he could speak to her but she would have none if it. If he had had the bearing or clothes of someone with power or connections the doors would have opened automatically. As he did not and was neither a friend, nor offering a bribe, she kept the doors locked against us. Bending down, Vitale tried shouting through the keyhole but she made it clear she wasn't listening. When she opened the door to let someone out Vitale tried again but without success. After ten minutes of this farce we went off and came back with the hotel administrator who curtly ordered the *dezhurnaya* to let us through.

We were over the first hurdle and now progressed to the second, that of finding a table. Those that make it through to the second round come up against the Soviet *maître d'*, invariably an imperious woman of middle age and a towering beehive hairstyle. She allocates tables and directs the waitresses with total authority. Within the confines of the restaurant she reigns supreme and no one dares cross her. Whether you get a table in the present or at any time in the future depends on your relationship with her. And with only two or three restaurants in a town, it doesn't pay to antagonise.

As in other areas of Soviet life, contacts and bribery in a restaurant are the norm. Bribery takes many forms. It is less likely to be roubles that change hands than products difficult to find, '*defitsit*' goods – scent, tickets for a concert, oranges, or East European products that are valued for their comparatively high quality. Bribes are sometimes given to the *dezhurnaya* to get through the door, to the *maitre d'* for a table and to the waitresses to secure vodka, wine, or better food that is kept tucked away in the kitchen for those prepared to pay.

'With money, anything is possible in this country,' Vitale told us. 'You can buy anything, even a tank.'

As the first foreigners to dine in the Volkhov Hotel a table was found for us immediately, even though others were waiting and the restaurant appeared full. The restaurant band struck up some Soviet rock songs and half the tables emptied while the diners gyrated on the dancefloor to the monotonous beat of such strains as '*Yulia, ya ne znaiu pachemo*' ('Julia, I don't know why') and a Russian variant of the lambada. At the end of the dance everybody returned perspiring to their tables and downed more vodka.

Apart from our weird hostelry in Leningrad, this was the first 'real' hotel we had stayed in, and we were more than content just to sit and watch the scene. Soon we were asked to dance. Howard and Gilles obliged, more out of courtesy than interest; it was easier, however, to accept an invitation than to disengage. Seated again round our table Gilles found the arm of his dancing partner extended, upturned, over his shoulder from the neighbouring table in an invitation to dance again. It not only appeared but stayed there despite every entreaty. Eventually Gilles gave up and turned back to his meal. Completely unabashed, his admirer kept her arm there while we continued our conversation. Whenever Gilles looked up the arm was still hovering there.

'She's not my type,' he commented, concentrating ever more single-mindedly on his chicken – very appropriate, we thought, that the Frenchman should be the first to score such a hit.

Before departure we went to the market to buy supplies. Novgorod market occupies a large concrete warehouse close to the bus station. At the entrance two women, swathed in layers like Egyptian mummies, sold gladioli. The building was three-quarters empty, deserted tables and scales neatly arranged in rows. All that was lacking was the hubbub and cry of market vendors, fruit and vegetables. Such vendors as there were sat in a row, huddled together for company, each of them behind pathetic little piles of wrinkled, spotted apples, the best of which, at five roubles a kilo, were clearly too expensive for most customers. A few men sat with a handful of spring onions and carrots laid out on a table before them, and that was all.

The real crowd was at the back of the hall, gathered round a butcher's block, the only one in operation. A few pieces of meat lay on one side but the queue looked as if it was waiting expectantly for parts of a pig's head that the butcher was trying to split with an axe. The first blow failed, and the second time when he brought both the head and the axe down together with a mighty blow, it split in half with a sickening crack.

We bought a kilo of apples each and stowed them away in our panniers; a few slightly rotten ones Howard tossed away. As we packed I became aware that not a single passer-by failed to notice them lying on the ground. No one stopped to pick them up but that they were noticed at all was enough to make me feel guilty about our wastefulness. Later, if we left anything of worth, I made sure to leave it where it would be found.

We left Novgorod on the Moscow Road. It was early in the morning and mist covered the flooded lowlands. Half-enveloped by mist, anglers stood on the riverbanks or fished from small rowing boats that stood motionless by the still, silver water. Our road, straight as a die, ran through flat fields of turned black earth and forests of silver birch, fir and rowan, the forest floor scattered with white anemones. It was as if a straight line had been drawn with a ruler on a map and the road built accordingly. But with no hills to avoid there was no good reason for the road to deviate left or right. For day after day the road narrowed to a speck on the horizon, which drew no nearer, no matter how many kilometres we covered.

What traffic there was consisted largely of buses and trucks, many of which appeared to be towing or transporting others that had broken down. Garages had no mechanical or repair facilities and when a vehicle broke down it had to be towed back to its home town, which could easily be hundreds of kilometres away. That there was a chronic shortage of consumer goods could be surmised from trucks on the road. Most had loads of timber, heavy machinery, industrial engines, metal and pieces of prefabricated concrete. Rarely were the loads tied down; lumps of concrete and metal bounced around wildly, but the police took no notice. They only appeared to be interested in drivers' papers.

We stopped in villages and towns to look around. No one seemed to notice us. People walked past without so much as a glance at us or the bikes. It made a curious contrast to the Indian sub-continent and Asia where I had bicycled with my brother and sister. There we had been constantly surrounded, almost mobbed, by huge, friendly crowds, curious and eager to talk. In the Soviet Union it was as if people were so used to foreigners that everybody had long lost interest in them. When we entered a village shop people fell silent or talked in hushed voices, as if a headmaster had entered a classroom. With the conversation abruptly curtailed and an unnatural silence reigning, the atmosphere was disconcerting. It was also strange, rarely being able to make eye contact with anybody. At first we shrugged it off but when it became the norm we began to feel peculiarly unwanted. We quizzed Vitale about this reaction, so different from the one we expected.

'The people have many problems in their lives – to find food, to find clothes. We have so many difficulties in our daily lives. All these things take a lot of time, so even if they want to talk they have no time.' There was some truth in what Vitale said but there was more to it than mere lack of time. We felt strongly that, for whatever reason, people did not *want* to talk.

We stopped in a tiny village for lunch, leant the bikes against the *stolovaya* and looked around. The dusty, unmade streets were quiet and deserted apart from a motley collection of dogs, so different the one from the other that it was hard to believe they could belong to the same species. A couple of women could be seen bent double working on their vegetable plots, white kerchiefs peeping above rickety wooden fences. Behind the *stolovaya* was the village church, cream and white, on a small hill. As the door was ajar I looked in. The interior was light, the roof having collapsed, and brick, masonry and fallen timber lay knee deep. Small trees sprouted from the debris. In the cupola and high on the walls the murals were still perfectly clear – Christ, St Philip and St Matthew, and the Virgin Mary.

I rejoined the others in the *stolovaya*. It was bare and uninviting, a hatch communicating with the kitchen. Gilles was taking photographs and the cook, red in the face, was yelling in a rage.

'Stop taking photographs! Photography's prohibited! You've no permission to be here! Get out! Get out!' Vitale tried to calm her down while Gilles put his camera away.

'What are you doing here?' she shouted.

'We've come for lunch,' Vitale replied, promptly.

'You're foreigners,' she continued, shouting. 'You've no right to be here! Where's your group?'

'We're four,' Vitale told her, calmly. 'We're a group of four, and I'm not foreign, I'm Russian.'

'Why aren't you with a group?' she shouted again.

'This is *perestroika*,' Vitale told her. 'You don't have to be in a group any more.' The cook, shaking with anger, subsided in the kitchen. We let her recover, then prevailed upon her to give us food. The shock of having to deal with foreigners had been too much for her. She was out of her depth. 'Maybe she is worried your photographs will be published in a foreign magazine,' Vitale said.

'Is that a problem?'

'Yes, it will land her in trouble.'

'But why?'

'Because it's not a very good restaurant.'

'If we photograph a big modern restaurant, then that's OK?'

'Yes, of course,' he said.

'Eat up and go!' the cook said. She wanted us out of her domain before catastrophe struck. But when we came out the sun was shining, so we stretched out in the grass for a siesta. Opening my left eye by chance I noticed the cook and two young kitchen assistants pressed up against a window watching us.

The intention was to take it slowly from Leningrad to Moscow to get used to the bikes, sort out teething problems and get fit. This stretch – Howard called it 'the blow-out period' – was 800 kilometres long and took us eleven days, an average of seventy-three kilometres a day.

In the late afternoon we would take a small side road and look for a site to camp. It soon became apparent that Vitale had a very different notion of what constituted a good campsite from Howard, Gilles and me. We preferred to camp in the open, or at the edge of a forest, to enjoy the evening sun and sunrise the following morning. But such places as we suggested were greeted with murmurs of disapproval by Vitale, who would plunge off deep into the forest until he found a spot completely hidden, well away from any forest track, where there was absolutely no chance of us being seen or overheard.

Howard, Gilles and I preferred not to be hidden away every evening in unrelieved forest. Having cycled all day with little contact with Russians we were keen to observe Russian village life but Vitale wanted to be well away, hidden, so well hidden that there was no chance of being seen or disturbed. This desire was not prompted by thoughts of trespassing; it was more, I think, an unconscious instinct of survival, or self-preservation, a deepseated need to be safe, beyond the reach of others, whoever they were. Other people spelt interference, intrusion, possibly trouble. Why invite it by camping in sight of a village or where someone might happen to pass along a farm or forest track? For the first few weeks we deferred to Vitale and then slowly broached the idea of camping near villages or even of accepting an invitation to stay should we be invited.

Gradually we became fitter but not before a few painful knee aches, hardly an encouraging sign with 400 kilometres behind us and 11,600 to go. Much of the landscape was dreary, forests of pine emerging from the water-logged swamp to left and right of the road, occasionally relieved by ploughed fields of clayey earth. So monotonous were both villages and landscape that by 27 April, after riding for only a week, Howard's entry for his diary began 'Another mundane day.'

We stopped at midday on the 27th at Valday, which before the Revolution had been famous for the church bells that were cast at its foundries. As it was warm, we carried our food out of the dreary *stolovaya* and ate in the sunshine in the square. Workers were erecting trestle tables and benches for the forthcoming May Day celebrations and people passed through the square but no one greeted us or came up to talk or look at the bikes. We went to investigate the church, the only building of any interest, and found fire engines parked in the nave.

Most Russian villages have at least two shops, one marked '*Produkti*' for food, the other bluntly marked '*Magasin*' or 'Shop', both so forlorn that, had one seen them in Europe, one would have assumed that they were abandoned. Built of grey bricks with a corrugated iron roof, they had a heavy metal door closed with an iron bar and padlock; the windows were empty, grey with dust, and spattered with cement and paint. Inside they were rudimentary and full of the shoddiest collection of goods imaginable. Anything of the least use or value had been bought up, while the quantity of unsaleable items grew over the years. There was no reason why these shops should have been clean or appealing. No entrepreneurs were competing for custom and prices were the same everywhere. There was but one place to go.

There was very little in the shops for us to buy other than bread, tinned fish and biscuits. Generally there was one type of biscuit available, which came loose in a large cardboard box behind the counter. (After a while we learnt that anything fresh or decent was kept out of sight behind the counter, reserved for friends and relations.) Round and dabbed on top with a little icing sugar these biscuits were as hard as stone and, if thrown, would have broken the dirty shop windows. The boxes from which they appeared had neither a date of manufacture nor a sell-by date – an alien concept, which meant no one had good reason to be disappointed.

Very quickly these biscuits became known as 'Leningrad bricks', but at that time we were not to know that they would be available, identical in size, shape and price, in a thousand village shops from Leningrad to the shores of the Pacific. I kept one of my very first Leningrad bricks and have it still, together with one bought six months later as I was about to leave. Not only are they indistinguishable but both are as 'fresh' as the day they were bought.

We expected to be stopped by the police on the road and asked for passports and documents, but between Leningrad and Moscow we were not asked for them once. In fact we were not asked for them until we were in the Urals, 2,500 kilometres from our starting point. We were curious to ascertain if the police at the roadside police posts knew about our progress and scrutinised their faces carefully as we approached, but they seemed so taken aback to see us go past that we felt this could not be the case. On rare occasions when we asked them for directions they sometimes asked where we were from and where we were going but more, we felt, out of curiosity than duty.

Late afternoon we arrived in Torzhok. As we cycled into town we waved to two girls on the bus in front of us and a few minutes later found them at the side of the road. Neither could speak a word of English but they insisted on giving us old medals with a portrait of Stalin.

With its sand-coloured town buildings and gardens falling down to the river and numerous churches, Torzhok had some character. In the centre next to the river was a rough hotel, the only one in town.

'Mafia,' Vitale told us, nodding at several suspicious-looking men lounging outside. 'We will have to be very careful with our things.'

Howard and I explored the far side of the town. On the hill opposite were two huge neo-classical churches, one dilapidated, the other seemingly restored. Our entrance was blocked by women in blue and purple uniform with epaulettes marked by crossed rifles. We explained in faltering Russian that we wanted to see the church.

'*Nyet!*' one said. We explained we were tourists. Just for ten minutes? five? Perhaps they could escort us themselves?

'*Nyet!* It is not a church.'

'What is it?'

'A meat factory. You still want to see inside?'

'Yes.'

'Only permissible with factory pass!' No doubt if we had slipped them a bottle of vodka we would have got in; we didn't and we got no further.

Above these churches was a monastery which we approached beneath a collapsing wall. Round the back were metal doors, through which we slipped, unnoticed. Inside was a scene of devastation. A massive mustard-coloured, neo-classical church with vast columned pediments sat amongst a pile of bulldozed earth and rubbish. Close by was another huge church, covered with wooden scaffolding that looked as though it had been in place for decades. It was a total ruin; floors, ceilings, stucco and windows had all collapsed, leaving only piles of rubble. Pigeons flew out in panic. It was no more than a brick shell.

The monastery living quarters were also in a pitiful state. In the corner of the monastery, forming a corner in the wall, was a tower that had been restored, its apricot walls picked out with lines in white, a green copper roof supporting a golden spire. The last church was in the most exuberant neo-classical style, once painted a pale creamy green and white, rising in tier after tier of rusticated stonework, columned façade, pediment, belltower and circular columns to an elegant, gilded spire surmounted by a cross. Peeling and neglected, with debris bulldozed up against the walls and surrounded by dilapidation, it looked like a wedding cake thrown out for the dustmen. Two bulldozers were parked beside it. We walked away, passing two little girls skipping outside the monastery walls. It was difficult to believe that this monastery which had evidently once been so beautiful could lie in virtual ruins. What madness could have prompted such wanton destruction?

We climbed up to a less impressive church at the top of a nearby hill behind bright blue railings, expecting further desolation. In fact, it was open and a service was in progress, the dark interior lit up by the gold light of innumerable candles.

The church was neither particularly old nor beautiful, and the nineteenth-century icons of no distinction, yet there was a great feeling of beauty and calm; coming from the devastated monastery it was a revelation to see a church being used for the purpose for which it was intended.

Entering a working Russian Orthodox Church for the first time, it was impossible not to be struck by the magnificence, the colour and richness of decoration. The icons breathed back gold and silver, shimmering and reflecting the dancing light of countless candles. The astonishing multiplicity of icons, the sheer quantity of chastened gold and silver icon frames, the almost cave-like interior illuminated by dozens of flickering flames was overwhelming. I hardly knew where to look, but was inevitably drawn to the wall of icons, the iconostasis, that separated the chancery from the body of the church, and to the priest. Clad in vestments of gold and silver thread, embroidered and decorated by hand in tiny and intricate patterns, his robes shone and dazzled in the candlelight. Long, lanky black hair, parted in the middle, fell onto the golden vestment. His eyes were large and sad, his face intensely pale, drawn and thin with long lips and prominent cheekbones. I watched him with fascination, almost mesmerised.

In Europe some priests elect to discard their religious habits in an attempt to convince a sceptical public that they too are normal; not so in the USSR, where the Church has suffered and priests have been so reviled. Visually, at least, it looked as though there had been no attempt to make the Church more amenable to the people, no compromise with modernity.

I found it difficult to see any point of relation between this man and the bleak Soviet world outside. His sad, ascetic features were so different from those of the plump, podgy and expressionless faces we had seen so far. Not only the priest but the whole interior of the church, brilliant with decorated metalwork, icons and candelabras, seemed to have no meeting point with the drab and dreary world outside, the scruffy grey apartment blocks, the forlorn streets, the endless cement and concrete, chipped and streaked. We had entered another world.

There were no seats or pews, and the congregation of old women and girls stood in a crowd before the priest, mournfully chanting in response to his intonations. Towards the back women prayed in front of darkened icons, murmuring quietly, lighting candles and crossing themselves repeatedly. Spellbound though we were, the continual intonation of the priest, the murmured responses, the smell of burning candles and incense, the darkened interior, the overwhelming mass of intricate detail and Byzantine decoration suddenly made me feel claustrophobic. We went back out into the fresh air.

As we walked back down the steep hill we heard a horrendous scree-ching sound and a car careered past us out of control. We jumped back out of the road and watched it head down towards the bridge, zigzagging across the road. It was badly dented, its headlamps and bonnet smashed in. Black smoke poured from the front tyre on our side where, bent at a crazy forty-five-degree angle, it rubbed against the chassis. We waited in suspense for the car to crash, half-expecting it to mount the pavement and collide with a house or tree. Somehow it made it to the bottom of the hill in a cloud of smoke and then, to our astonishment, not only crossed the bridge but began to climb the steep hill opposite. Eventually it dis-appeared from sight, screeching frantically, leaving a trail of smoke and an acrid smell of burning rubber.

Howard and I burst out laughing. Far from being out of control, it was merely a workable car in need of a little maintenance and patch-up work being driven home.

We rejoined Gilles and Vitale in the main square that was being tidied up and quickly repainted in time for the May Day celebrations. Red flags hung from balconies and walls to give a token festive feel. Outside the townhall hung portraits of Lenin, looking decidedly old-fashioned in Edwardian wing collar and tie, flanked by Engels and Marx with the air of successful Victorian businessmen. A large droopy banner proclaimed the universal solidarity of workers.

Torzhok, with a population of 150,000, had but one restaurant. It was Friday night and every table was full, that is to say that eighty people had managed to secure a place. As for the other 149,900-odd for whom there was no room, it was as well that they had decided to spend Friday night at home. At 7.00 pm we received the encouraging news that beer had arrived; at eight, when we went to the restaurant, it had long since gone. The rule in the Soviet Union seemed to be 'jam tomorrow and jam yesterday – but never jam today'. However, there seemed to be plenty of vodka and champagne around and most tables looked the worse for wear. Over a bottle of sweet Russian champagne, Vitale asked me if I knew a Russian story about English trade unionists.

'In the 1930s, a delegation of English trade unionists went to the big, the *famous* Soviet Union. They had a meeting with Stalin. They said how wonderful Soviet factories were and industrial production. Stalin was very friendly to them and the English trade unionists praised him and his country – so much production, such big factories and all for the workers! Then they noticed that on the table in front of them was a huge gold nugget, lying there, unguarded. They couldn't believe their eyes but it was real gold. They said to Stalin, "In our country you could not leave a gold nugget like that on the table or it would be stolen. A nugget of such value would be behind seven locks but here it is just lying loose on the table." "Ah!" said Stalin. "But in this country the wealth lies in people!"'

Later we heard another story about Stalin, this one true. The Soviet newspaper, *Robochaya Tribuna*, revealed that Stalin employed a 'double' who regularly impersonated him from the 1930s until his death in 1953. At Stalin's orders, the NKVD secret police were told to find a lookalike because of Stalin's obsessive fear of assassination and turned up a Jewish bookkeeper from the Ukraine called Yevsei Lubitsky. A team of doctors performed plastic surgery on him at a *dacha* outside Moscow to heighten the resemblance and then the doctors as well as Lubitsky's relatives were murdered. Lubitsky was himself jailed in a 1952 purge and died a short while after, having been released on Stalin's death.

When the band began to play , execrably, we left. It was depressing that this single dreary restaurant was all that Torzhok could offer its inhabitants on a Friday night. And although Torzhok may sound dismal, for us, after days and days of dilapidated wooden villages, each one virtually identical, and of being shunned, it was something of a highpoint. The town was tolerably attractive, at least in the centre; we had come across a church that was not in ruins; and two young people had actually come up and spoken to us. That evening Howard wrote in his journal: 'Torzhok gave us hope . . . the trip could be interesting after all. There has been nothing up to this point.'

The next morning there were clear blue skies. We were cycling along towards Kalinin, close together, Howard and Vitale ahead, Gilles and I behind in conversation, when a motorcycle combination began to overtake us. As it drew level the rider slowed down and swerved in, the sidecar wheel nudging Howard's front pannier. There was nothing Howard could do to extricate himself without losing his balance and the sidecar, instead of pulling away, edged further in and sent Howard flying to the ground. We were cycling at a fair pace and he hit the ground hard, damaging the bike, cutting his arm and leg and scraping off a large patch of skin. We helped Howard, cursing and swearing at the disappearing motorcycle combination, to his feet. There was no need for stitches but we pulled out the medical kit and bandaged Howard up as best we could, before looking at his bike. The panniers had been damaged but remarkably the front wheel was still true and the forks unbent. All in all, we reckoned, Howard had escaped lightly. We got him back on his bike, like Don Quixote on the plain of Montiel, and set off again.

'I think they were drunk,' Vitale told us. 'It's Saturday, the beginning of the May Day holiday, so they start to drink early in the morning.'

We came across the motorcycle combination and the three occupants further on at the side of the road. They appeared to be having problems with the engine and the driver was tinkering away with a spanner. All three were in their mid-twenties, oafish and extremely drunk. There was no question of them not knowing what they had done but they said nothing. Vitale harangued them fiercely, after which they looked sheepish and glum but remained silent. We were sorely tempted to tip the motorcycle into the ditch but to invite complications with the police at such an early stage seemed unwise. Ten minutes later one of them caught up with us and apologised. It had been unintentional, he assured us; his friend was drunk, that was all.

Over the next few months as we wound our way across central Russia we lost track of days of the week, but Saturdays and Sundays could always be identified by the number of drunken people around and on these days we were particularly wary of traffic. Perhaps the warning of trauma from the doctor at the hospital of Tropical Medicine and Hygiene was justified after all.

As we cycled along I talked with Vitale about the devasted monastery we had visited and the ruined churches that we had passed in larger villages.

'I have seen many devastated churches,' he said, 'in various stages of desolation, some miraculously intact and others transformed into warehouses, jails, clubs, cafés and military factories. From their childhood everybody knows that the Bureau of Religious Affairs is a department of the KGB. This is the only form of religion allowed by our state. And those people who dared to believe "on their own", that is without KGB consent, or unite in religious communities, were considered rebels, called "sectarians", and they quickly found themselves in concentration camps and jails. So plenty of them spent all their lives in confinement. Nowadays, it is said that a lot of these prisoners are being released but whether all of them are, I don't know. As for me, I never had a chance to learn much about religion. We were never taught it at school or by our parents, so we don't understand it.

'Do you ever go to church?'

'I have been a few times. I like to watch and to listen to the liturgy but I don't understand the ritual and can't get the words right.'

We cycled into Kalinin, a large city, the streets lined with dozens of brilliant red flags, splashing bright daubs of colour over the buildings. We approached the statue of Lenin, at the foot of which lay baskets of wilted flowers, dismounted and talked to two girls nearby who joined us for coffee.

We asked Helen, a university student, why so few young people appeared to be interested in meeting us.

'People here are not used to talking to foreigners,' she said, 'but the atmosphere in our country is better now. Soon the name of our city will be changed back to its old name, Tver. People are fed up with the old ways. The atmosphere is changing all the time; it began with Gorbachev four years ago but even in the last two years it has become better. Even two years ago you could have problems if you talked to foreigners. I know this because I have friends who were studying in the university at that time. Five years ago any conversation with a foreigner had to be reported directly to the KGB. And before that it was worse. Now it is possible for me to talk to foreigners without looking over my shoulder, to go abroad and study English at a foreign university. Five years ago that would have been impossible. Yes . . . now it is much more open . . . I think you can feel it, can't you?' She smiled and looked around her. 'When you leave the Moscow–Leningrad road I think things will be better – people will be more friendly and hospitable. I hope so.' We showed them our map and talked about our route and journey. 'Your trip is wonderful,' Helen said. 'This is something majestic!'

4
MAY DAY

AFTER A WHILE we began to establish a kind of daily routine. We emerged from the tents early in the morning and, stamping the ground with cold, gathered wood and built a fire. It was intensely invigorating to rise early, our breath caught in the cold air, and begin the day round a fire, watching the bright flames jump up from the frosted ground. Overnight our water bottles froze and our morning wash, in a nearby stream, was cold and brief.

The moment the first rays of sun touched our camp we turned the fly-sheets inside out and draped them over a branch to dry. We packed our panniers, filtered well or river water with Katadyn ceramic water-filters, and gathered round the fire for a breakfast of coffee and porridge. Once bowls and cooking pot had been washed in a stream of freezing water, the tents folded and stowed, and panniers and sleeping bags attached to the bikes, we were ready to leave. The final check of the campsite to ensure nothing had been overlooked became known as '*inspection générale*', whether due to a Gallic propensity to leave things behind or, on the contrary, to Gallic thoroughness, I cannot say.

As we set off we reset our kilometre gauges that recorded our daily and total distance. When possible we cycled side by side and talked, but from Leningrad to Moscow the road was generally too narrow and busy to do so. Mid-morning we stopped for a break of apples, bread and tinned fish, or Leningrad bricks, depending on what we could find.

At one such break we watched people at work building *dacha*s, the country cottages that Soviet town and city dwellers desire so desperately, both as an escape from the heat and pollution of the city in summer, and as a base from which to grow vegetables. We were surprised to learn that almost everyone who lived in a town appeared to have a *dacha* but the term covered everything from luxurious houses owned by the *nomenklatura* to small cabins no larger or more solid than a garden shed. Not only was the land crucial to grow supplies of vegetables for winter but it also appeared to fulfil a deep-seated need for millions of city dwellers who were only two generations removed from life on the land.

'Everyone has time for their *dacha*,' Vitale said. 'They just leave a jacket on the back of their chair at work. No one minds because everyone takes their turn. It's a kind of unofficial holiday.'

Between us and the *dacha*s the large field of a collective farm was being ploughed by a tractor which was being driven by two men – one to hold the steering wheel, the other to accelerate and apply the brakes? A man working on the *dacha*s waved at them to stop and, after a short conversation, accompanied by animated gesticulation, the tractor was driven over to a *dacha* plot which it proceeded to plough. Others, impressed by the speed at which their neighbour's plot had been ploughed, prevailed on the drivers to do the same for them. No doubt a few bottles of vodka changed hands and everyone left happy at the end of the day.

That the state farm remained unploughed was of little consequence. No one, it appeared, cared what happened on the collective farms, least of all those working on them, who are not held accountable for their work. Whether it ever occurred to them that the chronic shortages of food might, in minute part, be due to their own action or inaction, it was impossible to ascertain.

Most of the collective and state farms that we passed had chaotic collections of rusty and aging farm equipment, left out in the open air. Discarded tractor parts, rusting sheds and weathered buildings created a powerful impression of gloom and neglect. Along the muddy ruts that passed for roads, groups of men could be seen tinkering with old combines and tractors or standing about smoking, some of them red-eyed and sullen from the previous night's drinking.

'Soviet farm-workers are used to being told, "It's time to go and plough, time to harvest, time to use the rakes",' Vitale said. 'And if nothing grows it's not their responsibility.'

Because of the collectivisation of agriculture in the 1930s, in which millions perished, Soviet agriculture is a disaster story. Agriculture employs nineteen per cent of the Soviet workforce, and yet even in a good crop year the Soviet Union is compelled to import millions of tons of food, not merely grain but also meat, fruit, vegetables, sugar and other staples. The figures for grain production between 1981 and 1986 were so bad that they were simply suppressed. Even with massive injections of machinery, fertiliser and investment the USSR still lags far behind other developed countries in its labour efficiency, yields and livestock productivity. Rural social conditions are a major disincentive for people remaining on the land. Rural housing is poor, death rates are twenty per cent and infant-mortality rates fifty per cent higher than in the towns.

'No one wants to work on the land,' Vitale said. 'They have no incentive, no reason to work. Wages are low, only a hundred roubles a month and there is nothing for them to do, no facilities, even less than in the towns. Alcohol is all they are interested in.'

We stopped for lunch at a *stolovaya*. A meal in one of these places usually began with a thin, watery cabbage or beetroot soup, served with a dollop of *smetana* or sour cream, followed by potatoes, macaroni or rice with either meat *kutlets* or a meat stew. Boiled potatoes were difficult to spoil but rice was overcooked and macaroni congealed into a lump that had to be carved with a knife from a massive saucepan. Meat *kutlets*, which sometimes went under the misnomer of 'steak', consisted of a ground-up mixture of meat, fat and bread, with the latter predominating; they were normally fried and soaked in fat, the *stolovaya* kitchens being bathed in a haze of blue smoke. Not infrequently pieces of ground bone were the sole but reassuring indication that meat had actually been an ingredient. Due to their high bread content, these *kutlets* soon became known as 'breadburgers' and formed our staple diet for the next five months. Vitale's assurance that dog meat was sometimes added to make them go further did little to increase our appetite. But we saw no reason to doubt him.

Instead of 'breadburgers', what could loosely be called meat 'stew', a concoction of poor, fatty and gristly meat or a dish that consisted of unadulterated fried pork fat, was served with a spoonful of gravy. These culinary highlights were complimented by *chebouryeky* – lumps of dough with a scrap of onion and meat inside that were deep-fried. They came in two shapes and sizes, and became known, respectively, as 'greaseballs' and 'greaseburgers'. Famous Russian and Ukrainian dishes like 'Beef Stroganov' and 'Chicken Kiev' we never saw in 12,000 kilometres from Leningrad to the Pacific.

Cooked vegetables, other than potatoes, to accompany these dishes were rare. In *stolovaya*s we never came across cooked green vegetables or even root vegetables, which one might expect in Russia. Salads, as we knew them, were unheard of. For the first three months the only salad we encountered was a tiny plate of sliced cucumber with a spoonful of sour cream. In the summer, as they became available, tomato and cabbage 'salads' were to be found in the *stolovaya*s but all they consisted of was a single sliced tomato or a little sliced cabbage – with sour cream. Lettuce, endives, parsley, olives, celery, watercress and spring onions we never saw once in a *stolovaya*.

One thing that the Russians still know how to cook well is bread. Wholemeal brown and semi-brown bread, identical in shape, size and price, was available all the way from Leningrad to Vladivostock. At twenty and thirty kopecks a loaf (£0.008 to £0.012), bread is cheap, even for Soviet citizens. When fresh, it is exceedingly good but it gets hard quickly. In *stolovaya*s, as in restaurants and homes, bread was always cut into half-slices, to encourage people to take no more than they were likely to eat. The price was a kopeck a half-slice, 0.0016 of a US dollar or one tenth of a penny.

Of course there is no such thing as a Soviet diet, the Soviet Union being far too large and diverse to subscribe to one. The Southern Asian republics, Georgia, the Ukraine and other areas each have their culinary specialities. For most of our journey, however, we were in the Russian Republic and were subject to the 'Russian' diet: high in carbohydrates and fats, low in proteins, minerals and vitamins. *Sala*, a speciality eaten with great relish, consists of nothing more than pure lard or raw, salted pork fat. We were often offered it with bread and gherkins, accompanied by vodka or, as the main meal of the day, fried. Good quality meat was unobtainable in restaurants, *stolovaya*s or shops, the best being reserved for the *nomenklatura*, sold illegally, reserved for family and friends or stolen from the *stolovaya* kitchens by the cooks.

With such vast rivers we expected at least to find fresh fish in the Soviet Union but not once in our journey did we either come across a fish market or a fishmonger. Occasionally in a general store we saw a few trays of sad-looking frozen fish being sold off, so fossil-like that they could have been trapped in permafrost since the Ice Age. On the rare occasions when fish was available Vitale counselled us to avoid it altogether on the grounds that the rivers were usually polluted. Russians appeared to adore fishing and fishermen could be seen any hour of the day or week out on the riverbanks or floating downstream in boats with their rods. When we decided in Siberia to buy a fishing-rod to try and land some fish ourselves, we found that fishing-rods, hooks, bait and line were totally unobtainable.

For protein Russians depend mainly on eggs, milk and bread, as meat, fish and cheese were scarce, and nuts and pulses virtually non-existent. In six months we found cheese for sale only half a dozen times. On three of these occasions shop assistants refused to sell it to us, as it was reserved for war veterans and pregnant women.

The Russian diet is unbalanced most of all in vitamins and minerals. Most of the green vegetables that one takes for granted in an English greengrocer we never saw for sale in six months. In cities the choice was better, although many people could not afford the produce in the private markets. In June 1990 a kilo of tomatoes cost five roubles and of peaches seven, at a time when the average pension was seventy roubles a month and the average student grant fifty a month. The supply, quality and choice of fruit was extremely limited except in summer and autumn. In six months we saw oranges, though not for sale, on three occasions, a single banana once in a Moscow apartment, and lemons, limes and grapefruit never, although in the autumn melons, apples, grapes, peaches, plums and pears were available in the markets of the large cities of Siberia. To compensate for the scarcity of fresh vegetables in winter and spring, Russians pickle and bottle as much as possible, collecting mushrooms and wild berries in the forests.

Our impressions of Russian food were gained primarily from meals served in *stolovaya*s and restaurants but we were as dependent as the Russians on what food we could find in the shops when we were camping. The poor quality of food was the subject of much complaint. The Soviet newspaper, *Literaturnaya gazeta*, tried a range of sausages on thirty cats and found that twenty-four refused of the varieties they were offered, and five more refused most of them.

Naturally we ate better in private homes than we did in *stolovaya*s, but even in the best restaurants of the largest cities the quality of food is shocking, so much so that people go to a restaurant less to eat than to get drunk or to celebrate a birthday or graduation. Peasants who have their own vegetable plot, chickens and often a cow, are able to have a more varied and healthy diet than urban dwellers. The health minister, Yevgenii Chazov, told the 19th Party Congress in 1988 that the USSR had sunk to the thirty-second place in the world in terms of life expectancy, an important contributing factor being an inadequate and unbalanced diet. This diet must be primarily responsible for one overriding impression of our first month in the Soviet Union: the sheer unhealthiness of people – flabby, white, pasty-faced.

Forty kilometres from Moscow we stopped for the night and set up camp deep in a pine forest. The following day we planned to rise early and cycle straight into Moscow to witness the May Day celebrations in Red Square. It was a moonless night and we sat round a blazing fire, flames leaping up into the pitch black, tents and figures dwarfed by huge pine trees. Apart from the crackle and spit of the fire, it was quiet and peaceful.

'You remember Rust?' Vitale said. 'The German who landed his plane in Red Square?' This was the story of the nineteen-year-old German who had piloted his own plane, undetected over a 1000 kilometres of Soviet territory, to land outside the Kremlin. 'Everybody was very amused by him. We are always told what a strong and mighty country we have; how we must be prepared to defend the Motherland. And then this boy lands his plane in Red Square. How we laughed!'

'Didn't one or two generals lose their job as a result?' I asked Vitale.

'More than twenty, I think,' he said. 'It was very bad for military morale.'

'Have you done your military service?'

'Of course. Everyone must do it. It's two years, two long years and you learn nothing. I was lucky, I went to Hungary. I was a driver in the army, so when I left they said, "What can you do?" and I said, "I can drive." So I became a driver. I didn't want to. My father was a driver and I wanted to do something else, something better, but you know it is not easy to do what you want in this country.'

'What did you think of Hungary?'

'For me it was a big shock. I could not believe it. When I arrived and saw the shops in Budapest so full of food and clothes, I cried. How can it be possible that people can have so much, so many things? I asked myself. I had never believed it, though I had heard that things were better there. You never believe these things until you see with your own eyes. You know that everybody in the Soviet Union wants to buy East European goods if they can. They are always better quality than our own.' I was struck by Vitale's impression, for when I had visited Hungary in 1986 my own had been almost the reverse of his.

'Did you make friends with any Hungarians of your own age?'

'No, we didn't meet Hungarians much. We lived a life apart in the barracks and had little chance to meet them . . . and it was not encouraged. They were not very friendly towards us; you know why, I think.' We retired to our tents after sitting meditatively around the embers of the fire.

To reach the Kremlin we had to traverse the outlying suburbs of the city, past plains of identical apartment blocks, built from prefabricated slabs, grey and monolithic. May Day was a national holiday and the streets of Moscow were deserted, apart from densely packed buses and cars ferrying people to their *dacha*s outside Moscow. As we cycled in, Vitale pointed out a line of massive metal spikes in the shape of tank traps twenty kilometres from the centre of the city. They marked the limit of the

German advance on Moscow in the Second World War, from which point in 1941 German troops could see the suburbs of Moscow in the distance. It is a powerful reminder of how close the Soviet army came to losing the city. Gargantuan red metal letters confirmed our arrival in Moscow, a 'Hero City of the Great Patriotic War'.

As we drew near to the centre we came across thousands of policemen in grey raincoats lining the streets and caught up with the tail end of a large body of demonstrators. Our plan had been to cycle directly to Red Square to witness the May Day celebrations. We were therefore surprised when Vitale began to cycle in a direction that we felt instinctively must be away from the centre. We called him to a halt.

'Where are we going?' we asked.

'To the Sport Hotel,' Vitale replied.

'But didn't we agree to go to Red Square to see the parade and celebrations.'

'It's not possible for us,' Vitale said. 'There will be police, problems, difficulties. It's better to go to the hotel; you can come back in the afternoon if you want.'

'No,' Gilles said. 'We're going now. If we come back later, it will all be over.'

'It's not good,' Vitale told us, shaking his head. 'There will be many people, maybe problems and it's very boring.'

'But isn't this the first year that opposition groups have been allowed to take part?'

Vitale was reluctant to head for Red Square and looked unhappy when we insisted.

'There will be problems,' he forecast glumly, as Gilles, Howard and I turned round and made our way back to Gorky Street.

May Day celebrations in Red Square were one of the highlights of the Communist calendar and had traditionally been an opportunity for the Soviet Union to display its military might, with vast parades of tanks, rockets and armed vehicles. Thousands of gymnasts usually performed before the Soviet leadership gathered on top of the Lenin Mausoleum, shouting up to them, 'Glory to the Communist Party of the Soviet Union! Glory! Glory! Glory!' Portraits of Marx, Engels and Lenin were held aloft and carried through Red Square, in the way that icons were once paraded in religious processions of previous centuries.

1990, however, promised to be different. In keeping with the Soviet Union's rapprochement with the West, the withdrawal of Soviet troops from Eastern Europe, and the arms agreements concluded with the USA, the Soviet leadership had ruled that there was to be no military parade whatsoever. Nor was there to be the usual march-past of gymnasts, only the official parade organised by the trade unions. Even more astonishing in its departure from tradition was that permission had been given for opposition groups, ranging from social democrats and liberals to Christians, nationalists and anarchists, to march after the official parade. It was the first time since the Revolution that opposition groups had been allowed to take part in what had previously been the single most symbolic celebration of Communist power and achievement.

Dismounted, we pushed our bikes past a police cordon that was blocking half the road and found ourselves caught up in the flow of opposition groups, the official parade having already reached Red Square. People around us carried the yellow, green and red flags of Lithuania and hand-written placards demanding independence: 'Hands off Lithuania', 'Solidarity with Lithuania', 'Freedom for Lithuania', 'Shame on you. Stop the blockade' – a reference to the economic blockade that the USSR had imposed on Lithuania two weeks earlier following its declaration of independence. Thousands of police lined Gorky Street, and blocked access from sidestreets all the way to Red Square. Swept up by the crowd we advanced towards Red Square down Gorky Street and spoke briefly to a Lithuanian group.

'Most people here are Lithuanians,' one man said. 'But some of us are Russian. We're marching in solidarity with them as we believe Lithuania should have its independence back. The Soviet Union has no right to rule because of a secret pact between two dictators.' This was a surprise, finding Russians supporting the Lithuanian demand for independence. 'Perhaps thirty per cent of Russians in Moscow are in favour of giving Lithuania its independence but in the countryside many fewer.'

I peeled away from the group to take some photographs and, as the group swept by, a policeman put his hand on my arm and pulled me away to the side. He refused to let me go any further. I remonstrated fiercely but made little headway. Neither Howard, Gilles nor Vitale had noticed what had happened and very soon were lost to sight in the advancing crowds. In garbled Russian I tried to explain that I had to rejoin my friends, that I had never been to Moscow before, had no idea where I was, nor how or where I was going to meet them again – pleas that cut no ice. When I tried to set off, he grabbed me by the arm and steered me again in to the side. With little command of Russian, I felt powerless and vulnerable. If I was carted off in a police van, how would anyone know what had happened to me? Eventually we managed to come to a compromise and I was allowed to proceed down various deserted backstreets from where I tried to work my way back to Gorky Street, closer to Red Square. Every sidestreet was blocked with police but eventually I managed to slip through trying to look as nonchalant as possible and expecting every moment to be seized again.

Eventually, quite by chance, I met the others, their progress barred by metal barriers and police cordons. We were next to the central post office, draped with massive red flags and banners and a vast portrait of Lenin. Down the sidestreets hundreds of immaculate military trucks were parked bumper to bumper, full of security police in bottle-green uniforms. Gilles, Howard and I, determined to press on to Red Square, left our bikes with Vitale who was only too happy not to go any further, and proceeded on foot.

Very quickly a bottleneck built up of people who wanted to continue to Red Square, some arguing heatedly with the police to let them through but to no avail. However, we had a remarkable view of the proceedings before us, standing as we were at the top of a slight rise. Straight ahead stood the large, squat Historical Museum, a purple brick building in Russo-Victorian style, on which hung a massive portrait, covering three floors, of a smiling Lenin, one hand in pocket and the other giving a friendly wave, as if he was off to the races. To the right of the museum could be glimpsed the vertical Kremlin walls, the square red bulk of the Arsenal and the bright green tiled roof of the Nikolsky Tower, while to the left lay the yellow and green twirling dome of St Basil's Cathedral.

The fantastical architectural shapes and bright, almost garish, colours were extraordinary to a Western eye but the parade and demonstration were remarkable by Russian standards. From the bottom of Gorky Street a vast throng of people snaked across the huge open space of the Fiftieth Anniversary of the October Revolution Square, penned in on either side by a human chain of thousands of soldiers, behind which stood a further chain of police. Long before the tail of the huge parade had snaked into Red Square to the left of the Historical Museum, the first part had already exited, still between an avenue of soldiers, to the right. The unofficial nature of the procession, the presence of thousands of troops and the infectious sense of expectation gave rise to a heady and excited atmosphere. There was no sense of danger or fear but there was a certain tension in the air, a mixture of exuberance, expectation and uncertainty, as if everybody was conscious that they were treading new and unknown ground. The political nature of the parade was lightened by a genuinely festive feel, many people carrying gaily coloured balloons and placards. Instead of traditional stirring military music and patriotic songs usually played on such occasions, popular music filled the air.

A Christian group passed holding aloft a life-size crucifix, followed by

Latvians carrying flags of cherry red and white, Estonians with ones of blue, black and white. Instead of the monolithic and predictable pre-arranged parade of soldiers and gymnasts here were real people, individuals taking their grievances to the doors of power, voting with their feet. It was a heartening sight, especially after two initial weeks in which we had encountered little but political lethargy.

Eventually we were allowed through the barriers and Howard, Gilles and I made our way towards the Kremlin. The police had reopened Revolution Square to traffic and we were compelled to descend into Marx Prospect Metro station to take the subterranean passageway which, we were unnerved to find, was crammed with soldiers standing with their rifles at the ready. Their presence underground brought home vividly just how wafer-thin the new liberty on the street above really was, and how quickly it could be broken if it overstepped some invisible line. In contrast to the excited and good-natured feel on the streets, the hidden but waiting soldiers struck a chill.

Entry into Red Square itself was prevented by three cordons, of police in grey uniform, soldiers in green, and a paramilitary force in bluey-green. A crowd stood before the cordons, urging the police and soldiers to let them through. One short, well-dressed man, red in the face, was telling them they were a disgrace to the Soviet Union.

'So much for *glasnost*,' he shouted. 'May Day is our holiday, the people's holiday and you prevent us from going to Red Square. Why? What right have you? Why don't you let us through?' he demanded, addressing the officer in charge.

'Our orders are for no more people to enter the Square,' he replied.

'It's May Day,' he continued, passionately appealing to the crowd around him. 'Our holiday! Our country! Our Red Square! We have the right to enter.'

'They're clearing up now,' the officer told him.

'You're being deceived,' a plump, middle-aged woman shouted at the officer, waving her finger. 'That's not true! You can see that yourself! Why do you let yourself be deceived?' As we watched, thousands of soldiers lining the route into Red Square reformed and moved off with military precision, giving the impression that the timing and flow of the parade had been brilliantly managed to ensure that it was kept carefully under control.

'You will be allowed in at four o'clock,' the officer told the short, dapper man who had become spokesman for the group.

'That's wonderful,' he replied bitterly. 'Allowed in when it's all over and everyone has gone home! Do you think we're fools?'

'You should be ashamed of yourselves,' the middle-aged woman continued, taking up the cudgels and addressing the lines of police. But the passionate appeals of their countrymen had no effect whatsoever and after berating the police and soldiers in vain, the most vociferous amongst the crowd departed. When it became clear that we were not going to get in either, we retraced our steps and met up with Vitale.

The parade-demonstration had been large by Soviet standards, 40,000 people from opposition groups having taken part. But it was nothing in comparison to the massive demonstrations that had gripped Eastern Europe in the previous six months and brought down the Communist governments of East Germany, Poland, Czechoslovakia, Bulgaria and Hungary like a pack of cards. Given the first opportunity for seventy years to form their own groups and take part in the May Day parade, openly and legally to demonstrate in the very heart of Moscow in front of the Kremlin and the Soviet leaders, why, we wondered, had only 40,000 people out of a city of six million taken part?

It was only in the evening that we learnt, from the BBC World Service, that the demonstrators in Red Square had booed the President, an event without precedent in Soviet history. Clearly irritated, Gorbachev and other senior officials watching the parade had faced barracking by groups of protesters for more than thirty minutes before leaving the balcony of the Lenin Mausoleum. This had been reported on Soviet news in the evening and three days later Alexander Yakovlev, one of Gorbachev's closest associates in the leadership, conceded to journalists that the protests had forced Gorbachev's party to withdraw from Red Square.

Alexei had gone ahead to meet us in Moscow and that evening I asked him whether what he had seen differed greatly from previous years.

'Absolutely different,' he said. 'Now people come to the May Day parade from their head, spontaneously. Yes, what you saw today was a phenomenal event in our history.' Why, in that case, hadn't he taken part himself? 'I am a dissident in my heart and mind,' he said enigmatically. But this seemed to confirm what we had sensed in conversations so far: that although many people sympathised with those campaigning for greater justice, freedom and better living standards, it was an almost Herculean task to cross from being a spectator to being actively involved. Even though people might have liked to commit themselves to the fray, something powerful held them back.

We had not been in the Soviet Union long and had yet to appreciate the long historical legacy of oppression and submission that moulds the Russian character so powerfully. But at this stage we found the Russians' political disinclination to take advantage, at a collective level, of this historic opportunity incomprehensible and disappointing. We could not help but feel that the prevailing attitude was one of widespread apathy.

'Yes, maybe,' said Alexei, 'because for seventy years we were pressed, pressed, pressed . . . You have to understand that. You don't know what that is like in your countries.'

'But you respect the people demonstrating in Red Square?'

'Yes, of course. Not all, but most.' We gained a deeper insight into Alexei's reluctance to get involved only much later when he told us that his mother had been imprisoned for five years for campaigning for greater political freedom, and that she was still prohibited from living within a hundred kilometres of Moscow.

By chance we arrived in Moscow at a time when the city was in the throes of unimaginable political change which had affected the May Day parade in a fascinating way. Ten days before our arrival a radical university professor of economics, Gavriil Popov, had been elected chairman of the Moscow city *soviet*, in effect Mayor of Moscow. Up to this point Moscow city council had effectively functioned according to orders from the city Communist Party committees. In elections in March 1990, however, candidates backed by the Communist Party had taken barely twenty per cent of the council seats in Moscow and control of the council had been won by the 'Democratic Russia' coalition of radical groups. Although this coalition consisted largely of reform-minded Communists, they refused to take any further orders from the Moscow Communist Party. Thus, for the first time since the Revolution, Moscow had a non-Communist administration.

Having lost control of Moscow city council, the Communist Party quickly cancelled the arrangement whereby it published Moscow's two main newspapers jointly with the city council. By taking control of the capital's most popular dailies, the Communist Party thereby deprived the council of its principal media voice. Up to this point it had been the council that had had the power to authorise public gatherings in Moscow. However, no sooner had the Moscow council passed out of Communist control than Gorbachev issued a Presidential decree taking the authorisation of demonstrations and other public gatherings in the centre of Moscow out of the jurisdiction of the Moscow city council and passing it to the USSR Council of Ministers. Authorisation of the May Day parade allowing opposition groups to take part *had* been given but, it was widely believed, mainly to pre-empt the holding of a larger unofficial demonstration which might have clashed with the official parade.

Despite Gorbachev's claims that his policy of *glasnost* was to establish personal freedoms, a free press and the rule of law, the moment that the right to authorise demonstrations and public gatherings fell from Communist Party control to a democratically elected body, he acted swiftly to retake power by Presidential decree.

Leaving the Kremlin behind us we cycled to the Sport Hotel down enormously wide streets, four lanes wide in each direction. The Sport Hotel was a grey monolith ten kilometres from the centre on the Moscow ring road. Although rooms had supposedly been reserved, no one appeared to know anything about us. An hour's negotiations secured rooms and we managed to take our bikes to them, having overcome fierce opposition from the *dezhurnaya*s, the unrelenting duty women watchdogs that patrol the corridors and keep tabs on guests.

*Dezhurnaya*s are a classic Soviet invention, creating unnecessary work for hundreds of thousands of people across the country who could otherwise be doing something useful. The Sport Hotel had twenty floors and it is a strict rule of thumb that every floor of a Soviet hotel needs a *dezhurnaya*. Instead of being given a key at reception with which to unlock his own door, the guest is given a slip of paper recording his name, passport, visa and room number and the duration of his stay. This slip is handed to the *dezhurnaya* on the appropriate floor, who duplicates all the details already recorded at reception, and directs the guest to his room. Thus, at a simple stroke of a pen, twenty people succeed in duplicating what two have already done.

Apart from keeping a watchful eye on guests *dezhurnaya*s spend a good part of the day drinking tea in their offices with other hotel staff who have little to do. It is a cosy world that appears well suited to the Russian character; plenty of time, a sense of importance and no real duties or responsibility.

On the pretext of giving everyone a job to do, the Soviet system has institutionalised an old Russian love of doing very little. We could not help noticing that no one seemed to work hard in the Soviet Union, a character trait admitted by some Russians, and we were amused to see what the Russians considered to be hard work; they clearly had no idea of the way people work in the West. Despite decades of propaganda about production and 'shock work', Russians, it appeared, preferred to take it easy. In *Spring Torrents* there is a passage in which Sanin urges his friend Emil to stay. 'Like every true Russian,' Turgenev writes, 'he was delighted to seize on the first excuse which would relieve him of the obligation to do anything whatsoever.' Perhaps it is no coincidence then that a system has evolved that allows them to do just that, even if it does not guarantee a high standard of living.

In the Sport Hotel we each had our own room down a gloomy corridor that smelt strongly of cigarette smoke. The room was a narrow cell with a small bed, cramped and poky, and of the three lamps only one worked. In the bathroom there were towels, but no hot water, soap or bathplugs. After camping it made a pleasant change, especially when hot water became available for short periods at unpredictable intervals, but as one of the twenty best hotels in Moscow it left something to be desired. Who knows what the duties of a Soviet chambermaid are? The only onerous duty, that of making the bed, is left for the guest. Sheets and blankets are simply left in a stack on the bed. On our first evening Howard received a telephone call.

'Mr Cooper. This is the Foreigners' Registration Bureau. You and your friends are not registered in the Soviet Union. This situation must be regularised. When did you arrive in the Soviet Union?'

'Three weeks ago, at Leningrad.'

'This is a big problem, Mr Cooper. You should have registered on arrival in Leningrad and you have now been in the Soviet Union for three weeks. You have not arrived yet officially, so you will have to return and register at your place of entry, in Leningrad.'

'Well, we've just cycled from Leningrad, and I don't see us cycling back right away. Why don't you go ahead and register us here? We'll be around for a few days.'

And much to our surprise the registration was forthcoming within two days.

As SovIntersport had not arranged our accommodation it was almost impossible to eat in the Sport Hotel which catered to official groups of visiting and Soviet sportsmen, the foreign contingent largely made up of sports teams from the rapidly dwindling group of 'fraternal' countries. As we were not on the list of official sports teams circulated to the restaurant, it was even more problematic than usual to secure a table and almost impossible to get food. None of the waitresses wanted to know anything about us. In order to get anything to eat we were compelled to hawk ourselves around the restaurant, appealing to anyone who might be official and hunt around in the kitchens for a sympathetic waitress. This charade was not just reserved for the first evening but was played out every mealtime over the following six days. Eventually we found someone who agreed reluctantly to bring us some food. Just as in Leningrad, because we were not in the hotel in a standard capacity, the system could not cope. In the morning when we tried to order breakfast, the waiter disappeared for twenty minutes at a time, coming back first with some old rice puddings, then later with some pieces of cake and tea, then a little later again with sour cream and bread.

'What's the guy doing?' Howard asked, as food appeared in dribs and drabs.

'Looking for food in the kitchen,' Gilles replied.

'But this looks as though it has come off other people's plates.' When he came back we reiterated what we wanted – coffee, milk, bread, butter, fried eggs, and jam or honey, surely not too much to hope for in one of the best Moscow hotels. But the waiter was not even listening, his eyes wandering over to two Azerbaijanis who were striking a deal in whispered voices with another waiter. Ignoring everything we had just said, he continued:

'No. *My* question is, do you want to change money?' as if we had not quite understood that first and foremost he was a money changer and only secondly a waiter.

'No, what we want is br-ea-k-fa-st,' we told him, exasperated. 'Breakfast with coffee, bread, butter, jam, honey, and fried eggs.' He said nothing, disappeared into the kitchen and never returned. We saw him over the following few days but he steered well clear of our table. After a while we found the only reliable way to secure any food was to sit down fast at a table already laid for a fraternal sports team and eat their meal.

Everyone apart from us had their meals and accommodation paid for by an organisation, just as ours should have been by SovIntersport. However, we had to pay for our meals, the price of which ricocheted according to the waitress. One evening, Gilles ate alone and left a handsome tip in the hope of securing the same waitress the following day. But when we ate the following night, we paid less for a meal for four than Gilles had paid for his identical meal for one the previous evening. Breakfast for two cost more than breakfast for four, and meals with two bottles of wine or champagne often cost less than meals without them. After two days we began to send the bills back.

'It's too much,' we said. 'Make it less.' And the bills would come back halved. We soon began to make up our own bills, without reference to menus, which were non-existent, and merely called over a waiter to tell him how much we were paying; and instead of waiting thirty minutes for butter, jam or bread to arrive at breakfast, it was quicker to purloin what was left on neighbouring tables, a procedure to which the waiters made no objection. When it came to paying we merely explained what had been officially ordered and what we had acquired free from other tables.

Anywhere other than in the Soviet Union we would have made a strange sight, roaming the restaurant like street urchins, collecting dishes we liked the look of and ferrying them back to our table. Occasionally, for no reason, there would simply be no charge for breakfast at all. It was a Wonderland world, where anything happened and nothing should have surprised us.

However, it was no pleasure and no relaxation to stay in the Sport Hotel and instead of looking forward to relaxing over a meal we began to dread the prospect. The decoration and atmosphere of the restaurant were so depressing in any case that even had the meals been delicious and straightforward to order, we would have been hard put to enjoy them. As we passed out of the restaurant, a waiter would usually sidle over, crab-like, to ask in a whisper if we wanted to sell sports clothes. Prostitution, the sale of sports clothes and military badges appeared to be the hotel sidelines. In the hotel corners one could always find a Cuban basketball player, a North Korean gymnast or East German ice-hockey team member engaged in *sotto voce* conversation with Soviet black-marketeers, trading nylon tracksuits or synthetic sweatshirts for roubles or cheap Russian watches.

To escape from the Sport Hotel, we went to the Intourist hotel in Gorky Street, supposedly one of the best in Moscow, to find foreign newspapers and imported beer. Just to get into the hotel everyone has to run the gauntlet of half a dozen shady young men who lounge in the lobby and doorways carefully evaluating passing guests: Do you have anything to sell? Do you want to change money? Buy caviar? Ordinary Russians are pulled off to one side and questioned in a low voice about their business or are turned away by the mafia that control the foyer. To be Russian and get through the lobby into a 'luxury' hotel catering for foreigners demands a bravado, pugnacity and persistence.

Once inside, the hotel has about as much charm and salubrity as a Soho sex shop. You meet a world that ordinary Russians rarely see – plush carpets, glittering chandeliers, with French perfume, foreign drinks, newspapers and magazines for sale, though only for hard currency. Young women dressed to kill hang around the bars, the reception area and the restaurants. They are, we were told, a new breed of prostitute, christened 'Intergirls', who deal only with foreigners and accept only hard currency, their ambitions ranging from securing foreign luxuries to foreign husbands. While it was impossible to get a meal or a cup of tea without an interminable wait, two minutes were enough to find a woman for the night.

*

Our days in Moscow were designed for organising our trip, sorting out equipment, servicing our bikes and not sightseeing. We went to our respective embassies to inform them of our arrival and our revised itinerary for the next four months. I had written to the British Embassy before departure with details of the expedition and relevant personal information, and had asked a number of questions to which I had received no reply.

The British Embassy is situated in a magnificent location opposite the Great Palace of the Kremlin on the south bank of the River Moskva, in a fine nineteenth-century mansion, once the home of a prosperous Russian merchant. Such a prime location does the embassy have that the Soviet authorities have been trying to get the British to move for years, but without success. Despite the classical exterior, canary yellow and white, the inside is pure Pugin. For a moment I felt as if I had inadvertently stepped into the House of Commons. Dark oak panelling, ornate Gothic woodwork, portraits of Prince Philip and the Queen in heavy frames, a massive dog-leg staircase of darkened wood and heavy damask wallpapers combined to create a leaden atmosphere. Every detail created the setting and atmosphere of an Agatha Christie novel; I felt that a colonel must have been lying murdered in the library.

The bald receptionist was from Weston-super-Mare. He looked worried when I told him what had brought me to the Soviet Union, and even more so when I said I wished to speak to a consular official – not so much worried for my safety, or even health of mind, as to whom I should speak. I obviously did not fit the usual categories.

'I think you'd better see the Vice-Consul,' he said in a worried tone, in the way a GP might say 'I think you'd better see a specialist'. I heard him on the telephone. 'I'm sorry to bother you, Mr Coles, but I've got a young gentleman here who *says* he's going to cycle across the Soviet Union . . . Yes, he's with me now. I realise it's not very convenient . . .'

While I waited in the Gothic hall for him to arrive, Lady Churchill arrived for lunch. Diplomats sprang from the woodwork to greet her.

'Aah! How ni-i-ice it is to see you,' one said, without a trace of enthusiasm. 'I don't think you know Mr Appleby, do you? You don't? Mr Appleby – Lady Churchill. Yeees! I hope you had a pleasant journey. Aaah!' He looked about him, searching desperately for a subject of conversation. 'And this is our Third Secretary.' There was a lot of scraping and bowing. The Third Secretary looked at his watch, the diplomat at the grandfather clock and then everyone synchronised watches.

'He shouldn't be long now,' one of them said, after a long silence, which was followed by some awkward straightening of perfectly tied ties and clearing of throats. Handshakes were performed woodenly from a great distance as if everyone present was suffering from a contagious disease. Eventually Mr Coles appeared and led me into the library from where the body of the colonel had, it appeared, been removed.

'I haven't got much time,' he apologised 'what with one thing and another.' I explained the reason for my visit and mentioned that I had written to the embassy from Britain. 'Yes, I think we did have a letter, now you come to mention it. Perhaps you could fill out this form with your personal details, passport number, etc.'

'I gave all these details in my letter.'

'Yes, but there's no harm having them on the official form, is there?'

He could not believe that we had cycled all the way from Leningrad without being stopped by the police, nor that we had got as far as Moscow without our arrival being registered.

'No, the police must know who you are and what you're doing,' he said. 'Otherwise you'd have been stopped.'

'They seem most astonished when we cycle by,' I said.

'Oh no,' he said. 'I'm sure they know all about you.' The fact that we were setting off to cycle across the Soviet Union did not interest him in the least. 'Don't get into trouble,' he said. 'We've only got one consulate in the country and that's here in Moscow, so it will take a long time to help you if you get into trouble. So long as you register with the police every night and don't change money on the black market, you won't give us any problems.' The last thing we wanted to do was to report to the police every night; the whole purpose of the journey was to be as free as possible. It seemed curious, too, that such a restrictive procedure had been put forward not by the Russians, but by the British.

I enquired if it was possible to buy a few items from the embassy shop that were unobtainable in Moscow.

'I'd like to help, Mr Vickers,' he said, 'but I'm afraid we've got very strict rules on that, what with English teachers here and so on, otherwise we'd have everyone buying in the shop, wouldn't we? I'm sorry not to be able to help this time.' We shook hands outside the embassy but before he had time to get into his car a Russian woman with an intelligent, open face asked him if he could ratify that the English translation of her professional qualification certificate was accurate.

'No, I couldn't do that,' he told her, shaking his head sadly. 'Who made the translation?'

'I did,' she said.

'Oh no. We couldn't be sure that it's *correct*, could we?'

'But you can compare the official document from my Institute with the English translation; it wouldn't be difficult to check, I think.'

'Oh no, my Russian isn't good enough for that. You've got to go to the third administration department of the Ministry of Foreign Affairs and get them to ratify the translation first, then we can accept it.'

'But that will take months!' she said, looking crestfallen.

'I can't take responsibility for Soviet administration now, can I?' he said, before speeding off in a German BMW.

Back in the Gothic reception I asked to speak to the shop manager on the telephone.

'I was just speaking to Mr Coles about buying one or two things from the shop,' I said.

'Come straight over,' said a friendly woman's voice. As I left the shop I asked the manageress how she got on with the Russians. 'I get on well with them. I treat them rough and they love it. No point being polite. Treat them rough, that's my advice!'

When we met up we compared experiences at our respective embassies. Howard's and my experience had been similar but Gilles had a different story to tell. He had been invited in for coffee and croissants, and he spent a couple of hours talking about the journey to embassy staff.

'They're very excited,' he said. 'They want to help in any way they can. They think it's a great journey. The commercial attaché has been to some of the Siberian cities on our route and has told me which are the ones to avoid. He's also given me his home telephone number which we can use if we want to, and will help forward mail from abroad. He asked if we needed to buy anything from the shop and has said that anything we decide not to take we can leave at the embassy. He may even fly out and join us at Irkutsk for a few days.'

'The guys at the American Embassy just didn't want to know,' Howard said ruefully. 'They said they were here to help the Russians, not American citizens. Never *heard* such bullshit!'

'The British Vice-Consul doesn't want us to change money on the black market,' I said, 'so that the Embassy won't have any problems.'

'Strange,' Gilles said, 'the French Embassy said we *must* change money on the black market! They said anything else would be plain crazy.'

In Moscow our arrangements with Alexei and Vitale fell through just as they had at Leningrad. It had now happened so often that we began to despair at the hopeless unreliability of the Russians. When we made a decision with Vitale there was no problem, but when a second and then a third Russian became involved, even on the simplest matters, the discussion rambled on indefinitely, and God help us when there was a group of half a dozen or more! It was as though no one had any idea of how to come to a decision.

'No common sense!' Howard muttered angrily.

'A screw missing somewhere,' I said, shaking my head.

'More like a boxful,' Gilles said.

5
MOSCOW

THE WAREHOUSE BELONGING to Sofi, the Finnish company specialising in transport deliveries to the Soviet Union, was situated on a wasteland at the edge of Moscow, unmarked for security. Howard and I spent two days sorting through our gear, dividing up equipment and bicycle spares, vitamins, medical supplies, dried food and clothes. Sofi undertook to deliver our equipment safely to five strategically spaced cities we were confident we would pass through: Magnitogorsk, 2,000 kilometres from Moscow in the Urals; Barnaul, at the start of Siberia; Irkutsk, on Lake Baikal; Chita, the last city before we disappeared into the swamp; and Blagoveshchensk, where we hoped to emerge from it. The solitary Finn in charge assured us that the boxes would arrive safely but he could not guarantee fast delivery.

'We can deliver what you need to Aeroflot within twelve hours,' he said, 'but Aeroflot may take a day or a week to deliver urgent parcels.' He also generously gave us letters of credit so that we could send boxes internally at Sofi's expense. But they were viewed with incomprehension when we came to use them. How, Soviet officials asked, could they be sure that Sofi would pay? And they were waved away.

As we drove back to the centre we quizzed our driver about the occasional decent-looking block of flats and imposing new tower blocks. Without exception they were for members of the privileged élite, the *nomenklatura*. This one was apartments for high-ranking Soviet military; the other, just finished, with an impressive fountain, was for military intelligence. Others were for *apparatchiki* or high party functionaries; those three large glass cubes on the horizon were the new KGB buildings. It is not that the buildings were very luxurious, but in the Soviet context even a foreigner could hardly fail to notice that they were finished to a much higher standard, surrounded by high railings and were unique in having lawns and tended gardens.

'This very road, on which we are now driving,' our driver told us, 'was closed to ordinary people until last year. Between the hours of 7.00 and 10.00 am and 5.00 and 8.00 pm, it was only for the use of the *nomenklatura*, but now it is open for ordinary citizens. The *nomenklatura* have their own medical clinic in this wood to the left; it is very modern, very good . . .'

At Moscow airport we found the office for parcel collection which had a tiny window at waist height. The woman in charge was a typical Russian official. She made it clear she could not be bothered with foreigners unable to speak Russian fluently and ignored us. She told us to come back the next day, which would mean another twenty-four hours wasted. We pleaded, cajoled and persisted for twenty minutes until, sick at the sight of us, she let Howard through, glad to get rid of him. An hour went by before Howard re-emerged triumphant, clutching our box.

'It's chaos in there,' he said, as we pulled away. 'There's no system at all. Parcels and packages are mixed up together, irrespective of what airline they've arrived on, so we had to search through three halls as big as airline hangers. They don't use the cargo number to identify where the box is located, only to check that it really belongs to you once it's found. There must be *some* method in their madness but I'm damned if I discovered it! Simon, I need a beer.'

We went to the American Embassy compound where we got ourselves checked in past US Marines by a couple on their way out, and two minutes later we were in the bar. Considering that stringent measures had supposedly been put into effect, security seemed very lax; strictly speaking, only the diplomatic personnel of certain Western countries were allowed in on a Friday night.

'Hi there!' came friendly voices as we passed people in the dark on the way to the bar. Was that somebody saying hello? Someone I don't even know? I turned around in the dark to look at them. It was the first friendly greeting from anybody since we had left Leningrad, and we realised we were almost suspicious of their intentions. We looked at them in the manner the Russians had looked at us on our way from Leningrad – why are they smiling? Why are they laughing? What do they want?

After three weeks in the Soviet Union the bar of the American Embassy came as a culture shock. It was packed, it was noisy and people were laughing. People were crowded round the bar, round the dart board and the din of conversation was deafening. Every table was taken and a few people were dancing between the chairs and the bar. Here a couple were having a *tête à tête* in the corner, there a group was crowded animatedly round a table; up at the bar two guys were draining whiskies as fast as they could. People were laughing, shouting to make themselves heard, enjoying themselves. Even in Moscow itself we had seen nothing resembling this lively scene that we would have thought nothing of three weeks before.

'This is quite a party,' I said to the girl beside me.

'If you think this is good, you'll have to come to the Australian Embassy, that's real wild!'

The following day I took a break from expedition preparations to visit the Kremlin and walk around Moscow. Seen from whatever angle the Kremlin is an extraordinary sight, more intriguing than beautiful. From the Moskva it presents a combination of fairy-tale and Eastern exoticism, the gilded onion domes of the Uspensky, Blagoveshchensky and Arkhangelsky Cathedrals sparkling in the weak sunlight, sprouting from a forest of green trees. Walls of bull's-blood red are capped by medieval crenellations and punctuated by a bewildering variety of weird and eccentric towers, each different from the next. The immediate impression is that it is the work of a mad genius given free artistic rein. Much of the Kremlin was built by foreign craftsmen, but it is Russian in inspiration and spirit.

The walls and towers were designed by Italian stonemasons at the turn of the fifteenth century and the crenellations are those of early Renaissance Italy. The names of the towers and gates evoke the Kremlin's history: Redeemer's Gate, Trinity Gate, Forest Tower, Water-Hoist Tower, Tower of Secrets, Alarm Tower and Tsar's Tower, to mention but a few.

Within the Kremlin walls, the focus is Cathedral Square, where the three principal cathedrals are grouped, side by side. Nowhere in Europe does one find so many churches and cathedrals standing cheek by jowl as one does in Russia. It would be as if Westminster Abbey, St Paul's and St Martin's-in-the-Fields were all clustered within the walls of the Tower of London, with Buckingham and Kensington Palaces crammed in besides them. The proximity of the cathedrals to the seat of temporal power is, perhaps, symbolic of the relationship between the Russian Orthodox Church and the Russian State. It is ironic that the most famous and magnificent Russian cathedrals were built by foreigners, the Uspensky

(Assumption) by the Italian architect, Aristotle Fioravanti, and the Arkhangelsky (Archangel Michael's) by the Milanese Alevisio Novi. The style, however, is wholly Russian, Fioravanti having spent many years studying the religious architecture of the old Russian cities of Suzdal and Vladimir. Once built, the Uspensky Cathedral became Russia's principal church, serving as the burial place of the metropolitans and patriarchs of Moscow, and the coronation place of the tsars. Externally it is very simple, with walls of white limestone divided into recessed panels set off by columns and gables, and inside it is surprisingly light. All the walls are covered in frescoes, soft in colour, restrained and beautiful. It is the iconostasis that draws one's attention. Tier after tier of icons rise to the ceiling, bathed in a golden light that derives from the pigments, the layers of varnish and the use of gold leaf and paint. At its best, as here, the effect is mysterious and captivating. Nearby stands an intricately carved walnut throne, the Throne of Monomakh, which once belonged to Ivan the Terrible; overhead is a massive chandelier made from silver captured from French troops retreating from Moscow.

It seems hardly possible that at the time of the Napoleonic invasion French soldiers turned the Uspensky Cathedral into a stable and used the icons as firewood. When they left they carted away 288 kilos of gold articles and about 5,000 of silver, much of it exquisitely carved and decorated silverwork that formed an integral part of the richest icons. Napoleon even ordered the removal of the cross on top of the Bell Tower of Ivan the Great in the erroneous belief that it was made of gold. Most of it was lost in the course of the French retreat and never recovered.

The frescoes in the Arkhangelsky Cathedral are fascinating for their portrayal of scenes of battle and everyday life in seventeenth-century Russia, and the gilded and carved iconostasis is of unparalleled beauty. The Arkhangelsky Cathedral served as the burial vault of the grand princes of Moscow, and of all the Russian tsars from Ivan Kalita to Peter the Great, with the exception of Boris Godunov.

One of the curious aspects of the Soviet Union that we were to come across again and again was the Soviet obsession with size. Perhaps it is a natural obsession for a country that stretches over a sixth of the world's land surface, but one might think that this would be reason enough in itself to rise above such preoccupations. Schumacher would never have been a success in the Soviet Union. This preoccupation with size predates the Soviet period although, since 1917, it has been taken to extremes. But within the Kremlin walls one comes across at least two examples of the Russian obsession with size, the Tsar Bell and the Tsar Cannon. The Tsar Bell is the largest bell in the world and lies at the foot of the Bell

Tower of Ivan the Great. It was cast in 1733–5 in a special casting pit inside the Kremlin but during the Kremlin fire of 1737 several cracks appeared and a fragment broke off when cold water, used to extinguish the fire, fell on the hot metal. The fragment alone weighs over eleven tons, the bell as a whole well over 200. Only a century later was it raised from the original casting pit and placed on a pedestal.

Not far away from the Tsar Bell is the Tsar Cannon which has the largest calibre of any gun in the world. It was cast in 1586, weighs forty tons and is 5.3 metres long, with a calibre of 890 millimetres and a barrel fifteen centimetres thick. It used to stand outside the Kremlin where it covered the approaches to Spassky Gate and the ford across the Moskva. A special carriage was required to fire it and it was so unwieldy to manoeuvre that it had to be abandoned rapidly in times of battle.

Joining throngs of tourists I visited the Kremlin armoury that houses an astonishing wealth of military weapons, regalia and treasures belonging to the tsars. So vast had the tsar's treasure grown under Ivan the Terrible that when Moscow was threatened by the Crimean Tatars, 450 sledges were needed to move it to Novgorod. It was augmented by gifts from foreign monarchs and ambassadors, and was evacuated again to Nizhny Novgorod during the Napoleonic invasion.

The collections are stunning. The first hall displays two perfect thirteenth-century helmets and innumerable battleaxes, maces, coats-of-armour, muskets, oriental sabres and pistols. One of the earliest helmets, covered in embossed silver, belonged to the father of Alexander Nevsky and was found on the site of a battle which took place between Suzdal and Novgorod in 1216. Another belonged to Prince Ivan, the son of Ivan the Terrible, who was killed by his father at the age of twenty-eight in an outburst of anger. Case after case of ceremonial armour, Russian and oriental sabres followed, some inlaid with gilt and decorated with diamonds, rubies and emeralds.

Passing into the next chamber was like entering Aladdin's cave, a veritable treasure trove of Russian gold and silver: golden chalices and cups, bracelets, necklets, earrings, gold and silver dippers, golden bowls for toasting and drinking beer and *kvass*, some studded with jewels. From Novgorod came a fourteenth-century jasper chalice in a silver filigree case studded with precious stones; from Moscow a gospel, its golden cover inlaid with enamel, emeralds and rubies, a gift to the Cathedral of the Assumption in 1571 by Ivan the Terrible. Magnificent icon mountings of chastened gold adorned with pearls and diamonds surround dark icons of the Virgin, but the figures themselves have disappeared from many, such as that of the Virgin of Vladimir.

Reeling from such opulence and magnificence I passed into the third chamber, hoping for relief. This is crammed with jewellery, and ornate Russian Baroque and Rococo silver and gold work, lavish and exuberant: flamboyant silver candlesticks; collections of snuffboxes made of gold, silver, mother-of-pearl, tortoise-shell, ivory and porcelain, and decorated with precious stones and enamel portraits; silver samovars; golden dishes, plates and bowls of every shape and size; crowns of silver laurel leaves; gold and silver sculptures, clocks and watches, and Fabergé eggs. The outside of one silver egg was engraved with a map of the Trans-Siberian Railway and inside was a gold clockwork model of a Trans-Siberian express with a platinum engine, a ruby headlamp and windows of crystal.

In the Hall of Vestments, I found myself amongst costumes that had been worn by the imperial family, patriarchs and metropolitans. All were woven and embroidered with gold and encrusted with jewels and pearls. The velvet cape given to Metropolitan Platon of Moscow in 1770 by Catherine II is adorned with 150,580 pearls alone. Fleeing from this luxuriance I entered the Chamber of Foreign Gold and Silver – gifts to the tsars from foreign ambassadors – with its vast collections of Dutch, English, Polish, Swedish, Danish and German silver. The collection of English Elizabeth and Jacobean silver alone is unique; neither the British Royal Family nor any museum possesses anything as fine, most of it having been melted down in the Georgian era. The gifts of Richard Chancellor, the first English Ambassador to the Court of Muscovy, to Ivan the Terrible remain just as they were given in 1553.

Progressing to the next cave I came across the regalia of the imperial family with the thrones of the tsars: that of Ivan the Terrible decorated with ivory carvings; a second given to Boris Godunov by Shah Abbas of Persia, covered with gold and studded with 2,200 precious stones and pearls; a third presented to Tsar Alexei Romanov by Armenian merchants, known as the Diamond Throne and decorated with 1,223 precious stones and 876 diamonds. The last throne, Rococo and gilt, was used in the early years of the reign of Peter the Great when he shared power with his weak brother Ivan, and their sister Sophia was regent. There were two seats in front for the two tsars and a third, hidden at the back, where Sophia could sit unseen and prompt the responses they should make to ambassadors' questions. Of all the coronets and crowns the oldest and most remarkable is the Cap of Monomakh, which was made by Oriental craftsmen in the thirteenth or fourteenth centuries and is believed to have been given to the Grand Prince Vladimir Monomakh of Kiev by the Emperor of Byzantium. Made of finely wrought gold lace overlaying a band of gold leaf, it is surmounted by a pearl-tipped gold cross and edged with sable.

I emerged into Red Square, overcome by the beauty and opulence of these treasures. In Europe the gap between the royal families and the mass of the population was of course enormous, but in Russia it was so vast as to be unbridgeable. The tsar, even until the beginning of the twentieth century, was looked upon by the Russian peasantry as a father figure of semi-divine status.

It is difficult not to feel, as one walks away, that the tsars ultimately invited trouble and that a revolution was not only inevitable but desirable. Perhaps it is the intention of the Soviet authorities in exhibiting the tsarist treasures to encourage that very thought. While in Western Europe the power of monarchs was being gradually restricted by both the nobles and the landed gentry, in Russia it was expanding and becoming more abso-lute. In 1215 when King Stephen first conceded certain important powers to the English nobility the nascent Russian state was on the point of being subjected to a 250-year-long period of Tatar oppression. When in 1649 the English Parliament asserted its power and executed Charles I, the Romanov dynasty had only just begun. Some of the royal families of Europe saw which way the tide was running and began to accommodate themselves to the emerging order while others where caught out in the process. But alone of all the monarchies, the Romanov dynasty succeeded in arriving at the threshold of the twentieth century largely unchanged in nature from the sixteenth.

Had Ivan the Terrible been able to reappear in 1897, 350 years after he had acceded to the throne of Muscovy, he would have had little difficulty in taking up the reins of power, for in terms of the exercise of power little had changed. No other authority had arisen that could have prevented him from organising once again a special bodyguard like the *oprichina*, arresting and executing the nobles or the diminutive middle class, just as he had mercilessly persecuted the *boyars* (barons) in the sixteenth century. Nor, if he had reappeared in 1947, 400 years after he assumed the title of Tsar of All The Russias, would the situation have been very different. It is the absolute nature of executive powers in the Soviet Union that cuts it off from Europe and provides the frightening element of continuity in Russian history.

I met Gilles, Vitale and Howard in the Arbat, Moscow's 'alternative' street. It was Saturday and the street was crowded with people slowly strolling arm in arm. It was warm and sunny, and the feeling was relaxed and carefree; the lime trees were covered in a gentle shield of young green leaves – there was a distinct sensation that winter was finally over and spring was in the air.

Despite the Arbat's popularity, there were just two cafés to go to. In search of coffee we descended to the first, in a basement. It was cold, large and gloomy; we emerged, relieved that it had no coffee, and set off again. We walked to a nearby restaurant-café, but when we arrived the scene resembled the first day of the Harrods sale, with 200 people waiting in a scrum round the closed doors. We had not left before the doors opened and the crowd surged forward eagerly, bursting through the door like peas from a pod. There was no point, we were told, in joining the fray. Had we waited an hour or more for a table, we would have had to wait another hour for a waitress, by which time all food and drink would have run out.

We were hungry. The choice remained between the Arbat Restaurant with seating for 2,000 or a hideous kiosk in the Arbat itself, masquerading as a Russian log cabin. Outside it were three small tables. Naturally enough there was a queue and we waited our turn. Three items were available: ice cream, fruit juice and 'cocktails'. We ordered all three, only to find that 'cocktails' consisted of fruit juice and ice cream mixed together.

Nudging a drunk off the end of a bench, we settled down in the sunshine. We had walked from one end of the Arbat to the other and back again, and had seen all there was to offer in the way of cafés and restaurants. And the Arbat was the most popular and 'liveliest' street in Moscow, the capital. Simple café pleasures were out of the question. The ice cream was not bad but there was no choice and in six months we never came across any other flavour than vanilla. Russians would not believe that Americans have ice-cream parlours with thirty or forty different varieties on sale, or that one can walk into a café or restaurant and be shown to a table straightaway.

In the afternoon, at the suggestion of some American students, we went in search of a 'Bob Marley concert' that was being put on by West Indian students in a park on the fringes of the city near the Third World Institute. We took the Metro to the end of the line, arriving on the outskirts of the city amongst a wasteland of apartment blocks and derelict building sites. It seemed a fitting location for a Third World Institute but none of the Russians waiting at the concrete bus shelters had so much as heard of it. Some pointed to other towerblocks in the distance, others in the opposite direction. We took a bus one way and walked into a cold, biting wind, stopping to ask for directions until we saw some African students. They too were under the illusion that the concert was to be held in a park next to the Institute. The 'park' turned out to be a patch of rough woodland that had miraculously escaped destruction, full of undergrowth and brambles. It seemed extremely unlikely that a concert of any description could take place in such a wilderness and eventually we extricated ourselves and returned, scratched, to the Institute.

Appropriately enough the Third World Institute was a meagre, concrete building, grey and streaked by the winter of its twenty years, with doors half off their hinges, and a depressingly abandoned look, in all these essentials not so very different from other buildings round about. Inside it was dirty and gloomy, most of the lights devoid of light bulbs, but there was a bar serving ice cream and sweet sticky buns. Apart from our group, which included three Russians and a few other West European students, there were about 200 West Indian and African students. The time of the concert had changed and we went off in search of food. Naturally enough, it was not a question of 'popping round to the corner shop' and we found ourselves on a marathon walk. Following directions we took two buses a total of eleven stops, changing direction in the middle, and then headed for a modern, if ugly, concrete building on the top of which unlit neon signs proclaimed 'Café. Food. Pharmacy. Pizzeria'.

Here at least we would find sustenance. Grey dusty windows did not deter us, familiar as we were becoming with Soviet shops, but the building, only five years old, turned out to be abandoned and in a dilapidated state. The steps were broken and used as a latrine.

Accompanied by Russian friends, we asked the locals for further directions and we set off again by bus through a residential area, passing block after block of apartment buildings ranged in rows and labelled with numbers: block 37, block 38, block 39. After descending from the bus and walking for ten minutes we checked directions, continued for a further five, checked again, then another five, but the elusive food shop and café never seemed to approach. Like Alice and the Red Queen, no matter how fast we went we never managed to get somewhere else. To our chagrin a new set of passers-by then pointed us in a completely different direction. Even our Russian companions began to lose hope and we gave up, making our way back by bus to the Third World Institute, empty-handed, after a journey of well over an hour.

'Seventy years have shown us that socialism is a failure,' commented Valodiya as we returned by bus. It was hard to think of consoling words.

'It is impossible for you as a foreigner,' Oksana said, 'to imagine how much effort and nerves it takes to solve the simplest problem in our country; how many authorisations you have to submit and so on and so forth. But facing all these problems makes us stronger and adds to our surviving power. You cannot do without it in this country.'

By the time we arrived back the concert was in progress and two Soviet policemen wielding truncheons were hanging around the main entrance, looking as though they would rather not be there. Talking to the African students, we found that instead of them being fraternally grateful to the Soviet Union for its cheap education, they were heartily sick of living where they were largely shunned and discriminated against. The 'international fraternity of working people', which had ostensibly just been celebrated on May Day, hardly extended to African and West Indian students who felt they were regarded as second-class citizens in the USSR.

'Russian racism and nationalism are strong but subtle,' one student confided. 'They say nothing but their looks say it all. Sometimes it's difficult even for us to get served in shops.' Seeing what it was like to be served as a Russian and even as a Western visitor I dreaded to think what it must be like for them.

The interior of the Third World Institute was ramshackle and dilapidated, and as there was no auditorium or lecture hall the concert was held in a big classroom. As a concert it was far from remarkable, but memorable for the atmosphere of infectious enthusiasm, so clearly at odds with the sombre Soviet world outside.

In the evening we met a young man, Sergei, of about our age, the first, and one of the few, professional black-marketeers that we met on our trip. Smooth-looking and dressed in the uniform of Soviet black-marketeers and mafia, he wore American jeans, a black leather jacket and new foreign 'docksiders'. Dropped down in Western Europe or the USA he would not merit a glance but in Moscow his clothes immediately identified him as somebody with influential connections and money, somebody who could fix deals and obtain the unobtainable. He showed me his address book stuffed with the addresses of hundreds of American visitors to Moscow. He spent his time hanging around the Intourist hotels in Moscow where he casually got into conversation with tourists, offering them caviar and black-market rates for their dollars. He had started by selling caviar bought illegally from state foodstores; he could get hold of icons and furs. Through an American tourist he had succeeded in getting three computers into the USSR illegally, each of which had cost him 6,000 roubles, the total cost being equivalent to four years' average salary. Through his contacts, he had sold them to a Communist Party office in the Ukraine for four times the price, by lying about the price he had paid in the first place.

'So who's being robbed?' I asked him.

'No one,' he replied, surprised. 'They would have paid more.'

'But ultimately whose money was it that the Communist Party paid out – the people's?' He shrugged his shoulders and said nothing. That transaction alone had netted him the equivalent of twelve years' average salary.

'He's smart,' Gilles said later. 'If I lived here I'd do the same. What's the point of working on a collective farm or in a factory for 200 roubles a month?'

As we walked down the street, Sergei recognised and greeted half a dozen acquaintances, dressed like him, in leather jackets. We went to a private Georgian restaurant where he had reserved places; without him we probably wouldn't have got in at all, but Sergei knew the patron, the waiters, the man on the door. The cost by Soviet standards was prohibitive – the equivalent of a month's pension, but Sergei didn't bat an eyelid.

I asked him what he thought about *perestroika* and *glasnost*, and whether he felt the Soviet Union was changing for the better, but he wasn't interested in the future of the Soviet Union.

'We don't believe in Gorbachev,' he said 'and we don't intend to wait for him.' He wanted to make money and to leave the country, but to make money, if possible, without working, by outsmarting the system. He hoped he would get permission to visit his friends in the USA and, once there, he would not come back.

It seemed the country faced a bleak prospect if Gorbachev's proposals for the total restructuring of society and the economy held no appeal for the young.

Sergei left the restaurant early, excusing himself, saying that he had to get up at five the following day for 'business outside Moscow'. Rare are the Russians who get up at five o'clock, let alone for business! He must have been onto a good deal.

I found it enervating to talk to young Russians like Sergei. I always came away feeling that there was no hope for a country with such disillusioned young people. In the Soviet Union everybody plays the black market to some extent; they rely on it to get essential everyday items, to arrange things in an emergency, to get supplies of vodka or caviar if they are having a celebration. The black market is a part of life, as indispensable as air itself. But the professional black-marketeers and the 'mafia' (as they are continually referred to by ordinary Russians), milk the system for all it is worth, and in a system that has both endemic shortages and corruption, the opportunities are endless.

*

Having taken the bikes apart and thoroughly cleaned and regreased every part, we reassembled them and divided the gear equally by weight, Howard taking a tent, water-filter, spare derailleur, and medical kit, Vitale a second tent, spare chain, derailleur, sugar, coffee, tea, stock cubes and dried foods, Gilles cooking pots and pans, firelighters, axe, spare derailleur, chain, brake and gear cables, spokes, axles and bearings, and me the cooking primus, fuel bottle, pump and tool kit. Food that we later bought along the way we would split up between us. Despite the intention to reduce our gear we found little we could do without and as it was still cold morning and evening we kept all our clothing. In terms of equipment we took even more with us than we had had between Leningrad and Moscow, our first equipment drop being in Magnitogorsk, 2000 kilometres away in the Urals. As we were testing out revolutionary wheels, we took enough spare spokes to rebuild a conventional wheel from scratch should the eventuality arrive. After six days in Moscow we were keen to get under way and strike East.

Although to be in Moscow was exciting at first, the sheer ugliness and uniformity of Soviet architecture we found intensely depressing. We heard of one Swedish architect who had cut short his visit to the Soviet Union and returned home, so overwhelmed was he by the overpowering impersonality and ugliness of Soviet architecture. Moscow of course has more to offer than any other Soviet city; it dominates political, economic and cultural life to an even greater extent than Paris or London do France and Britain, so much so that part of the punishment for dissidents and criminals is that they cannot live within one or two hundred kilometres of the capital. Elsewhere in the Soviet Union there is a great desire amongst young people to move to Moscow, often of the erroneous opinion that Muscovites have a better standard of living than they do. On a number of occasions we met people in the countryside, far from Moscow, who assured us that the Soviet authorities looked after Muscovites, keeping their shops well stocked, but did not care what happened to them, the peasants. Despite the enormous building programme of the last twenty years there is still a huge housing shortage in Moscow and serious overcrowding. And this has developed in the face of a system of internal domicile registration that makes it both difficult and illegal for people in other parts of the country to uproot and come to Moscow in search of work or better living standards.

Like other Soviet cities Moscow is redeemed by the trees that line many of the streets or survive haphazardly amongst the building developments, quite apart from its parks. But as municipal flower beds and private gardens are virtually non-existent, trees take on an importance in Soviet cities far greater than in European ones. Apart from a display of tulips beneath the Kremlin walls, there were few flowerbeds of spring flowers and little attempt to beautify the city. With an artistic eye, a small degree of flair and a modest budget these forlorn areas of wasteland criss-crossed by beaten-earth trails could have been turned into attractive gardens and communal parks, enhancing life for people, yet nothing was done. The trees, giving shade and breaking up the monotony of the soulless architecture, lent something of the beauty of nature to what, without them, would have been an unredeemed desert of ugliness.

Before leaving, I went to a performance of *Iolanta* at the Bolshoi Opera House, a vast pink classical building, built by Bovet in the spate of construction following Napoleon's burning of Moscow. One-rouble tickets were being sold outside to foreigners at five American dollars each, a mark-up of three thousand per cent, indicating no little appreciation of free-market economics.

The interior is astonishingly rich and magnificent, scarlet seats and balconies with ornate gilt sculptures and decoration rising in tiers to a dizzying height, the atmosphere still one of opulence and luxury. The opera house was full to overflowing and the mood excited and expectant, even if the production was stilted and old-fashioned. Used to the boldly inventive stage sets of English opera companies, this set was unimaginative. The singing itself was excellent but acting was, it appeared, of secondary importance. The female characters were well-built Russian women who looked most improbable playing the part of young maidens. Each time a new character appeared on stage on appreciative murmur of excitement rustled through the rows as the costumes and jewellery were surveyed intently through opera glasses. The arrival of the heroine, an exceedingly plump, pasty-faced matron well into her forties and draped in robes of shimmering white laced with silver, brought gasps of admiration from the audience, some of whom rose to their feet in appreciation.

The feeble acting and the old appearance of characters did not detract one iota from the audience's enjoyment. Essentially the Russians are sentimental people, and the melancholy and romanticism of Tchaikovsky's fairy-tale world goes straight to their hearts. Improbabilities and the unreality of a production are hardly noticed; it is the spirit of the production and the tale that count, and in this they are rarely failed. The more exotic the costumes, the more romantic the music, the more extravagant the sets, the more melodramatic the emotions, the more they enter into another world of make-believe and fantasy totally removed from normal life. At the end came a deluge of applause that went on and on, unrestrained and wildly appreciative. Roses were tossed through the air, landing on the stage and in the orchestra pit, and on the way out people talked eagerly and enthusiastically about their emotions and the behaviour of the characters, especially the heroine.

In spirit, I found myself thinking, the Russians are much closer to the Italians than to the British or Germans; emotion comes before efficiency or practicality; personal warmth is more important a quality than success or brilliance. The Russians use the terms *sukhovaty* – dryish – to describe someone who is too cold, too careful or reserved. *Sukhoi* – dried-up or arid – is worse and *sukhar* – meaning as dry as an old crust of bread – is the worst of all. They are not as extrovert nor as lively and boisterous as the Italians, but just as emotional. In Russia, as elsewhere, the English have the reputation of being meticulous, restrained, secretive and rather puritanical – like Sherlock Holmes who is, oddly, immensely popular.

On our last day in Moscow we happened to walk past a motorist who had been stopped by a policeman close to our hotel. The car was a Mercedes which in itself was evidence enough that the driver was some-one with both connections and money – a ten-year-old Mercedes in Moscow being rarer than a vintage Bugatti in London. Just as we passed him, the driver handed over a US dollar bill and we were close enough to see the denomination – five. Instead of pocketing it straightaway the policeman held it up to the light like a bank clerk to check the watermark, and only once satisfied did he put it into his pocket. Normally the cost of some infringement of the traffic code, real or imaginary, is ten roubles; but someone rich enough to have a Mercedes could obviously pay in dollars.

We went round to the offices of the Moscow sports newspaper to give an interview at their request but when we turned up as arranged no one was there. The offices were close to a synagogue, so we went in. There was no service in progress but there were a few Jews in the hallway who looked at us anxiously until we explained who we were. They told us they were expecting a pogrom the following day instigated by the Russian nationalist organisation, Pamyat, and as they could not rely on the police for protection they expected serious violence. Their attitude to Gorbachev and *glasnost* was ambivalent but, like most Russians, largely sceptical and mistrustful. To a certain extent things had improved in that emigration had become easier, a record 65,000 Jews being allowed to leave in 1989, including some long-term 'refuseniks'. Official persecution had also diminished; it was now not so crucial that people hide their Jewish origin or faith.

Over the twentieth century until *glasnost* began in 1985, Jews had Russianised their names; now they were changing back, something that could only be validated at the synagogue. *Glasnost* had allowed the Jews to produce the first Jewish newsletter for seventy years. The very first copies had arrived a few days earlier and we were given a copy of the first issue. But permission to publish the newsletter, they believed, stemmed not from a truly more enlightened policy of religious freedom but from the desire to improve relations with the United States. The journal was aimed at the White House, not at the Soviet Jewish community. They pointed out that there was still only one synagogue for the whole of Moscow, a city of eight million, and that permission to build more was continuously turned down. Unofficially, therefore, Jews meet in their own apartments for illegal services, but these have to be conducted as discreetly and quietly as possible.

But while official persecution has diminished, the threat from the Russian nationalist anti-Semitic organisations, like Pamyat, has grown. Fear of the future was leading Jews to emigrate in larger and larger numbers. In 1990, 30,000 Soviet Jews left every month for Israel, an unprecedented exodus that would reduce the three-million Jewish population in the Soviet Union to zero over a ten-year period, if the scale of emigration continued at that level. And opinion polls show that three-quarters of Soviet Jews wish to leave.

In order to ensure that the anticipated pogrom received maximum publicity, the Jews had alerted foreign press correspondents. Probably because of this precaution, it failed to materialise.

6
THE HUNGRY REGIONS I

WE SET OFF from Moscow on 7 May, cycling through industrial and residential suburbs, vast and grey. Moscow appeared to have no old quarters other than in the centre of the city. Everything was new and yet slightly decrepit, built on a giant scale, a maze of high-rise apartment blocks laid out geometrically like military barracks. In the middle of a roundabout on the edge of the city stood a gargantuan metal statue of a menacing soldier clasping a rifle. A group of schoolchildren stood before the war memorial, red Young Pioneer scarves floating in the wind.

'I had to do the same,' Vitale said, 'all propaganda. It was so boring.'

'What do they tell you on such visits?'

'We learned about the defence of the Motherland, and how we defeated the Hitlerites in the Great Patriotic War, and the sacrifices we had to make. I was a member of the Young Pioneers but never a member of Komsomol. But there's a lot of pressure to join; it's considered unpatriotic not to.' It became apparent that Vitale knew almost nothing about the vast quantity of American and British aid to the USSR that had made victory possible, nor about the Normandy landings, nor about the campaign in North Africa. 'When did Britain join the war?' I asked him.

'In 1943–4, I think,' he said, hesitantly.

When I told him that Britain had declared war in 1939, two years *before* the Soviet Union, Vitale was astonished.

Although Communist ideology is meant to unify and bond Soviet citizens together, the unifying power of the Great Patriotic War legacy is far more powerful, and it is used unremittingly by the Communist Party to foster allegiance and support for the system. It was startling to see and hear so many references to the war in official speeches, in the newspapers and bookshops where there were large sections devoted to the Great Patriotic War, just as there are to Lenin and the Communist Party.

On the stretch from Moscow we stayed one night with a teacher who had an English textbook for the eleventh form of secondary schools. It was entitled *Feat in the Name of Life* and subtitled *Stories about the Great Patriotic War*, and had just been reprinted. After a quotation from Lenin came chapters entitled 'Soldier's Glory', 'The Death of a Hero', 'Soviet Army Men Liberate Allied Airmen', 'Commander of Unbending Will', 'Soviet Children – Heroes of the War: How Shura Kulikov Made the Fascist Invaders Retire on Foot', and so on. 'Soviet Army Men Liberate Allied Airmen' is worth quoting:

> Major-General Sizokrylov was driving in his car looking at the endless columns of Soviet troops. The soldiers of the victorious Soviet Army were marching to the West. Crowds of liberated people were moving along the roads. A wave of pride rose in him. He was happy that Soviet troops, led by Communists, were liberating the world from fascism. He considered it natural, just as natural as the fact that Communists were at the head of a partisan movement in all enslaved countries. Communism was a force, liberating the world. The Soviet people were an example to all others in the fulfilling of their internationalist duty . . . Soviet troops began preparation for a final offensive to capture the capital of fascist Germany . . . the British and Americans were eager to capture Berlin themselves. [Sizokrylov then passes a German prisoner-of-war camp, full of Allied soldiers, that has just been freed by a Soviet tank that is too busy to stop.] The British and American airmen asked all the Russian officers to find out at least the name of the commander of that tank. It was funny, of course, that these British and Americans considered the saving of 200 Allied airmen almost as the greatest victory of the war. The Soviet officers did not think it was important. They answered simply, 'Oh, well, what does it matter?' The Allied officers thanked the Soviet command for the liberation, and the friendly and comradely treatment . . . and surrounded the Soviet general and other Soviet officers. They shouted, 'Thanks, boys, long live Russia!' But they went quiet when they heard the Soviet Army was going to capture Berlin. Group-Captain Sir Reginald Tangley was smiling too. He was looking at the well-trained and well-equipped Soviet Army units, at the new powerful Soviet-made tanks and artillery . . . Tangley remembered his long conversations with other British officers about Russia and the Soviet Army. They were all of the opinion

that Russia would come out of the war weak and the Soviet Army would be tired and weak, too.

'It does not look like this,' he thought now, and suddenly he felt a growing disquiet. 'They have gone a long way into Europe!' Sir Reginald Tangley stopped smiling. He had even forgotten for a moment that it was the Soviet Army that had liberated him from a fascist concentration camp . . .

The vast propaganda machine is still at work, partly because it is so extensive and so deeply embedded that it is difficult to order it to stop, and partly because some of the propaganda has taken hold and is now widely believed to be reality. Just as a fully charged supertanker needs miles to slow down and stop, so too does Soviet propaganda. Nevertheless, *glasnost* has encouraged a reassessment of Soviet history, which although only partial, is real and encouraging.

However, at the time we were in the Soviet Union, a Supreme Soviet Commission revealed that nearly 845,000 victims of Stalinism had been posthumously rehabilitated during 1988–9 but that local officials were not implementing a high-level decision to erect memorials to such victims. Just as we arrived in the USSR mass graves were discovered near Chelyabinsk, containing 80,000 corpses, as well as others near Donetsk, and in Karelia and Byelorussia.

A leading Soviet demographer estimated that altogether 9,400,000 peasants had died during Stalin's collectivisation programme in the 1930s, a figure that for the first time approximated Western estimates.

During June, as we approached the Urals, more mass graves were discovered near Kharkov in the east Ukraine and at Mednoye near Kalinin in Western Russia, through which we had cycled on our way to Moscow. A local KGB official confirmed that the graves outside Kharkov contained the remains of Polish officers as well as the remains of Soviet citizens executed by the NKVD in the Stalinist purges before the Second World War. But even though the evidence was being uncovered and a blanket admission of responsibility made, only Stalinism, the NKVD chief and his subordinates were held responsible.

We cycled into Kolomna through old red Kremlin walls, found a *stolovaya* and carried the bicycles up the broken steps into the foyer. As we did so, we met two language students and invited them to join us for lunch.

'We have only four restaurants in this town,' Alexander said, 'and that is for 170,000 people. And of the four at least two of them are usually closed. The situation for food is not good, as I expect you have noticed.'

I was curious to know if you could tell, from labels on canned foods or boxes, the origins of the food inside, and whether it came from the Ukraine or parts of Byelorussia affected by Chernobyl.

'No, of course not,' Alexander said. 'We have no information about this. We have been told that the area has been cleared up now, that is all, but I do not believe it. It is very difficult to be a student here,' he went on. 'First of all we have very little money. Our grant for the month is fifty roubles and you know how much it costs for food – seven or eight roubles for a kilo of tomatoes in the open market. It is enough for food if we buy it in the state shops, and no more. Our hostel costs us eleven roubles a month [US$0.70], so that leaves us thirty-nine roubles for everything else. We could not afford to eat in this restaurant even if we wanted to. Nor can we afford beer, but we are lucky there – there is no beer in Kolomna!'

'What do people think of Communism now? Do they still believe in it?' Howard asked.

'Russians once believed in Communism – my parents' generation, and their parents. But now we don't believe in Communism. And we don't believe in religion. We don't believe in anything any more. I just want to leave this country. Russia has developed into a model of how people shouldn't live. I am interested in the Bible but I have no money to buy one because they cost about 150 roubles – three months of my student grant. (We calculated that if a Bible in England cost the equivalent of a student grant for three months it would come to something like £1,000.)

'What do you think of the Church?'

'I think it's good! Especially right now because there is disbelief everywhere in the Soviet Union. We must believe in something. And it will be better for us if we believe in God.'

'What about young people like you?' Howard asked. 'Are there still young people who believe in Communism?'

'Hardly at all – not among young people. Nearly everyone wants to go abroad to work or to live. We are envious of the East Germans who have been given Deutschmarks for their own currency and are now part of West Germany. Perhaps the United States could do the same with the Soviet Union – give us dollars for roubles!' He laughed uproariously.

'If you wanted to, couldn't you set up your own business here in Kolomna under the new law allowing private businesses?'

'No, it's impossible. The mafia would extort payments from us.'

'What mafia?'

'The mafia are connected to the *nomenklatura*. They deal in stolen goods, foreign luxuries. They are powerful and use their connections to secure deals.'

'Couldn't you report them to the police?'

'No, the mafia have friends in the police. They are corrupt. The mafia would take revenge, that's certain.'

'Do you talk with your friends and other students about these problems, and how to overcome them?'

'No, we are sick and tired of these problems already. We talk about nothing: pop music, girls, films . . .'

'Not about organising a demonstration to demand change?'

'Rarely . . . Never! I'm not interested in it. I'm not going to struggle here in the Soviet Union, because I think it's useless to do so against the Communists. It's very difficult. No one knows when change will come but we believe it's possible, it's inevitable. But it will take many years, maybe fifty, maybe a hundred. We're tired of the regime.'

'So you just want to leave?'

'Yes, like you do.'

'We've just arrived!' we remonstrated, laughing together, but aware of the yawning gap between our Western experiences and the limited room for manoeuvre open to Alexander and his friends.

'We've been struggling since 1917 – for seventy years . . . '

'What do you feel about Gorbachev and *perestroika*?' Gilles asked him.

'Some people think that he just talks and does nothing. As for me I think he was useful in the early years of *perestroika* but now he is exhausted. We want someone more radical like Yeltsin or someone else. I'm not sure who. I'm not interested in Soviet internal policy.'

'But isn't this important for you, for the future?'

'Maybe it is important for me but I just want to go abroad. Many people of the older generation do not approve of Gorbachev because of the new cooperatives and the high prices. They are used just to state prices in shops. Most people do not like the new cooperatives, the private businesses. They prefer to have no goods with low prices than to have goods with high prices – this is just a habit of Soviet people . . .'

'For them, life was better under Brezhnev?'

'Twenty years ago people said things were better under Stalin, then under Khrushchev. Now people say things were better under Brezhnev – because we had more food and more goods in the shops. In twenty years' time,' he said, smiling bitterly, 'people will be saying things were better under Gorbachev.'

After thirty minutes a waiter finally arrived; after another twenty our miserable meal. 'Normal Soviet life,' Alexander said. When I mentioned

Sholokov's *Quiet Flows the Don*, he reacted violently. 'Typical Russian realism!' he spat out. 'A story of life in a poor Russian village. We are sick of it.'

As we ate, a small event, seemingly trivial, caught our attention. The restaurant was large and cheerless. A mere dozen people, spread far apart, added to the gloom. At the table closest to us were two men, one in military uniform, the other in civilian dress. The officer's uniform was immaculate bottle green, covered with gold braid and decorations. When he walked to his table three rows of huge gold medals clanked against each other, and he removed his tall gilt hat and white gloves with a certain self-satisfaction. Towards the end of the meal a waitress brought him a plateful of oranges. There was a moment of hush in the huge room. We hadn't seen any oranges since we had arrived in the Soviet Union and we called the waitress over to order some too.

'*Nyet*,' the waitress told us, 'there are no oranges.'

'But the officer has just been brought some,' we said, pointing out the table nearby.

'There are no oranges!' she repeated bluntly and walked off. This blanket denial of the incontrovertible was becoming typical of our experience in the Soviet Union. We were told restaurants were closed when they were open, that there were no vacant rooms in hotels when they were half-empty, that it was impossible to send telegrams when we had already done so, that there was no hot water in a hotel when we had already had a hot shower in the hotel staff's bathroom. Black was white and white was black.

It seemed absurd but the existence of a few oranges had created a little *frisson* in the restaurant. Oranges, it appeared, were reserved for people of consequence. We questioned Alexander about the rows of medals the officer was wearing and discovered that their proliferation is in part due to the practice of issuing a new war medal every ten years. For a start, the four standard ones can be multiplied by a factor of four, celebrating the tenth, twentieth, thirtieth and fortieth anniversaries of the end of the war. Then there are campaign medals. Even young officers, far too young to have been in the war, seem to have collected strings of medals, their appearance lying somewhere between Idi Amin and Baron Munchausen. Nor would Russians be content to wear just the medal ribbons, bright though they might be. There had to be big shiny medals, and the bigger the better. But not only soldiers wore medals. Millions of civilians wore their war medals permanently pinned to jackets. The national obsession with medals was taken to its extreme by Brezhnev who awarded himself four gold stars as a 'Hero of the Soviet Union' for bravery in the Second

World War which, even *Pravda* admitted, he did not deserve. To them, he had added the Order of Victory, reserved exclusively for military commanders who gained important wartime victories. Such was his love of decorations that when he died more than 200 awards and other distinctions had to be carried behind his coffin.

Alexander could tell us little about the Chernobyl disaster. Russians suspected that the problems were far greater than they had been led to believe but officially Chernobyl had been cleared up and the region outside the thirty-kilometre exclusion zone declared fit for human habitation. Only in the West, and amongst a handful of Soviet scientists, is the extent of the catastrophe known. According to the Soviet government, thirty-one people have died from radiation, 200 others have received serious doses of radioactivity and 135,000 have been evacuated from the exclusion zone. The Soviet government has never altered this assessment, first presented at an international conference in Vienna in August 1986 at which Valery Legasov, one of the architects of the Soviet nuclear programme, declared, 'I am profoundly convinced that our nuclear power stations are the pinnacle of achievement in power generation.' In 1988, two years after giving this optimistic appraisal, Legasov hanged himself.

The first foreign scientist to visit the 'Sarcophagus', the huge protective structure of steel and concrete built to contain the remains of the No 4 reactor, reported that it was far from being hermetically sealed and that Soviet scientists had inadequate radiation-monitoring instruments and protective clothing. They had no easy means of measuring alpha-particle radiation – the radiation given off by plutonium, the most toxic material at Chernobyl – their protective clothing was very primitive and gave them meagre protection, and the radiation surveillance of each individual for body contamination was desperately poor.

The scale of the catastrophe is only slowly becoming apparent. In 1990, the Chernobyl Union, an unofficial organisation of those involved in the clear-up operation, estimated that of the half-million people who had worked in the thirty-kilometre zone, 5,000 had died from radiation and up to 350,000 might be suffering from sickness due to radiation. In Byelorussia and Northern Ukraine around three million people are now believed to have received serious doses of radiation. 'It would be difficult to exaggerate the scale of the Chernobyl catastrophe,' according to Dr Zhores Medvedev, a Soviet biologist. 'The economic costs are almost incalculable and they will continue to grow well into the next century.'

Soviet scientists have evidence that places exist outside the exclusion zone where radiation counts are as high as inside it but officially this is denied. The inhabitants of these contaminated areas have not been evacuated, continue to till the soil and have not been given even basic information on how to avoid the effects of eating and inhaling radioactive food and dust. They continue to eat vegetables from their gardens, to gather and pickle mushrooms from the forests and hunt deer which feed on lichen, a vegetable that absorbs caesium.

By a decree enacted on 15 May 1986 all information about radioactive contamination was classified as secret, a ban that was extended on 27 June to doctors, who were forbidden to link any illnesses to the effects of Chernobyl's radiation. As a result, not a single person out of the half-million people who have worked within the exclusion zone has ever been diagnosed officially as suffering from any form of radiation sickness. The absence of a genuinely free press means that those most directly affected by Chernobyl are the least informed.

Our meal took so long to arrive that, by the time we had eaten it, it was mid-afternoon. So we accepted Alexander's offer to spend the night in the student hostel.

From a distance the hostel looked modern but as we approached we could see it was shoddily built and surrounded by a sea of mud, through which the students had to pick their way. Inside, the guardian, a flabby, suspicious woman ensconced in a little glass box, tried to stop us from entering, before being pacified.

Four students shared a small room, large enough for two bunk-beds and two desks, with a wooden cupboard each for their belongings. On the walls were advertisements torn from European magazines and photographs of Western and Soviet popstars. Down the corridor were communal showers and bathrooms in a state of extreme squalor. The walls and floors of the shower rooms were made of tiles, half of them broken, with rusty metal pipes running around the room at floor level. Moss grew on the walls; the floor and wooden duckboards were slippery with old sweat, of which the room smelt powerfully. The communal kitchens looked as though they too were cleaned rarely and perfunctorily. No kitchen equipment was provided by the hostel, everyone having their own saucepans and utensils in their room, and the kitchen consisted of four gas-fired stoves and a big plastic dustbin for slops and rubbish. The lavatories were unspeakable, with the filthiest stench, broken pipes, cracked lavatory seats and general ordure. One of the windows had been smashed to allow some aeration.

Witnessing the conditions in which they had to study, the state of the town and their talk about Russian history, it became easier to understand the students' pessimism about the future. One student, Natasha, believed that Russia had developed differently to the rest of Europe both because of the size of the country and the influence of the Russian Orthodox Church. She went on to say that the size of Russia and the vast, unexplored and unsettled territories in Siberia meant that Russia had always focussed Eastwards, away from Europe. This suited, and was encouraged by, the Russian Orthodox Church which held that it alone was the repository of true Christianity after the fall of Constantinople to the Ottomans in 1453. As a result, Russia had missed out on the Renaissance, and all the Greek and Roman scholarship, philosophy and culture that to the Orthodox Church was so much pagan learning.

The Church has always prided itself on the unchanged nature of its teachings and doctrine. When Russia adopted Orthodoxy in the eleventh century from Byzantium, the religion of the Greek Church had been established for nigh on a thousand years, so the books, the doctrine, the music, the paintings, the monastic system and even the architectural style were taken over wholesale, ready made. All these elements were viewed as aspects of a perfect whole, directly transmitted from Christ and therefore incapable of improvement, 'Orthodox' meaning 'that which guards and teaches the right belief' and admits of no alteration. Seeing itself as the guardian of true Christianity and Moscow as the Third Rome, the Church had no reason to allow pagan heresies – classical writings – or Christian heresies – Catholicism – to penetrate Russia. The Orthodox Church therefore ensured the isolation of Russia from Europe; preventing the development of any alternative culture, Russian culture remained synonymous with that of the Orthodox Church. It was largely from the Church that there also developed the indefinite but persistent belief that Russia had a world mission to fulfil, a quasi-religious mystique that merged with Marxism-Leninism and re-emerged as the role of the Soviet Union in establishing Communism worldwide.

In the sixteenth century the tsars, powerless to vanquish the Western kingdoms of Poland, Livonia, Sweden and the Crimean vassals of the Ottomans of the South, defeated the weak successor states of the Mongols and made themselves supreme in Russia itself. No regional and provincial autonomies, nor any corporate cities, were allowed to develop and when the tsars found autonomous corporations already in existence, as in the city of Novgorod, they destroyed them. So the struggle against royal absolutism, which in Western Europe so often took the form of a defence of regional and corporate autonomies, lacked in Russia one of its strongest bastions.

The Church was the one body that had the authority to counterbalance the power of the tsar, but in all civil, and many ecclesiastical matters too, the Church acknowledged his authority and, following the Byzantine tradition, preached his absolute power. Once Ivan the Terrible had destroyed the power of the old noble families, the tsar was left in the sixteenth century with absolute power. From the end of the fifteenth century the tsars had begun quietly to assume the mantle of the Byzantine emperors, Ivan III adopting the double-headed imperial eagle of Byzantium and, from about 1480, using the title of 'tsar', at first only in relations with his weaker neighbours. Little by little the tsar's historical claims grew until Ivan the Terrible assumed the title in 1547 of Tsar of all the Russias, a claim that the Turks, the Holy Roman Emperor and the Poles rejected outright. The universalism inherent in the idea of the Third Rome developed rapidly into a uniquely Russian blend of imperialism that suited the tsar and the Orthodox Church perfectly. Even by the sixteenth century Western visitors to Russia remarked on the extremes of Russian xenophobia. Ideally, the Church would have liked to cut the country off totally from the schismatic West but the tsars encouraged a small number of Western professionals, such as engineers and architects, to enter the country. The intention was never to absorb their experience of the European Renaissance, rather to take advantage of European technical advances and discard the rest.

The following day we cycled 114 kilometres to Ryazan across flat, ploughed farmland punctuated here and there with pine forest. In the city, it was Victory Day with parades, speeches and more red flags celebrating the end of the Great Patriotic War. We continued through Ryazan and set up camp on a river bank in the shade of some old willows. Not far away was a railway embankment towards which a steady trickle of people made their way at twilight, passing through the field of grass we were in. They were families from Ryazan who had come out to tend their gardens and spend the public holiday in their *dacha*s; the train stopped on the embankment to let them clamber on, clutching rope bags and vegetables, and whistled before moving slowly off, taking them back to the city. Overhead flock after flock of geese in V-formation flew towards the West and the setting sun, the occasional mournful honk intensifying the silence.

Gathering old rotten willow trunks we built up a huge fire, flames casting a red glow onto the gnarled and twisted trunks of the willows. Long after the rumble of the last train had passed away, and the geese had been swallowed up in a pitch-black sky, we sat silently, staring at the red embers, aware of our solitude on the Russian plain, listening to the hoarse croaking of unseen frogs on the riverbank.

The next three weeks we spent cycling across the vast Russian plain that stretches 2,000 kilometres from Moscow to the Urals, a flat expanse of arable land with slight undulations that do little to relieve the monotony of the landscape. The pine forests north of Moscow give way to forests of silver birch that had burst forth into a brilliant, tender green. The fields were huge and open, stretching away to the middle distance, lacking any kind of natural physical feature, farms, barns or outbuildings.

One fascinating aspect of the Russian landscape, novel to the European eye, was the unenclosed nature of the farmland. Apart from the tiny garden-vegetable plots next to the village houses and *dacha*s, all the land belonged to the state, being farmed either as a collective or a state farm. With no private land to speak of there was no need for any to be fenced in and demarcated; fields stretched on and on without any boundary. Day after day passed without our seeing barbed-wire fences dividing up fields; in fact, in the entire 12,000-kilometre distance from Leningrad to Vladivostok I did not see a single barbed-wire fence other than those running along the national borders.

On the way to Shatsk a lorry pulled over to the side of the road and a young man jumped out. He waved at us to stop, and ran across the road with two loaves of bread, still hot from the bakery, and gave them to Gilles. 'Tell your friends this is a present for them!' was all he said, climbing back into his lorry and departing with a wave. We were glad to have them in the next village, which was decrepit in the extreme. It had no café or *stolovaya*. At the village shop we bought tinned fish, milk and boiled sweets. There was nothing else to buy, most of the shelves being half-empty. We sat outside in the sunshine on a dilapidated bench and ate hungrily. Close by, a few yards away, was another bench where four men in their thirties sat, while a fifth stood, gazing about him. They were badly dressed in what looked like second-hand, cast-off clothes such as one might pick up in a charity shop. It was midweek, and the middle of the day, but they appeared to have nothing to do. Our arrival and presence didn't bother them, nor did it create a flicker of interest. They neither greeted us, nor looked at us or the bikes. Worn patches of earth and a few birches separated us from the deserted road. Nothing came and nothing went apart from a horse-drawn cart that drew up at the shop. Over a wooden fence we could see three peasant women in white kerchiefs and brown coats talking; sometimes they appeared to be about to move off, but whenever I looked up they were still there in conversation. I glanced back at the men; they sat still and hardly spoke. Occasionally one looked about him in a bored way, but not at us. Their hair was tousled and unkempt, and they stared ahead of them in silence, vacantly.

We must have been the first foreigners ever to stop in their tiny remote village, we were five yards away, and yet not one of them seemed the vaguest bit interested. Then I realised where I had seen that vacant, dulled, withdrawn expression before: on the faces of prisoners in a television documentary on prisons in Australia.

'They have nothing to do,' Vitale said, 'you can see for yourself that there is nothing to do in the village.'

'Don't they have any work?'

'They probably work on the collective farm but no one does much there, the wages are very low.'

'What would they earn on a collective farm?'

'Maybe 120–50 roubles a month; it's nothing, *nothing*. It's hardly enough to live.'

'So they sit around instead?'

'They do a little work, of course. The important thing is to turn up to work in the morning; if they do that they get paid. The collective farms are so badly run that when harvest comes people from the city must leave their offices to work in the fields.' I remembered Olga, a professor at the Leningrad Academy of Sciences, saying that she too had to go to the fields round Leningrad in September to dig up potatoes by hand because there weren't any potato-harvesting machines. 'Food rots in the warehouses, because no one is held responsible. It makes no difference to the warehouse manager if it all rots. His wage stays the same. But the peasants store their own produce very carefully, so that they can sell it in the spring when the state shops are empty.'

(In 1990 alone it was estimated that the Soviet Union lost twenty-nine million tons of grain, a million tons of meat, and one third of all fruit and vegetables during collection, processing and storage.) 'I know from a cousin that there was a good crop of potatoes last year in the Sverdlovsk region, but there were not enough potato sacks, nor vehicles in which to transport them, so many were wasted.'

'Why does nobody mind if so much gets wasted?' I asked Vitale.

'Nobody cares because it's not their own,' he replied, 'everybody knows this.' Khrushchev had tried to do away with the private plots, cutting them to a maximum size of half an acre, but under Brezhnev this reverted back to an acre, and figures showed that private-farm output rose as a result.

We arrived mid-afternoon in Shatsk, a one-horse town with a dusty, fly-blown highstreet. Gilles felt unwell, so we decided to stop for the night and sought out the hotel, a shabby building of grey brick that looked as if it had been built by Sunday-school children. We let Vitale go in first to ask for rooms, as the sudden appearance of three foreigners sometimes caused an administrator into denying that there were rooms available. There were no showers and no hot water, the latter having been switched off from 1 May to 1 October. We set off for our first Russian *banya*.

For twenty kopeks we gained entry past a vast *babushka* on door duty. Having purchased our tickets from her we came to a man two yards further on whose job was to collect them. Beyond him we entered a changing room, dilapidated and dirty. Stripping, we collected an aluminium bowl and entered the second room, hot and humid, where men were busily washing and scrubbing themselves. Leaving our bowls behind, Vitale led the way into the steamroom and as he opened the door we were knocked back by the wave of hot steam.

Gasping for air we entered, just able to make out glistening brown figures enveloped in a cloud of steam, sitting on steep wooden steps.

Seated and hardly able to breathe, we started to pour sweat. Now and then someone would get up and throw a bowl full of water onto the red hot stones, to create a mushroom cloud of steam, each one intensifying the searing heat, until another shouted, 'Enough! Enough!' The Russians next to us, only just visible, were whipping their bodies with bunches of birch branches. At Vitale's order we lay down on the red-hot boards, while he proceeded to thwack us methodically with birch branches given to him by his neighbour.

After five minutes Vitale directed us back, red as lobsters, to the washroom. Huge men sat soaping themselves up, scrubbing vigorously with loofahs and plastic scrubbing pads, as though cleaning a dirty saucepan. Following Vitale's example we filled the bowls with ice-cold water and tipped them over our heads. The effect was electrifying – my whole body sprang alive, tingling and burning. After a good dousing we went back into the steamroom and repeated the whole process.

The atmosphere was more convivial than any we had experienced, the baths appearing to double up as club and meeting house. But the tile floor was dirty and broken in many places, and the metal pipes were rusty and encrusted with blisters. The walls were covered with peeling paint, and the tiles were broken, cracked and clumsily repaired. Vitale said the *banya* had been built before the Revolution. Seventy years had passed and no one had built a new one.

When Vitale's neighbour realised we were foreigners he told us that he had been a teacher and had recently retired after forty years' service. All his life he had taught history but it was only in the last five years, with *glasnost*, that he had realised that everything he had taught was false.

'Only now do I know that what I taught was not the truth,' he said sadly. He seemed a kind man, a well-meaning schoolteacher in a small provincial town who had given the best part of his life to his profession. And then just as he retired, when he should have been able to look back with pride on his life's work and achievement, he had learnt that what he had taken on trust and taught was not true. It made a mockery of everything he had done, a mockery of his entire life. And it appeared no one could be held responsible.

We left the *banya* feeling a certain melancholy after the teacher's tale, but nonetheless physically invigorated and unbelievably clean. For us, these *banya*s were a life-saver.

In Shatsk there was one very new white-brick building, a new Communist Party headquarters, and a few shops stocked with curious odds and ends. In the dusty square a few *babushka*s sold onions, garlic and parsley from a trestle table and nearby a man sold apples from the back of a van; but at six roubles a kilo he had very little business, large and crisp as they were.

'They're very expensive!' Vitale expostulated, reluctant to pay such an exorbitant price. But we had plenty of roubles and as there was nothing other than apples available I insisted we brought three kilos. 'They're almost certainly stolen from a collective warehouse,' Vitale commented as we walked away.

There wasn't much to buy in the food shops – lard, some fatty sausages, butter, tinned fish, Leningrad bricks, bottled apple juice with a thick layer of sediment at the bottom, glutinous jam, coffee substitute, green pickled tomatoes, sugar (to Vitale's surprise) and milk which we could not buy as we'd forgotten our own container.

'Simon, I told you our country is crazy. Don't ask me to explain it. I cannot.' As we walked back, I asked Vitale about the proposed law to grant Soviet citizens passports that would enable them to travel abroad freely.

'Even if the law is passed,' he said, 'many people will not be able to get these new passports.'

'Why not?'

'We think we will have to pay for them in hard currency, in American dollars.'

'Which you do not have?'

'Of course not. Where could we get American dollars? It's illegal to have them. So even if we could get them, when we handed them over there would be trouble. People would ask, "How do you have dollars?" The mafia have dollars, of course, but they will find a way round the regulations somehow – they always do.'

The next day a friendly cook, Tamara, let us into the hotel canteen an hour before it officially opened – an impressive accomplishment. She fussed around us, bringing us food, spoiling us as much as she could, probing to find out if we were married.

'Not married?' she squealed in delight. 'Nor the American? Nor the Frenchman?' She couldn't believe it. Her laughter affected the other cooks and servers who up to then had been dour-faced and had kept their distance. Everyone suddenly cheered up.

'What's the coffee like?' I asked Howard at breakfast.

'Tastes like mud.'

'So appearances aren't always deceptive.'

From the beginning of our journey we succeeded in confusing Howard totally over the girl's name, Svetlana, and the Russian word for sour cream, *smetana*.

'Get me some more Svetlana will you,' we would tell Howard in a *stolovaya*, and his request for one, two or even four more Svetlanas inevitably brought screams of laughter from the kitchen.

Sometimes, to convey what we wanted, we ventured into the kitchens and mimed out dishes that our Russian was unequal to describing. Such forays were periodically successful, especially when we found bags of meat, eggs and vegetables the staff had purloined to take home, but not infrequently a tremendous din from the kitchen would precede Howard being chased by powerfully built Russian cooks weighing more than the four of us together.

Although Howard had assured me that his command of Russian was 'good enough to get by', he was soon turning to Gilles and me for Russian words. In *stolovaya*s and people's homes, Howard would launch forth enthusiastically and rapidly exhaust his Russian vocabulary. His reply, which he gave irrespective of the question put to him, was 'Me? *Amerikanski*.' Over six months the distinction between '*Amerikanyets*', an American, and '*Amerikanski*', the adjective, continued to elude him.

When we left the 'Tourist Hotel' in Shatsk, Tamara gave us each a hug, shyly pulling out a chain with a crucifix from around her neck, and asking if we were Christians.

We set off through vast pine and birch forests along dead-straight roads that stretched to a pinprick in the distance. We were probably the first Europeans to have passed through these towns and villages, but we could have been the last for all the interest in us. If anyone looked at us from a distance they would turn away as we drew close and not look again. Cars overtook us but rarely did anyone turn round to examine us.

Not so long ago involvement, even a conversation, with a foreigner spelt trouble; two generations back it was tantamount to treason. As foreigners we were dangerous material, hard to handle. Both the state and the

Russian people have a deep-rooted suspicion of foreigners, especially those that visit their country. What are they doing? Why are they here?

Contamination with foreign ideas has always been the dread of Russian rulers, tsarist and Communist alike, and they have done their utmost to prevent their entry and limit their circulation. Russian nobles who pursued the remnants of Napoleon's army back to Paris were so impressed by French civilisation that they returned to Russia determined to reform their own country along more enlightened principles. But the Decembrist plot was discovered; some were executed, others exiled to Siberia, and the power of the autocracy was intensified. Throughout the nineteenth century the tsarist autocracy fought to prevent the diffusion of foreign liberal and revolutionary ideas and, under Stalin, sympathy for them was enough to secure heavy sentences in the labour camps. Deep xenophobia, stemming from ignorance and prejudice, is a historical Russian trait that a few years of *glasnost* is unlikely to eliminate.

This ingrained fear of foreign contamination has astonishing ramifications. One Russian woman recounted how, as a teenage girl, her mother had been caught in Odessa on the Black Sea at the time of the Nazi invasion and occupation of the city. She was sixteen, uninvolved in the Soviet war effort and had never had any contact with the occupying German forces. Many years later, when she wanted to study, at the Foreign Language Institute, the fact that she had been in occupied territory during the war was held against her, as it was when it came to finding a job. It wasn't a question of collaboration with the Germans, or even sympathy with them, but the mere fact of having been in close proximity to them.

All three of us found this idea of guilt by association intrinsically repugnant, even more so when extended to children, as it had been in this case. But we heard of many like it.

7

THE HUNGRY REGIONS II

SUNDAY WAS WARM with hardly a cloud in the pale blue sky. We passed two churches, both in ruins. The fields grew ever larger, black earth stretching away to the horizon without interruption. We paused in a village after sixty kilometres of wheatfields to draw water from a well. It was quiet, and old men and women sat on wooden benches just outside their cabins, facing the empty road. Behind the houses were wells operated by a huge wooden beam balanced on a fulcrum. The white blossom of the hawthorn confirmed the arrival of spring, intensely white against the bright green of newly unfolded leaves. Here and there men were ploughing their private plots with horse-drawn wooden ploughs, one furrow at a time. It was quiet and peaceful with hardly a sound in the air.

We turned down a rough track to a village marked Dubityel in search of lunch; the café was open but deserted, and we lunched on bread and tinned fish. As we prepared to leave a little crowd of women and children gathered. 'Are you Estonians?' the boldest woman asked. They were as astonished to learn we were French, American and British as we were to learn that they were not Russian but Mordivinians and Udmurts, both Uralic ethno-linguistic groups related to the Finnic people, and that we had unknowingly entered the Mordivinian Autonomous Republic. From them we learnt that we had passed not only into a new republic but a new time-zone and we advanced our watches by one hour.

Another sixty kilometres brought us to Zubova Polyana, a dusty town well shaded by birch trees. We went first to the *stolovaya*, to slake our thirst, and then to the hotel where we met the first secretary of Komsomol, the Young Communist League. He invited us to join him for dinner, returned at seven o'clock with a car and took us to the same *stolovaya* we had stopped in. The staff were surprised to find us back so quickly in the company of a local Communist Party official. This time, instead of eating in the bleak canteen as before we were led up stairs to a private dining room with its own bathroom, padded chairs, glass cabinet, and a large table laid with a clean tablecloth and attractive china. When the second secretary of Komsomol arrived, dishes, champagne and mineral water appeared with unaccustomed speed, served by a uniformed waitress. The first dish to arrive was *okroshka*, a cold summer soup made from cucumber, chives, cream, chicken stock and *kvass*, a traditional fermented rye drink popular in Russia. Followed by tender beef, fried potatoes, salad and coffee, it was the best meal we had eaten for weeks.

Keeping off politics the conversation went fine; but we were more interested in their attitude to Gorbachev than local hunting and fishing. Our first question about *perestroika* froze the air and both secretaries appeared acutely embarrassed. Yes, they were for *perestroika*, they said, cautiously.

'We want to vote for reformists to the Supreme Soviet,' the first secretary said, speaking gingerly and glancing at his colleague. 'But since *perestroika* began, every candidate claims to be in favour of reform, so it's impossible to know who is speaking the truth. The military candidate says he wants to reform the army, the agronomist is for agricultural reform, the Communist Party candidate for reform of the Party! Nobody knows if these people want real change or just cosmetic changes, which will leave everything the same.'

'What does your work as first secretary of Komsomol consist of?' Gilles asked.

'Propaganda,' he replied, 'is the most important part. And I organise competitions, sports, meetings and talks for young people.'

'Do young people play sports every weekend?'

'No, sports competitions are held on national holidays. We had one recently on Victory Day.'

The directness with which he assured us that his primary role was propaganda took us aback, but we found that 'propaganda' has a very different connotation in the Soviet Union to the West. Whereas to us it is a pejorative term, in the Soviet Union it is still largely seen as something positive and praiseworthy.

'We have three new electronics factories here,' the second secretary then said, 'and they are all "ecology free".'

'Ecology free?' I asked, puzzled.

'Yes,' he said. 'They do not pollute.'

Breakfast the following morning was interrupted by the arrival of the second secretary clutching a magnificent chess set in a wooden box with an inlaid picture of the Virgin Mary and Christ on the lid.

'A present!' he told us. 'Now you can play chess in the evenings.' Wondering what the religious imagery meant to him I asked if he went to church. 'No, I'm interested but do not believe,' he replied.

His friend, a man with blue, humorous eyes and the air of a joker, introduced himself as a guitarist. Zubova Polyana was a small town, hardly large enough, I thought, to justify a professional musician.

'Is there enough work for you in Zubova Polyana?' I asked.

'I have a contract with the Komsomol organisation,' he said with a knowing wink.

'Are you a professional guitarist?'

'Almost,' he said with a grin. 'I was. Now I paint houses from time to time because I have a wife and son. Even a musician has to earn a living, you know! Normally, I sing – yes, I sing too – in Russian, but I have a new song in English because everybody is international now – even singers. My hero, my inspiration, is Vladimir Visotsky, because he represents the little man.' When we said goodbye and rode off, our chess set strapped to the back rack, the guitarist smiled enigmatically.

'I think we will meet again,' he said.

'I hope so,' I said.

'I think so.'

For days and days our road stretched as straight as a pencil across the European plains of Russia, huge horizons to left and right. Either side of the road was a broad swathe of emerald-green grass scattered thickly with golden dandelions. Set back, one hundred yards on either side, was a wall of tall silver birches, that gave the illusion of having entered an avenue leading to a Chekhovian country estate. Every treetop was filled with crows that cawed noisily and rose up as we cycled past. From morning to night the only sound was the caw, caw, caw of crows and the rustling of the wind. The land undulated gently and even a slight rise could give a distant view of fields stretching away without end. The only objects to stand out in the landscape by virtue of their size were the shells of ruined churches, so many destroyed that it felt as if we were witnessing the aftermath of war.

With little traffic we cycled side by side, talking, or spread out, absorbed in our own thoughts. Our natural pace seemed about the same, no one lagging far behind. We cycled slowly, rhythmically, soaking up the hot spring sunshine, feeling stronger and more invigorated as the weeks went by. It felt intensely good to be alive, tiny pinpricks lost on the vast map of the Soviet Union, inching our way East. We were not in a hurry; summer and autumn stretched ahead of us. We were young, fit and free to go as we pleased and ahead lay unknown territory.

Wheatfields stretched without a break for ninety-six kilometres until Nizhniy Lomov, a dilapidated town with pot-holed streets where we came across a collection of metal cabins marked 'Motel'.

'They call this a motel!' Howard said, looking around him, laughing. 'I must be the only American who'd recognise it as one.'

It took half an hour to persuade the adminstrator to allow us to bring our bikes into the compound. Once inside, Howard, who had nominated himself expedition chief at the start of the journey, began to prepare a vegetable and pasta stew. As usual, we had not been able to find meat.

'I take it no one's invited a girlfriend,' he said, sitting cross-legged, peeling potatoes, 'so we'll have plenty of garlic, OK?' Vitale, Gilles and I went for a *banya* while Howard continued with supper, and came back after forty minutes to find him swinging the door to-and-fro while smoke poured from the cabin.

'Smells good tonight, Howard. All well?' I asked.

'Close,' he said. 'The stove set the rubber floor alight. I had to toss it through the door and stamp the fire out.'

'Not the stew too?' Gilles asked, alarmed.

'Christ, you guys are lucky to have anything! My shoes almost melted putting out the fire. I just hope that dragon doesn't have a sense of smell.'

The next morning the administrator inspected the cabin, sniffing suspiciously, but noticed nothing, Howard standing like a schoolboy with his foot covering the hole in the floor.

Sixty-five kilometres brought us to Mikhailovka where we stopped beside a huge, red-brick church. All the roofs had caved in and a massive crack snaked down the front of the church to the doors which were propped up with huge timbers.

Inside, virtually all the stucco had fallen off and the ground was churned up, tractors having entered not through the main door but through holes in the walls. Heaps of fertiliser and old wheels lay around; pigeons flew out as we explored.

Outside, I asked a boy wearing a red Young Pioneer scarf how old the church was.

'Four hundred years,' he told me, but it looked more like mid-nineteenth century to me. He did not know when it had been closed. I sat down on a knoll opposite and looked around. It was yet another, dusty, chaotic-looking village of poor wood cabins, village pumps along the main street and a few mangy dogs. A wooden cart driven by a white-haired man and pulled by a grey horse hove into view and passed the church, its wooden wheels creaking and groaning. It could have been a sight from a hundred years ago.

We moved on. Eventually Penza came into view – a large modern city, with tall white and red apartment blocks rising straight from a shoulder of dense pine forest.

As we entered the town we passed a jet fighter impaled on a concrete plinth in the centre of a roundabout, a monument to the Great Patriotic War. At the hotel the administrator said there were no rooms. We had heard that rooms in hotels are always kept back in case they are needed by visiting *nomenklatura* who appear unexpectedly and demand a room. For forty-five minutes we waited outside in the cold, then we were allowed to bring the bikes in and wait inside. Another hour passed before we were asked for our passports. After another fifteen minutes Gilles and Vitale were allocated rooms, after thirty Howard and I were. No explanation was given as to how four rooms had suddenly become vacant in a full hotel and no Russian would have expected one.

From the moment of arrival to the moment we got to our rooms had taken two and a quarter hours, and that at the end of a hard day's cycling, having covered 120 kilometres on a lunch of thin, watery soup, gristly meat, congealed rice and biscuits. Exhausted and hungry, we just wanted to get to our rooms; we did not care that the curtains were stained, the furniture was old and mismatched, there was no hot water, no plugs and the bathroom sink was half detached from the wall. Gilles had diarrhoea – but none of our bathrooms had any lavatory paper. At reception they apologised and said that none was available, neither in the hotel, nor in the city. There was a *defitsit* that month.

Most of the Soviet Union's lavatory paper is made in Lithuania. With the economic blockade, supplies were running low throughout the entire country. The Lithuanians, it appeared, were making the rest of the Soviet Union pay a heavy price for the blockade.

From my room, I tried to put a call through to my sister in England. On the eighth attempt, I got the international operator.

'You will have to wait for a line,' I was told.

'How long?'

'Four days.'

I gave up, and descended with Howard and Vitale to the restaurant. Inevitably, it was closed for repair, but in the café we found some cold roast beef.

'Let's get at least a kilo,' I said to Howard.

'Simon,' he replied, with great deliberation, 'we're taking it *all*.'

So we bought it, over three kilos of best cold beef, to the amazement of the woman behind the bar. It cost us sixty roubles, the equivalent of a month's pension, and it was money well spent. We would have paid three times the price, even traded in the very shirts we were wearing. Like all Russians we had money in our pockets. For them and for us it was the same story – finding something to spend the money on. We also found cheese, the first we had seen in 1,500 kilometres, the first since Leningrad. Howard was excited.

'I don't believe it. I just *don't* believe it.'

'We'll take the cheese too,' I told the dumbfounded woman. 'And those chocolate sweets . . . yes, all of them.' We double-checked to ensure we had not missed anything, and returned to our room.

'Amazing!' Howard exclaimed, shaking his head. 'This is *real* meat.'

Howard, Vitale and I went for a walk in the evening to get the feel of the town. Penza had a more prosperous air than any we had seen. In search of a coffee we tried to get into a restaurant.

'*Nyet, nyet,*' came the familiar response as a woman blocked the door successfully with her ample body. We asked directions but most people were non-plussed by the question. They had no idea. Eventually we found a café, baldly illuminated by striplights. Outside were plastic tables and chairs, round which people sat in near darkness. Howard and Vitale sat down while I ordered coffee for three.

'Coffee *nyet.*'

'Tea?'

'Tea *nyet.*'

'Beer?'

'Beer *nyet.*'

'What have you got?'

'Ice cream and biscuits.'

We sat in the dark with ice cream and biscuits. We could just make people out in the dark. Although they were young, they talked barely above a whisper, as people might during a church service. There was no music. It was almost as if conversation in public was not approved of. It seemed hardly surprising that the Russians' favourite pastime seemed to be getting drunk; there was very little else to do.

I had asked Vitale what he did of an evening after work, and he told me that he normally met up with friends, not at his house – it was too small – but at his friends' houses. They went to the cinema from time to time but never to cafés or restaurants – they were too expensive and bad – and at weekends they went to the country, to his *dacha*.

As far as we could make out, this 'café' was one of the few places open in Penza in the evening. After an hour sitting in the dark, we wandered back to the hotel. An Armenian in a room opposite ours invited us in for a drink; there was a bottle of vodka and another of cognac open on the table, and the air reeked of alcohol. He was there with two girls, a pretty Ukrainian and an Armenian, and all three were slightly drunk.

'I'm a businessman,' he told us proudly, tapping his chest.

'Great,' I replied laconically, shrugging my shoulders. 'What kind of business?' He dragged out a pile of bleached and crinkled jeans from under the bed.

'American,' he said. They were crudely made and sewn with an imitation American brand logo, the work of a cooperative near Kharkov in the Ukraine, of which all three were partners.

'How much do they cost?' I asked him.

'Four hundred roubles.' That was a handsome sum, well in excess of the average monthly salary of 250, the equivalent of an eight months' student grant. There clearly would not be many students at Penza University wearing these jeans.

'Don't you have a problem selling them for so much?'

'No, we can sell as many as we can make. The problem is finding material to make them with. Come and join us.' But the prospect of another bout of drinking was more than we could bear. We said goodnight.

The following morning we sent off a few telegrams, a process that took an hour and a half. We left and cycled for days across vast plains, passing nothing but wheat for 200 kilometres.

Seeing the gigantic area of cereal production it was hard to believe that there wasn't a massive abundance of food in the Soviet Union. Thinking back to earlier travels in Pakistan, India and Bangladesh, I wondered what the people of those countries would make of such a landscape. In Bangladesh every patch, every square inch, had been cleared, worked and planted. The land was intensively cultivated, tiny areas producing enough food to support a family when cyclones and floods did not intervene. In Northern Pakistan and India the hillsides had been terraced for centuries, staggering physical toil that could make all the difference between hunger and sufficiency.

Nothing could have made a greater contrast to the carefully husbanded rice paddies of the Indian sub-continent than this Russian sea of wheat. That the country could not even feed itself seemed a mockery, a cruel joke, an absurdity. And when I saw the half-empty shops, the queues, the ration cards, it seemed more like a crime.

Beyond Kuznetsk we stopped in the late afternoon at a shop next to a tiny village. Apart from pasta shells and tinned white fish with an unpleasant smell, there was nothing to buy. Luckily, we found three huge women at the roadside selling onions and potatoes from an old red pram. They laughed heartily at our bright, tight-fitting cycling clothes and declared we were Martians.

Asking in the village where we could pitch our tent a man showed us the way to a patch of grass beyond his garden fence. Noticing that our clothes were covered in mud, he told us to bring them all up to the house, where we washed them in his courtyard. He was called Nikolai, and had just turned sixty and retired the previous week from his work as a mechanic on the collective farm.

When Nikolai came to bring us a handful of onions we asked him about the remains of a brick church on a nearby rise.

'It was burnt in the Revolution,' he said, 'but there was a much more beautiful one in this village built entirely of stone. But that too was destroyed after the Revolution, and there's nothing there now, nothing at all.'

Will another one be built one day?'

'No,' he replied. 'There is a church in Kuybyshev, 200 kilometres away.' We had a bottle of vodka with us and it did not take much persuasion to get Nikolai to have a drink. His tongue loosened by a few nips of vodka, he asked if we were married, and about what we did back home.

'Are your parents rich?' he asked Gilles.

'No. Well . . . no! It's difficult to say. They have a restaurant and a farm in France . . . They work hard and they live well but they're not rich.' Even answering such an ostensibly simple question was remarkably diffi- cult because the words themselves conjured up such different images to Nikolai and to Gilles. Wealth is relative and, like beauty, varies in the eye of the beholder.

'I welcome you to the Soviet Union,' Nikolai said, solemnly toasting us with a glass of vodka. 'How would you like to come and live here? We will give you land if you come.'

'Well, that's very kind,' I said, conscious that nothing we had seen in six weeks could possibly induce me to take up residence in the Soviet Union. 'But I think that would be . . . difficult . . . We haven't seen any girls in the village.'

'That's easy to arrange,' Nikolai said. 'Don't you worry!'

The following day we cycled towards Zhigulevsk, close to the River Volga. Vitale told us that Kuybyshev was a 'closed' city, because of military factories which we would have to bypass. It poured with rain all day, grey skies and rain combining to turn bleak villages and towns into living nightmares of mud and water. At lunchtime we entered a *stolovaya* up crumbling concrete steps through a dirty, wooden door, dark with grease. Water poured from us and squelched out of our shoes. Inside were the usual plastic tables, surly cooks, the same miserable fare: foul-smelling soup, a pink and uncooked pork hash, and macaroni like rubber. It was all inedible but there was nothing else and we tried to eat something to gather energy for the afternoon. The decrepit concrete building doubled up, unbelievably, as a hotel but the prospect of spending a night there was infinitely worse than that of continuing in the rain.

'Oh my God!' Gilles groaned, biting into another stodgy dough-ball, drenched in cooking-oil. 'Can this be real?'

'I guess this trip must be tough for you,' I said, 'being used to French cuisine.'

'Well, maybe ... it's tough ... yes, it's a tough trip,' Gilles said, grinning tiredly. 'You don't miss dumplings, Simon? Boiled beef and peas? You should be used to this. But then you've lived in France, too. It's not so bad for Howard, he's used to American cooking ...'

'Gilles, on the ranch, we eat steaks this big,' Howard countered wearily, holding his hands over a foot apart. 'T-bone steaks you wouldn't believe.'

'I don't understand this country,' Vitale reflected. 'Really I don't.'

Water poured down, drowning all other noises, and steam rose from our clothes. Suddenly we were all laughing, laughing hysterically at everything and nothing in particular, laughing to release the strain, the absurdity, the hopelessness of it all, until our shoulders ached and it felt as though our collar bones were about to break. The cooks and those eating looked at us as if we were mad. Then we climbed onto our bikes and cycled off, chased by wind and sheets of rain.

Why *do* you do it? many people wonder and a few ask, perplexed. There were moments when I asked myself the same question. I couldn't say I *enjoyed* that day; we were soaked to the skin, our eyes screwed up against the rain. Occasionally we were drenched with muddy water by a passing vehicle, the landscape was monotonous, the villages more bedraggled than ever, the side roads of earth turned into a sea of mud, grey concrete merging with grey skies. But to travel only in ease and comfort is to cut oneself off from all that is most immediate and vital in the world.

After 120 kilometres we cycled into Zhigulevsk through roads drowned in water. The hotel there was one of many that decided they were full the moment we arrived. As it appeared half-deserted we prowled around the corridors opening doors, found several unoccupied rooms and led the grumbling administrator back to see them.

We carried the bikes upstairs to a large room with four beds, past a large oil painting of Lenin relaxing over a cup of tea on a terrace in amiable conversation with Maxim Gorky. Like so many others, the hotel had no bathrooms and no hot water. To get clean we had to go out to the public *banya*; tired, wet and hungry we walked there in the rain. At the *banya*, there was a queue of nearly twenty men ahead of us, waiting for their turn to enter. They were sitting, most in silence, a few talking quietly as if round a deathbed. We took our places. As we edged forward slowly one man aged about fifty came up to us and whispered furtively with a smile about his lips:

'How do you like our queue?'

'It moves desperately slowly,' I replied.

'The result of our Revolution,' he whispered. 'Our silent experiment . . . made by the Jews.' His look was conspiratorial.

'But aren't the Jews good people too?'

'That', he replied, with a thin smile, 'is a complicated question! Do you see we don't talk? It's better not to talk in our country. Forty-six million people were killed by Stalin. Are you surprised? Our culture has been destroyed and our people drained of their spirit.' And then he was gone, as suddenly as he had arrived.

Our turn came and we went in. Never had hot water seemed more welcome. One man talked to us, inviting us to join him for breakfast the following day.

Alexander Vasilivich lived in one of those concrete apartment blocks that are so omnipresent that they could symbolise the Soviet Union. He ushered us into his neatly decorated flat, introducing us to his wife, Galina. Alexander had had a special reason for talking to us in the *banya*. He had been released from a concentration camp near Bremen in 1945 by British and American troops. He had been taken prisoner as a boy by the Germans near Smolensk in 1941 and had spent four years in a German camp for Soviet and Polish women and children. He was only thirteen when taken to Germany and as a Russian had been compelled to wear a white armband to indicate his nationality.

'At the beginning of 1945 Bremen was very heavily bombed and as our camp was close to the city, we were bombed too. English, American and Soviet planes bombed Bremen, but of course we knew which planes were which. We feared the Soviet bombing raids the most because they bombed indiscriminately, while the English and American planes bombed specific targets in the town – factories, the railway yard, bridges. I don't know why the Russians bombed blindly – maybe because they were more angry at the Germans. Of course, we didn't know what was happening in the war until one day we found that the German troops guarding our camp had left! Not long after English and American troops arrived. Suddenly we were free. I would like to be in touch with those soldiers. Maybe there are organisations for veterans in your countries. . .? I wanted to go home after the war but I met an uncle in Byelorussia who advised me not to go back to Smolensk as everything had been destroyed there, so I went to work on a collective farm. Now I am an electronics engineer in a factory making aircraft pieces; I earn 160 roubles a month.'

'What do you feel about the German people?' I asked Alexander.

'I think there are good people in Germany but the two Germanies should not be reunited. As I was only a child in the war I was occasionally allowed out of the camp and I begged German women for bread and sometimes they gave it to me. Yes, there were good people.'

While the conversation turned on the war Galina was happy, but once it turned to politics she began to look worried and twice cautioned her husband to be careful in what he said. Alexander seemed happy to answer our questions, however. At first he had liked Gorbachev but now he was not sure. He felt that the *nomenklatura* were responsible for preventing change, and that Gorbachev was having difficulty ousting the old deputies who clung onto their positions and privileges. The longer we had been in the Soviet Union the more apparent it became that the pressure for change came from the non-Russian republics – the Baltics, Georgia, Armenia, Kazakhstan, the Ukraine, but never from Russia. Howard asked why nothing similar seemed to be happening in the Russian Republic.

'Russia is the poorest republic,' Alexander replied. 'For seventy years we have built up the other republics. Now that they're rich they want to leave. And Russia has helped so many countries abroad; this aid should be stopped and the money spent at home. We must stop helping Cuba and the African countries . . . The Revolution was for a good future but what happened later was something else . . . At the moment we have no motivation to do anything as everything is *ours*, not mine.

'Do you think people are prepared to pay the price of change to a market economy or do they prefer to stay as they are?'

'No, most people do not want to change to a market economy. We are afraid that if we change we will not be able to pay for food. Pensioners receive seventy roubles a month, you know what that will buy today . . .'

A short ride took us to Togliatti on the other side of the Volga, one of the vast Russian rivers, that flows south into the Caspian. To get to the city we cycled over a massive hydroelectric power dam, the kind of mammoth engineering project Russians delight in. After industrial suburbs we penetrated a wasteland of raw apartment blocks and beyond them the city centre, past vast propaganda murals and Soviet factories. Against the grey concrete buildings they were a welcome relief. But nothing could have made a greater contrast with reality than these pictures of clean, organised factories being directed by white-coated foremen holding portable phones. I wondered how the Russians reconciled such propaganda and the political slogans in giant letters that are ranged along the top of buildings with what goes on around them.

'We don't notice these things any more,' Vitale told me. 'They are just like trees or bushes in the landscape.'

In the city centre we came across three German businessmen who advised us to stay in the Lada Hotel. 'It's the only place to get a reasonable meal; elsewhere there is nothing.' Togliatti, it turned out, was the site of the Soviet Union's largest Lada car factory, which owned the best hotel for visiting businessmen. We secured rooms with the help of a smooth, fast-talking, American-educated Sudanese businessman representing a Qatar-based company which had the monopoly for Lada cars in the Middle East.

'I'm not here to help myself. I'm here first of all for the Russians, to help them, and only then to make money,' he told us. 'I've got a lot of friends here. We're honest with the Russians. We lay our cards on the table. We say we will show them how to make money and we promise to give them a dollar for every dollar we make. You couldn't have anything fairer than that, could you? There are 280 million Russians and they need 280 million things. They have everything here: technology, minerals, resources. They don't need our help, you're mistaken if you think that . . . they just need to be educated. But they have a brain, oh yes, they have a brain.'

His conversation appeared to be intended for his Soviet companion, a Lada representative, but the longer he talked the greater the impression he left that he was taking the Russians for a ride. From the less verbose British director we learnt more. Their company bought Ladas for $3,000 each and resold them in the Middle East for $10,000, mainly to be used as taxis. They were cheap, strong and reliable, if basic. The Lada factory had been built by the Italians and had the latest technology. Lada dominated the city: there were Lada schools, Lada shops, special Lada holiday camps for employees, and wages were higher here than elsewhere. It was strange to come across foreign businessmen after the previous few weeks. They looked ill at ease, incongruous in their well-cut suits, especially in the presence of the Russian Lada officials in their lumpy, shapeless Soviet clothes.

'Lada Hotel' or not, one meal consisted of tough beef, greasy chips and sweet Russian champagne. Company directors of foreign firms found, to their shock, that they were on a Soviet diet, even if the hotel was the best in town. That evening we made a curious assortment of people at the bar – American, Japanese, German and the British businessman who looked as though he was hating every moment of his stay.

'There's one thing the Russians are good at,' he told me, over a rough Georgian cognac, 'which, if they could export it, could make them billions – wasting time. They're past masters at it. No one ever makes a decision. When I was in Moscow I waited for one hour outside McDonald's and people queuebarged all the time. In Britain there would have been blood on the streets but here no one said a thing. They are used to being subjugated; it's in their nature. I've never had so much wasted time.'

Talking to a Japanese delegation I found a slightly different perspective.

'We have to treat them just like children,' a Japanese businessman told me. 'They know nothing about business, nothing at all, so we always have to start from the beginning and keep it very simple.'

No one looked as though they were enjoying their stay in Togliatti except for Hamlet, a well-built and handsome Georgian, the director of a factory in Tbilisi employing 5,000 people. Warm, sympathetic and affectionate, he joined us for meals and insisted on paying for everything. Hamlet proposed endless toasts – to our happy meeting, to absent families, to beautiful women, to our gathering together, to our meeting again. At the end of the meal he and a Yugoslav broke out into song at the table, to the embarrassment of the Russians. Twice we had heard Russians singing in restaurants, punch-drunk, in slurred voices that verged on the maudlin. But Hamlet was far from drunk; he sang out of pure pleasure. And his deep-seated contentment was clear for all to see. How different was his face from the Russian physiognomy: placid, imperturbable, from which one could divine so little. On Hamlet's face could be read all his emotions; his delight in listening to our stories, his disappointment if we refused a cognac, his earnestness in inviting us to Tbilisi. By the time we said goodbye to Hamlet we were all keen to visit him in Georgia, Vitale included.

We spent the next day in Togliatti and I suggested having a look around the town.

'You can do what you want,' Howard laughed, 'but I saw all I wanted to as I came in. I'm staying right here!'

'You're a sucker for punishment, Simon,' Gilles said, and Vitale felt the same way; I went on my own.

At the edge of the huge, empty square were four rows of large black and white photographic portraits, a metre square in size. The figures were dressed in severe black clothes, men and women alike with medals pinned to their chest, and all had the most lugubrious expressions. We had come across similar portraits before in other towns and invariably the people wore the same grim expression. It turned out they were a Soviet method of rewarding individuals for having fulfilled production quotas and the like; but they looked so miserable that we had mistaken them, at first, for police photographs.

For a couple of hours I wandered around the city centre; it was exceedingly small. People queued to buy ice cream or *kvass* from a small truck at the roadside. Out of curiosity I entered some shops where there were few people, and fewer goods; the staff knew the shops might as well be closed for all the amount of business they were going to do. I came to another deserted square with the townhall on one side and a grand but locked 'House of Culture' on the other. Working my way back to the centre I came across a cinema. Apart from that there was nothing: nothing attractive, nothing of historical significance and as far as I could see no other focus of interest. After nearly two hours I was back, footsore, having found nothing whatsoever to justify my outing.

'Enjoy yourself?' Howard asked, looking up with a wry grin.

'Tell us all about it,' Gilles added.

'OK, OK,' I replied, 'we all make mistakes.'

The next day we left, cycling for ten hours in steady rain. For 122 kilometres we did not come to a single village, nor a single café, nor a single restaurant, nor any buildings at all, nothing but wheatfields stretching away into the distance. At the end of the day we finally came to a village and stopped for the night.

It was a sea of mud, the earth roads dissolved by the day's rain, prefab concrete blocks set amongst the boggy lanes. There was nothing fresh to buy in the shop except eggs and tomatoes. As we negotiated with some villagers for milk and onions, a girl of twenty appeared and introduced herself as the village English teacher. She invited us to spend the night in her apartment, so, surrounded by her pupils, we pushed our way through the mud to her home. Mud washed right up to the open communal door and the interior hallway at the bottom of the stairs was strewn with earth and rubbish that hadn't been cleaned out in years. A wooden plank had been put down from the doorstep to the first step of the stairs so that those who lived upstairs could avoid the mud and debris. It was more like walking into a cow-pen than a block of flats.

Tatiana had already spent a year in the village and had been given the apartment by the village council. With three big rooms and a small kitchen it was surprisingly spacious but sparsely furnished with rough wooden furniture. Her bedroom had neither a wardrobe nor a chest of drawers in which to store her clothes, which were hung up on nails in the wall.

After graduating from the Pedagogical Institute in Kuybyshev the year before, Tatiana had been assigned to this tiny village. She had played no role at all in the choice of where she was to be sent; the Pedagogical Institute decided where her first three-year posting should be. It turned out that this was normal procedure; without it no one would volunteer to go to run-down, bleak villages such as this one. Tatiana was lucky in that her home town was only 100 kilometres away; some of her friends were 1,000 kilometres or more from their homes. After three years she would be free to find her own posting and she hoped that it would be back in Kuybyshev.

The rooms were shoddy and badly decorated, no attempt having been made to redecorate the apartment before she moved in. She had asked the village leader if it could be repainted but he had told her there was not enough paint. There was neither hot water nor a shower, summer or winter. In the bathroom there was one cold tap. The lavatory was stained and broken; she had to flush it using a metal bucket. The bathroom was cold with a raw concrete floor, a small plastic mirror and lacked any kind of cabinet. The kitchen had a single cold tap, a tiny basin, a minute stove, and two saucepans, one with a broken handle. The walls were stained and dirty, there was no fridge, no kitchen cupboards, only a rough table. Pictures of cars and models torn from a German magazine had been stuck to the walls. We were horrified to learn that she had already been living in these conditions for a year. Couldn't she redecorate it herself? we asked.

'No, I have no money for that. I do not have money for a radio or cassette either, but I have a television.' Later we saw the television; the pictures looked as if they were transmitted from Mars.

There was nothing to alleviate the starkness of the surroundings. There was nothing, she said – literally nothing – to do in the village. We believed her. To us there had seemed precious little to do in the cities, but compared to a village like this, the cities were sophistication. What astonished Gilles, Howard and me, however, was Vitale's comment that the apartment was 'not bad'.

While we were preparing our evening meal Tatiana asked if some of her pupils could come in to meet us. No foreigner had been to the village before. Ten children aged twelve to sixteen filed in, dressed in rough clothes; some of their faces had a rather thin, pinched look about them. They did not look healthy or hardy. I asked them about their history lessons.

'We don't study much history,' one replied.

'What do you think about Stalin?' I asked.

'Stalin was bad,' one of them chimed.

'And Lenin?'

'Lenin was good.'

'What do you do in your summer holidays?'

'Work on the collective farm.'

'What do you get paid for that?'

'150 or 200 roubles a month.'

We were astonished. This was far more than Tatiana earnt as a teacher, as much as the Doctor of Physics we had met at the Leningrad Academy of Sciences! Tatiana confirmed it was correct; the collective farm paid extra labour very well at harvest time, although the normal wage on the farms was very low.

After a while Howard asked them if they had any questions about the United States.

'No,' replied one of the older boys. Howard, unabashed, proceeded to tell them something about his life back in Colorado, rounding up the steers on the ranch, the branding, the barbecues, the long days in the saddle. Still no questions.

I was curious to find out what they knew about England – if they knew anything at all. There was silence for a while, until a small boy shouted out 'Sherlock Holmes'.

'Sherlock Holmes had a pipe,' a second contributed.

'The weather is terrible and very changeable,' said a third.

'Is it true that English people would always give their last piece of bread to an animal?'

'Is it true that English people don't talk to each other on the train?' Yes, that I had to admit was basically true. And that was it – no further questions.

It seemed an extraordinary hotchpotch of information to have reached this forlorn, bleak village on the Russian plain 1,000 kilometres from Moscow, 2,000 from the Polish border. How, I wondered, had this muddled picture filtered through? How had the exploits, or at least the name, of Sherlock Holmes become the knowledge of Russian schoolboys who knew neither that Britain was an island, nor that we still had a queen? It was Gilles's turn. He asked them what they knew about France. Apart from the fact that the capital was Paris, they could think of nothing at all.

Many times after we had settled down to sleep the door opened and the light was switched on as curious villagers came to look at these strange foreigners visiting their village. Having been thoroughly exhibited the light eventually went off and we fell into a deep sleep.

The next day we cycled 106 kilometres again without seeing any villages. Wheatfields and copses of silver-birch trees stretched away interminably over a flat landscape. Without villages on the horizon there was nothing to look forward to, nothing to aim for. The fields were devoid of wildlife. So far, we had seen only a handful of 'prairie dogs', small, worried-looking creatures that resembled woolly hedgehogs, and magpies, crows, one kingfisher, one sparrow-hawk and, for the first time, a single hare. We came to the conclusion that so many wild animals must have been shot or trapped during the famine of the 1930s or during the war that they had never recovered.

We camped at the edge of a silver-birch copse, looking out over emerald-green fields scattered with dandelions. Grey rain clouds melted away, the pink, setting sun streaking the evening sky with delicate pastel shades. Sitting round the embers of the camp fire we listened to the BBC World Service: Gorbachev had announced a referendum on reform to a market economy, saying such a move was not possible without popular support.

'Which way would you vote, Vitale?' I asked.

'For a market economy, for change, of course. But older people will vote against it. For instance, my parents – they will vote against it. They don't want such change.'

'And what would be the result nationwide?'

'Most people will vote against change. Both my parents are retired. My father's pension is seventy roubles a month, my mother's is sixty; 130 in total. Meat in the private market now sells at ten–twenty roubles a kilo. They cannot afford to buy it but there is nothing in the state shops. So what do they do? They don't eat meat, except very rarely. But for them this *is* the market economy that Gorbachev is always talking about. If we change it will mean real hardship for millions . . . hungry people. I think there are some who are hungry already. Do you know how my father spends his days, now he is retired? He spends it looking for food to buy, walking round Moscow with his bag. He goes out after breakfast and looks for food, that is all.'

After a night of rain the winds were right behind us, allowing us to cycle thirty to forty kilometres per hour on the flat and as fast as fifty to sixty downhill. Egged on by the wind we raced each other, overtaking horse-drawn carts and a few old Zaporozhets, the smallest Russian car that putputs along like a lawnmower.

The only villages were located far off the road but eventually, hungry and thirsty, we were compelled to turn off to find food and water. After ploughing around in the mud we found the *stolovaya* set amongst dilapidated buildings. At the back was a bakery producing cream-covered sponge cakes. We ate two huge cakes between us and set off with two more strapped to our back racks. With the wind behind us we sailed into Oktyabrisky, cycling to the main square lined by Stalin-era buildings, heavily monumental and surmounted by wedding-cake decoration. Stalinist architecture was invariably vulgar and grandiose, the inevitable result of a narrow mind dictating the course of culture. Any such central square in Europe would have been lined with cafés, restaurants, banks and newsagents, the heart and soul of the city, alive with people. In Oktyabrisky the square was empty.

We were given a suite in the hotel with a kitchen and a living room.

'*Nomenklatura* suite,' Vitale remarked, impressed by the glass cabinet full of crockery. 'We only get this because you're foreigners.' From the window on the second floor we looked directly out onto a statue of Lenin, arm outstretched over the deserted square.

As usual there was no hot water, nor could we go to the baths, which were reserved that day for women; to cap it all, the hotel restaurant was closed for repairs.

The sole viewing on all three television channels was of Gorbachev making a speech that dragged on for just under an hour. Vitale lost interest and walked off after the first two minutes, even though the speech was of major significance. In it, Gorbachev was presenting to the Supreme Soviet his latest proposals to transform the Soviet economy. All through the summer and autumn of 1990, a battle raged in the Soviet Union as to which economic programme leading towards a free-market economy should be adopted. The radical plan, devised by Stanislav Shatalin and known as the '500-day programme', envisaged sweeping privatisation of state-owned property. Large enterprises would be converted into shareholding companies, small businesses and shops put on the market, and land would be offered for sale to peasants. Shatalin's programme also proposed the gradual deregulation of prices and the creation of a free market in hard currency.

After appearing to have accepted the 500-day programme, Gorbachev proceeded to water it down, trying to merge it with his own Prime Minister's plan, in the light of statistics showing dismal economic performance. But his attempts to merge the two fundamentally incompatible programmes were greeted with despair by Nikolai Ryzhkov, his Prime Minister, and dismissed by Yeltsin, who said it was 'like trying to mate a hedgehog with a snake'. Shatalin stressed that his radical programme could not be combined with the government's. But Gorbachev backed away completely from 'shock therapy', fearing a nationwide backlash of strikes and social unrest.

Central to the transition to a market economy was price reform. Soviet prices reflected neither the real costs of production nor world price levels, and ignored the relationship between supply and demand. Incredibly, Nikolai Ryzhkov told the Supreme Soviet that many prices for goods and services had stayed unchanged since the 1930s. But his announcement that the government would raise prices from 1 July sparked a nationwide wave of panic buying, compelling Gorbachev to make a televised address to the country to try and calm fears about the reforms.

Chelyabinsk in the Urals was torn by rioting caused by a shortage of cigarettes – and even bread disappeared temporarily from the shelves in Moscow. Panic buying swept city and countryside alike, and Moscow City Council had to announce a temporary ban on the sale of food and consumer goods to anyone unable to produce a Moscow residence permit. The effect was to exacerbate further the breakdown in the distribution system; officials in the neighbouring regions of Kalinin, Smolensk and Vladimir retaliated by ordering food supplies to Moscow to be withheld as local people were then prevented from travelling to the capital in search of food. It was an indication of how precariously balanced the Soviet economy was.

8

THE URALS

THE FOLLOWING DAY we left Oktyabrisky for Ufa, the first of the large
industrial cities at the foot of the Urals, the mountain chain traditionally
thought of as the border between Europe and Asia. The Urals are in fact
disappointingly small, not real mountains at all, only gentle, low-slung
hills that run north-south for 2,000 kilometres, falling away in the North
into the frozen Arctic and losing themselves in the South in the salt flats of
Eastern Kazakhstan.

They are not a geographical barrier and have never impeded the ebb
and flow of people across the Russian plains. It is only the complete
absence of anything more impressive in any direction that enables the
Urals to be called mountains, and therefore the 'frontier' between Europe
and Asia. One, two and even five thousand kilometres further east in the
Russian Republic, architecture, food, clothes, customs and life itself are
the same as in that part of Russia west of the Urals. Logically, it seemed,
the frontier between Europe and Asia belonged much further west.

For the first time in six weeks we had hills to climb – hills of blood-red
earth, very gently rounded, scooped and eroded over thousands of years,
smooth hills that rose up to a lip as though giving onto a plateau, beyond
which were further waves as the land rose and fell like an ocean swell.

In the afternoon, when we turned off the road in search of food for our
evening meal, we came across three women in bright floral dresses and
kerchiefs sitting beside the dusty road. They were large, powerfully built,
cheerful women and the largest beckoned us to follow her if we wanted
eggs. We came to a neat blue and white wood house behind a high wooden
fence.

'Come in, come in!' she called. Vanya! Lyena! Visitors!' Out of the house tumbled her husband, a Stan Laurel lookalike, a wispy, scarecrow character, as thin as she was fat. Vanya must have been asleep. His hair stood on end and he had a lost, puzzled expression. Instead of being given eggs, we found ourselves seated at the table being served large bowls of chicken soup, cold duck, tea, bread, and fresh cream which we ate straight out of the bowl with a spoon.

'Eat, eat!' she told us enthusiastically, beaming as she watched over us. When we told her our nationalities, she told us she was German.

'German?' How did you come to live here?'

'I'm a Crimean German. We were moved here in the war, in 1940. This village is half-German, half-Tatar. We were moved here at the same time. Many people were moved to this region. I was only a child at the time. I came with my parents but they died shortly after they were brought here. It was too much for them.'

'Do you still speak German?'

'I remember only a little now. I cannot always understand it when I hear it on television. And Lyena doesn't know it. We have lost most of our history, our language.'

'Can you go back to the Crimea now?'

'I cannot now. I have three daughters, two who are married living nearby and Lyena who is still with me. I do not want to leave them.'

'So this is now your home?'

'Yes, but we have never really settled here. We never felt settled. We have always felt that maybe, one day, we will be moved again. When we came we did not think it would be forever. We always thought we would go back, so we did not seek to establish ourselves permanently. We just lived for the day.'

'When you were moved,' I asked 'how much warning did you have that you were to be moved?'

'They came in the morning and we were moved that evening.'

'The same day?'

'Yes. We had a few hours only.'

'Could you take your clothes, your tools, your belongings?'

'Nothing. We were allowed nothing.'

'But your personal possessions . . .'

'Only the clothes we wore, nothing else.'

'So when you arrived here you had no tools to work with?'

'No. We were moved by truck, brought to this spot.'

'And what was here when you arrived – there was a village here already, I presume?'

'No, there was nothing. We had to build our own houses, but first we had to make ourselves tools. The government gave us nothing and of course we were not popular because we were Germans. Those were difficult times.' She lifted the corner of her apron and dabbed at her eyes. 'My parents died soon after.' She sighed, breathing heavily, her whole body rising and falling.

Looking at this kind, blameless woman I remembered the recent 'rehabilitation' of the Crimean Germans. An official announcement had been made to the effect that they had not been responsible for the crimes Stalin had accused them of – sympathising with the Germans in the Second World War. Their name had been cleared, they were innocent after all. It had all been a mistake . . . Stalin was to blame. That was all. Then silence, a silence that rang, as if an apology could put right the injustice, the fear and suffering, the ruined lives. It wasn't just a few families that had suffered but entire nations – the Volga Germans, the Crimean Germans, the Crimean Tatars. Only sitting in that small whitewashed house on the edge of the Urals, listening to Maria's quiet sobs, did the horror of the Soviet experience come fully home.

When we rose to leave, Maria insisted on giving us twenty eggs, far more than we needed, as well as onions and parsley that she pulled from the garden. We cycled along in silence, sobered by our meeting, before pitching our tents under some tall silver birches off the road. Gilles and I cycled to the village to collect water. It appeared deserted, the wide street dusty and silent. We entered a dry, dusty yard lined with wooden out-buildings and a prolific vegetable plot. We called out and knocked at the door but without response. Tall hollyhocks grew at the front of the house, its cream wooden walls half-shielded by dappled sunlight piercing through the birches. The silence seeped into every corner, merging with the afternoon heat, creating an overpowering somnolence. No one appeared. We lowered and winched up the bucket twice until our containers were full and were on the point of leaving when a motorcycle combination bumped into the yard. It came to a stop, the man swinging out of the saddle, a small peasant woman climbing out of the sidecar. Apologetically, we explained our presence, which didn't seem to perturb them in the least.

'Ah, that water from the well is no good. I'll fetch you some good water,' the woman said, taking our containers from us, smiling gently.

'*Fkhaditye! Fkhaditye!*' ('Come in! Come in!') her husband told us, beckoning us inside. 'Leave your shoes on.' He gave us strong black tea, and we talked a little, learning to our astonishment that our watches were two hours slow. We had traversed two time zones since leaving Moscow, which explained why it was already so light by the time we rose. Soon his wife returned with our water; thanking them we returned to Howard and Vitale under the birches.

How naturally they had welcomed us, how at ease they seemed, even coming home to find two tall, strange foreigners in their courtyard! In Britain would a husband and wife in their sixties have taken it quite so calmly? In Russia, a deep underlying fear and a disarming trust, a childlike innocence, seemed somehow to coexist.

Huge wheatfields accompanied us all the way to Ufa. As we approached we came to the first private cooperative restaurant we had seen. Bright, attractive and clean, it was a world apart from our habitual eating places, but with prices five times those of a *stolovaya*, Vitale didn't know who could afford to pay. Apart from us it was empty.

Heading for Ufa proper, Howard's expedition jacket fell from his bicycle. A passenger in a passing car motioned to us that we had lost something but by the time we had cycled back it had disappeared. A workman indicated that someone had jumped out of a passing car and picked it up, before speeding off.

'The son of a bitch!' Howard cursed, kicking the gravel. 'I'm going after the bastard.' He picked up his bike, glaring at a disappearing vehicle.

'He's not going to stop just round the corner. It's gone. You won't see it again.' After this incident Howard cycled along slowly, morosely, in silence. As we came in through the dusty suburbs I tried to change the subject.

'Pretty warm, isn't it?' I ventured.

'Fucking hot as hell!' Howard spat. Vitale looked puzzled.

'It's American for "It's too hot to be cycling",' I explained.

Ufa was desperately ugly. We cycled to the centre, hoping to find some redeeming architecture, something to look at, an old quarter perhaps. But we found nothing. We bounced over railway tracks, past heaps of metal and concrete, archaic-looking factories with broken windows, rusting metalwork and leaning fences. Black clouds streamed from blackened chimney pots of brick; yellow buses, their windows blotted out with dust and grime, lurched over the tramlines, where queues of people waited patiently, poker-faced.

In the centre, beyond a vast mural of a purposefully striding Lenin, we came to the Hotel Tourist, a shabby building of grey brick, grey cement and peeling metal window casements. Dozens of bored army officers lounged in the foyer. Once in our rooms, we threw ourselves onto our beds in exhaustion. That evening we went down to the restaurant. A plastic chair blocked the door with a scrawled message 'Closed'.

I looked inside. The kitchen staff and the waitresses were sitting round

s, chins resting on arms propped up on the tables. 'Forget it,' I
d, 'we're not getting anything here.' There was one other hotel
aurant in the city.

aking a taxi,' Howard said with determination.

are no taxis,' Vitale reminded us as we walked out of the hotel.
We walked until we succeeded in flagging down a private car. At the
Intourist hotel the door was closed from the inside and another hand-
scribbled sign announced it too was shut but we could see tables that were
laid and people eating. So we forced the door open and found a table.

The restaurant was the usual scene. A five-man band, all in flared
trousers and imitation leather jackets, played the same popsongs we had
heard in every city since Leningrad, in a bored, lifeless way and looked
about them as though they no longer heard the music while garish lights
gave the place the look of a brothel. In the centre, at a large table, a party of
girls sat celebrating their graduation. At the edges sat the men, faces
puffed and heavy. Empty vodka and cognac bottles littered the tables.
From time to time virtually everyone rose to dance drunkenly, swaying on
their feet. Men, invariably drunker than their partners, manhandled
women on the dancefloor as if shifting lumps of timber. Often it was only
having a woman to hang onto that kept the men on their feet.

One man, unsteady and flushed, went up to the students' table, sat
down on an empty chair and put his arm round one of the girls. She tried
to move away, pull back from the leering face. He went on murmuring to
her, trying to get her against her will onto the dancefloor, but had
difficulty standing up. The other girls tried to persuade him to desist; they
did not, however, appear to be angered by his behaviour. Eventually, he
retraced his shaky steps to his table. No matter how boorish and drunken
the admirer, girls sometimes seemed to like this sort of attention.

'I'd like to see him try that in France,' Gilles said, shaking his head.

'In England, he'd be nursing his cheek by now.'

'He'd be nursing more than that if he tried it in the States.'

'I don't like these drunk people,' Vitale said, 'but this is probably the
only place to go in the evening. People don't come here to talk, they come
to drink.'

When I mentioned such behaviour to a girl in Siberia she told me that
relations between men and women was one of their most painful
problems.

'"Rude ugly mugs" is the only nickname for our men – but not for all of
them, of course. But between men and women we have rather strange
relations. You know, the greatest wish of any woman today is to feel
herself tender, weaker and softer. But we can't be such. We have to prove

today that we can do the same things that men do. And today there are few people whom we could call gentlemen. And if you come across such a man, you think, "Oh, what a crank he is!" So, you can imagine the situation.'

We were glad to leave Ufa and looked ahead in vain for the Urals. Pausing in a village beside new log cabins, a young woman appeared from nowhere, handed us each yellow tulips and irises of bright blue, wished us well and disappeared as quickly as she had come.

An ancient wooden cart rumbled up the mud street, driven by a red-faced peasant who stood upright, the reins in his hands as if it were a chariot. Despite the heat, he wore a blue padded jacket and a large black fur hat. He stopped beside us, unloaded half a dozen milkchurns, readjusted the halter and set off, giving the weary old nag a flick of the whip. In the *stolovaya* we queued up to order sixteen cups of tea to quench our thirst. A thin soup, bony, dessicated fish and congealed macaroni masqueraded as lunch.

In the late afternoon we arrived in the village of Archangel where, according to our map, the road stopped. The shop was surprisingly full and noisy, but the moment we walked in the conversation ceased. There had been a delivery of macaroni and boiled sweets, and a queue snaked round the shop, everybody with their *avoshka*s – their just-in-case bags – at the ready. The moment we closed the door behind us conversation took off again. It was like playing a game of grandmother's footsteps, except that when we turned round it was conversation that froze.

The only hotel in the village had been open one year and from a distance it looked quite attractive, built in the style of a Swiss chalet, but disconcertingly out of proportion. Outside, rubber tyres painted white demarcated what was presumably a garden. As garden ornamentation, there was an old army helicopter, its controls ripped out, impaled on a concrete spike, set back from the hotel.

'A fine piece of socialist realism,' Howard said.

'No, this one's just realism,' Gilles told him.

Although it had opened a year earlier, the hotel was not finished and it was clear that it never would be. Along with unfinished concrete balconies outside, raw concrete stairs, ham-fisted cement and mortar work characterised it inside. There was no hot water, the doors were too small for the door frames and the restaurant appeared to have fallen down. The hotel had also been built in such a way that virtually no light entered our room. We requested extra light bulbs, as only one worked, and as there were no spares the manageress directed us to take one from the next-door room occupied by a Russian. The cook in the kitchen had no food, no assistant and, apart from us, no clients. They managed somehow to get us a bowl of meatballs. We sat, waiting for them, in the dim light of a single bulb.

'This is the Third World,' I said, shaking my head.

'It's the Fourth World,' Gilles replied.

We were hungry but when they came the meatballs smelt high and we disposed of them in the garden, behind the helicopter. We walked to the village *stolovaya* and ate disconsolately, writing our journals. From time to time people came in to eat. They usually said nothing to the cooks, just collected their food in silence, took it to a table and ate, head down, silent or staring in front of them. They neither looked around nor spoke. They ate mechanically, as if unaware of what they were eating. It was eating reduced to its most basic duty, no more: to keep the body going.

I suggested a stroll round the village before the sun went down to shake off the depression that had overcome me.

'Think you're going to find something new?' Howard looked up. In twenty minutes we had walked to the end of the village and back again. A single dusty street, wooden log houses to either side, corrugated iron roofs, vegetable plots, leaning wooden fences, a few mongrel dogs sniffing each other, a solitary figure down by the river with his rod: that was it. What more should one expect?

The new road from Archangel was rough and unfinished, made of uncompacted stones and hardcore, making cycling almost impossible. Instead we took our bikes into the fields and cycled there, plunging into troughs ten feet deep. Before Ufa we had entered the Bashkir Autonomous Republic, the Bashkirs being an Altaic people of Turkic origin, but it was only after Beloretsk that we came across them.

To all intents and purposes they have been Russified, all visible signs of their culture having disappeared. They live in the same wooden houses as the Russians, wear tawdry Russian clothes instead of their traditional costume and work on the same collective farms.

Although subject to the same law of uniformity, Bashkir villages were neater and more prosperous than Russian ones; the Bashkirs themselves seemed better dressed. Their mosques had been destroyed with as much ruthlessness as the Orthodox churches but when we used the Muslim greeting of '*Salaam aleycum*' we invariably got a friendly response. The Bashkirs also appeared to be more kindly disposed towards us, happy to chat and full of questions. We stopped and talked to an old man squaring a felled tree with an axe. It was to be used as a top-beam in a new wooden house, and this beam alone would take him sixty hours to square.

Whitewashed log cabin near Magnitogorsk.

Half way across the 3,000 kilometre Kazakhstan steppe.

(*Left*) Gilles Mingasson.

(*Middle*) Simon Vickers.

(*Below*) Maksim Sokolenko (*right*) and Sasha Klebalin (*left*).

(*Opposite top*) Gilles Mingasson (*left*), Simon Vickers (*centre*) and Howard Cooper (*right*), pausing in bear-infested Taiga near the Chinese border.
(*Opposite bottom*) For days our Siberian trail turned to liquid mud. Gilles Mingasson (*left*) and Howard Cooper (*right*).

May Day 1990: the first unofficial demonstration for seventy years enters Red Square in Moscow.

(*Right*) Russian friends at Kulunda.

(*Above*) A river serves as our route near Yerofey-Pavlovich, Siberia.

(*Right*) Impassable swamp forces us to push along the Trans-Siberian railway.

Captured Soviet tank near Vladivostok.

Simon Vickers discussing our route with Soviet army officer at Dzhalinda on the Chinese border.

(*Left*) Ruined church at Mikhailovka in the 'Hungry Regions', European Russia.

(*Right*) Maksim Sokolenko on a dirt road near Nerchinsk, Chitinskaya oblast, Siberia.

(*Left*) Repairs on the Russian steppe.

Negotiating ice-cold rivers in Amurskaya oblast, Siberia.

'Our problem,' he told us, 'is that all the young are going to the towns. We're virtually all pensioners here now. I don't know who will do the work in the future.'

'Would people come back if they were given their own land?'

'We need new houses and good roads to bring them back, not land. You've seen the state of the road, you know what it's like. But before they come back they must have somewhere to live and houses are too expensive for them to build.' Out of curiosity I asked how much an average log house would cost to build new – 15,000 roubles (about $1,000) or five years' gross average salary, a proportion comparable to that in Europe. Considering that wood covered the Urals and logging was the main industry of the region, it was far from cheap.

A Bashkir farmer directed us to a glade beside the river, bidding us goodnight, with a warning to watch out for bears. The following day we pushed over a wide, swaying wobbly suspension bridge and turned off down into another village in search of bread. This was one Russian and more chaotic. Old men, dressed in baggy trousers and old jackets, were sitting around the village shop waiting for it to open, all with empty glass jars to collect cooking oil. After the initial conversation we asked what the village was like before 1917 and whether it had changed much since then. This seemed to set them going. Before the Revolution there had been two iron-smelting plants owned by a Frenchman and a German, and worked by Russians.

'When the Revolution came they fled and the Communists took over,' said an old man wearing a worn jacket with a military order pinned to the lapel. 'But things did not get better. Now we know that Marx and Engels, Lenin and Stalin were wrong and that Communism is impossible. But before we thought it was possible.' When we asked him what had happened at the time of collectivisation, there was a moment of silence.

'In the 1930s this village lost many people under Stalin.'

'Who was it that was taken – rich farmers, teachers?'

'Everybody. I'll tell you a story. There was a man who lived here, a friend of my father's. He had three cows and three horses and he was a good farmer. One day, at the time of collectivisation, the Communists came and said that he must give them to the collective farm. Everybody had to do so. He shouted at them, "I refuse, and if anyone tries to take anything of mine I'll shoot the cows and horses, and burn my hay." The next day the Communists came for him and took him away. No one saw him again. And there were many like him in this village. That's so, isn't it, Alexei?' His neighbour nodded and grunted in assent. 'But it wasn't just here – it was all over Russia, and the best people were killed, the most intelligent and educated. Churchill and Roosevelt knew that Communism was a bad thing. Now we must live in peace and be brothers,' he concluded abruptly. The five other men had listened, made an occasional nod, but said nothing. It was difficult to tell what they were thinking. Then the shop opened and everybody crowded in. The group split up and we were left on our own.

Surrounded by pine forests we wove our way through the Urals. Here and there baby violets and cowslips nestled in rocks at the roadside and cattle strayed across the near-deserted road. Not long after a siesta in a sunny glade we came across a police car going in the opposite direction. The moment it saw us it drew up; there was no doubt in any of our minds that it was looking out for us. The policeman asked for our papers and passports, and seemed put out that we weren't on the main Ufa–Chelyabinsk road. Hadn't we seen the sign prohibiting traffic? The road was in the process of being built and it was dangerous because of lorries. Vitale assured him laconically that we had been in much greater danger in this respect between Leningrad and Moscow. After noting down all the details he handed our passports back and twenty minutes later he overtook us heading in the direction he had come from.

It was curious that it should be here in the Ural Mountains that the police asked for our papers for the first time. But the fact that we had covered over 2,500 kilometres before being asked for them was more surprising. I remembered the British Vice-Consul's recommendation to register with the police every night, something this policeman didn't even mention.

In the fields outside Beloretsk the town's population had been mobilised to plant potatoes. Trucks, buses and cars ferried out the unlucky citizens to the fields which looked as though they were covered with swarms of locusts. Vehicles were stuck in the soft mud, and people pushed and pulled, shouting directions. It must have been the most inefficient way to set about planting a field, but if the people of Beloretsk wanted to eat potatoes, they would have to plant them.

Beloretsk was hideous but at least the hotel had hot water, the first for two weeks. Howard, Gilles and I were charged twenty-five roubles each for our room, Vitale three, but we couldn't be bothered to argue the toss. We all felt uplifted to have been cycling in hills for the first time.

Drunks crowded the restaurant. One, a Brezhnev lookalike, wandered around talking quietly to himself and making the sign of the cross. Twice a waitress steered him out of the restaurant and twice he wandered back. At the end of the evening policemen with truncheons came in, as usual, to steer or haul away the remaining laggards.

Listening to the BBC World Service we learnt that Boris Yeltsin, the radical politician, had been elected President of the Russian Republic. Like Gorbachev he had a reputation as a tactician and a pragmatist, but unlike him he had enormous popularity. Gorbachev was almost universally disliked. We had heard virtually nothing in Gorbachev's favour, nor were we to hear much more in the following months. But Yeltsin seemed to touch a chord with ordinary people wherever we went, in towns and villages, and his election renewed people's hope for change.

According to our map the road from Beloretsk to Magnitogorsk was metalled all the way. Not a bit of it! A new road was in the process of being made, forcing us to cycle on hard core and rubble. The gradient of the new road was impossibly steep. Instead of twisting up gradually, making maximum use of the natural gradients of the hill, it cut up, straight as a pencil. Even from the highest pass through the Urals there were no peaks to be seen, no more than a rounded protuberance of crumbling red stone that barely rose above the pines. Beyond the ridge lay protected valleys of emerald grass, enlivened with swathes of cowslips and dandelion, and dotted with clusters of silver birches. So perfectly grouped were the trees, so gentle the gradients, so short and perfect was the grass that these valleys were more like English parkland landscaped by Capability Brown.

Beside the rock road was an earth track used by horse and carts, extraordinarily smooth, although it rose and fell continuously in gentle swells. In the space of a few hours we left the Urals behind and could make out a huge cloud of smoke hanging over Magnitogorsk. As we approached it grew worse, thicker, and a powerful acrid smell became apparent. We arrived in the centre of the huge industrial city as the evening sun sunk low. The view over the river was weird, surreal, mesmerising. An infernal panorama of grimy iron foundries, factories and belching smoke stretched far up and down the river, a maze of gigantic blackened buildings and huge chimney stacks sending forth black, grey, white and a poisonous-looking yellow-orange smoke. The chimney stacks were too numerous to count, half of them lost in drifts of orange smoke. The air above the city was itself transformed into a yellow grey. Curiously the city, even the main square, was orientated to face the factories on the far side, as though they constituted a fine view.

None of us had seen such pollution before. It was as close as the imagination could get to dark satanic mills. The air itself seemed dry, brittle and after a couple of hours it began to affect our throats and eyes, making them sore and achy.

There were but two hotels in this vast industrial city and both were five kilometres from the centre. No one knew which was better. No one had ever stayed in them. We cycled to the Hotel Asia which was situated across the river, directly behind the vast steelworks; appropriately it was the hotel connected to the steel foundry. We circumvented the factory, passing innumerable propaganda hoardings that listed the accomplishments of the city, production figures and future targets. It was 8.15 pm by the time we arrived at the hotel, a hideous building, sunk in grime. To the side was the main entrance to the steelworks, surrounded by metal panels of heroic Soviet workers and dominated by a large statue of Lenin cast in black metal with arm stretched out pointing to the steelyards.

No, there were no rooms. We could wait if we wanted to. While Gilles and I guarded the bikes outside Howard and Vitale scouted around inside trying to find the elusive director of the hotel. Eventually two Georgians intervened on our behalf and rooms were forthcoming, but by this time our lips were cracking from the polluted air. The skin seemed to tauten and our throats were sore. There was no hot water in the hotel so we accepted an offer from a young man to take a shower in his flat.

Osip was half-Russian, half-Jewish, with a keen, intellectual face, such as we hadn't seen for a long time, and he was eager to talk. His flat consisted of three rooms, virtually devoid of furniture or possessions. He had a mattress, a suitcase full of clothes, a television and a Sharp video cassette recorder. It looked as if he had moved in the day before but he had already been there for three months. I asked him if he worked for the steel factory.

'No. I don't work for the Communists,' he said bitterly. He had trained as an engineer, but there was no point in working as one as the salary was pitiful.

'So what are you doing here in Magnitogorsk?'

'I show VCR movies: I rent them out or sell them to hotels, to clubs, to the *nomenklatura*. That way I survive.'

'How did you get the Sharp video cassette recorder? They must cost a fortune here.'

'They do. This one cost me 5,000 roubles. That is two years' salary. Of course, you can only buy them on the black market. But it is an investment. I can always sell it for twice what I paid for it. It is a miserable life. I hate the system. I hate what I do, but what else is there? Do you know about Magnitogorsk, about its history?'

'No. Very little.'

'We call it the City of Bones. It was built by slave labour in the 1930s. Hundreds of thousands died in the process. Everybody knows that. Magnitogorsk is famous even in Russia for the number of people that died here. You can ask anybody.'

'Yes. It's true,' Vitale added.

'The main industry here is steel. Magnitogorsk has always produced steel – at least this century. But do you know that it is such bad quality that the West won't buy it? We can only sell it to Third World countries and then only cheaply. This city is corrupt. Everything is corrupt in this country. People know this, but no one dares to say anything, to complain. It is too dangerous.'

'What do you mean exactly when you say dangerous?' I asked.

'I will give you an example. People wait for ten years, for fifteen years for an apartment. You know that? Well, if that person writes a letter, criticising the way things are organised or managed, let alone suggesting corruption, they lose the apartment they have been waiting so long for. It's as simple as that. And what have they gained? Nothing, because their complaint means nothing, changes nothing.'

'So the élite, the *nomenklatura*, can punish those that protest without using the law?'

'Of course. The Communists control everything. The law is the last resort; they hardly need it.'

'So in the end no one dares protest?'

'Almost no one. To a great extent the Russian soul died under Communism, under Stalin. People are too scared to speak out and lose the little they have. In the war people here had nothing to eat, remember, whereas you in France, in England and in America, you had food. We had nothing here. Now these people have an apartment, even if it is small, and they don't want to lose it. Our system is based on fear. But people have to protect their families as well as themselves. Very few dare criticise, especially if they have a family.'

Talking to Osip I was confronted yet again by the crushing limitations imposed on the Soviet people by the system. Highly intelligent, alert and articulate, it was easy to see Osip in the West as a university professor, a successful businessman or barrister. He inspired confidence and was clearly a man who could make a success of almost any field. And yet here he was, renting out worthless, illicitly copied American videos to hotels and dingy clubs, 'surviving' from day to day, able to plan no further ahead than the next couple of months. He put a video on for us to watch: Schwarzenegger's *Running Man*, a voyeuristic thriller in which excited crowds pay to watch fights to the death as a form of titillating entertainment, the latest invention to revive jaded palettes bored of horror movies. On the few occasions when we saw American videos in the Soviet Union they were invariably drivel. If Russians needed insult to add to injury, this was it – to be treated to such garbage after all they had been through!

In the morning we went to the airport to collect the first box we had sent ahead. It had arrived, although the warehouse was in chaos. A smiling black-marketeer in a leather jacket watched us unpack our equipment, gave something discreetly to the doorman, and disappeared. We extracted spare tyres, inner tubes, vitamins, puncture-repair kits, pumps, mosquito repellent, skin creams, repacked the rest and requested that the box be sent on, handing over our letter of credit that stated that Sofi would pay the necessary charges. The women in charge had never seen a letter of credit and puzzled over it for a long time, phoning other people for their advice. Eventually they said they would need three copies, as well as the original.

'Can you photocopy them?' we asked.

'We have no photocopy machine. You must do them.'

But there was no photocopy facility at the airport in any of the offices. Even in Magnitogorsk we would have to get permission from the city authorities to use a photocopier and the office would be closed by the time we had returned to the city. We would have to do it tomorrow and come back again, another round trip of sixty kilometres by taxi.

'Forget it. We'll pay ourselves,' Howard snapped in frustration. It had already taken us all morning to get as far as we had.

We couldn't get out of Magnitogorsk a moment too soon. Our throats and lips were parched and our eyes smarted. It was a relief to be in the countryside again, breathing properly. It was dead flat, the Urals having disappeared completely, more fields of young wheat stretching away to left and right. When we came to a clean river overlooked by a high cliff we stopped, crossing on a suspension bridge and setting up camp on a rise immediately above the water. From the clifftop we could dive down to the river thirty feet below, into cold clear water that cleansed us of the pollution of Magnitogorsk and the dust of the road. Our tents were pitched on a bed of wild thyme that scented the evening air; we ate silently watching the blood-red disc of the sun slip below the horizon.

In the twilight a horseman approached, riding a mare behind which trotted another mare and two delicate springy foals. The rider looked Mongol or Tibetan to us, with high cheek bones, jet-black hair and Eastern almond eyes. He swung out of the saddle, and came and crouched beside the fire. We greeted him, happy to have his company out on the plain, even though none of us felt in the mood for talking. Kazakhstan lay ahead and he was the first Kazakh we had encountered. After a while he rode off but appeared again, bringing us a dozen eggs, a pound of salt and fresh *kumass*, fermented mare's milk. I tried it first. It had a tangy, rich and slightly bitter taste, unsavoury, but with some curious fascination.

'It's the idea of drinking *kumass* that you find attractive,' Gilles assured me, 'and the taste that you find repellent.'

Gilles later maintained that Howard and I paid the price for drinking *kumass* the next day, but I have no such memory. The following morning Howard mixed the remaining *kumass* into the porridge, giving it a none too pleasant flavour. But it was the headwind that was primarily responsible for our slow progress, not the mares' milk.

The riding was dull and, with the wind, hard, dispiriting work. Downhill we could manage to work up a speed of twenty kph, but uphill we managed no more than ten. We cycled right behind one another to minimise wind resistance, taking it in turns to front the full blast. We speculated wildly. Ten kph and 9,000 kilometres to go, that meant 900 hours' cycling at the worst. At perhaps eight hours of solid uninterrupted cycling a day, that meant 112 days of continual cycling. Allowing eight days for rest, servicing the bikes and emergencies and that was exactly another four months. It was 4 June, which would make arrival date 4 October; snow would be falling in Siberia . . . In truth, we needed more than eight days for servicing the bikes, resting, collecting and sending parcels. To send a single parcel sometimes took half a morning . . .

Drained of energy by the wind we turned off into a bleak village and asked a massive, pot-bellied man where the shop was.

'There's nothing in the shop. Come in.' We weren't in the mood to refuse any invitation, any respite from the cursed wind. Inside it was stiflingly hot. The house seemed to belong to two huge brothers, both truck drivers, and a long-suffering wife who immediately started to prepare a meal. Sausage, bread, cake, milk and fried eggs were placed on the table. Although only midday both brothers had been drinking vodka, which they pressed upon us. We declined; the prospect of vodka on top of *kumass* porridge didn't bear contemplating. Igor sat down beside me.

'*Tchut, tchut!*' ('A drop, a drop!') he whispered, nudging me with his massive arm, winking.

'*Nyet, spasiba!*' I assured him.

'*Tchuuut, tchuuut!*' he whispered again with another powerful nudge. To change the subject I asked him about his yellow sweatshirt, marked France and the USSR, telling him Gilles was French. He seemed delighted. 'French?' he asked Gilles. A moment later he had stripped off the sweatshirt and handed it to Gilles. 'A present, for you to remember us.' He was adamant, Gilles had to take it. He was built like an ox and his back was tattooed with a magnificent scene of a medieval castle complete with castellation, drawbridge, knights in armour and ladies mounted on horses. It was astonishingly well drawn. He sat there shirtless and continued talking. 'It was done in prison,' he confided before noticing that none of us was drinking the vodkas that had been poured for us. 'I have another on the inside of my lip. See!' And he turned down his lower lip to prove it. It was true alright.

Eventually we cycled on. After twenty minutes a lorry overtook us and swerved in dangerously close, just missing us, and jammed on the brakes. Igor jumped down with his son.

'We must have a photograph of you with my son, Kolya!'

Worn out by the wind we slept beside the road for several hours. In the evening we dragged ourselves into a village and wearily set about seeking food, Gilles searching for onions, Howard for eggs, Vitale for potatoes and me for milk and butter. For some reason no one wanted to know us that evening and we were getting desperate when we heard voices and laughter coming from behind a tall courtyard wall. We knocked at the door.

'*Fkhaditye!*' came a clear woman's voice. We laughed. Little did they know who it was at the door. Perhaps they were expecting a friend, a relation . . . We opened the small wooden door and entered, leaving the bikes outside. Inside a dozen people were standing talking, including an attractive woman holding a baby. She stared in amazement for a moment, laughed and called us in. We explained our story and that we were trying to find food to buy. 'Come. Sit down. You will eat with us. We have been to the cemetery today to remember our dead family but after that we always celebrate. We have already eaten but there is plenty of *shashlik* for you.' We were introduced to her husband, Nikolai, a policeman, her parents, brother and sister-in-law and neighbours; a table and chairs were brought out into the courtyard for us. Suddenly, far from being shunned, we were the centre of attention. It all happened so quickly, so naturally. A tablecloth was spread, in the middle of which was placed four loaves of good brown bread and a large samovar and a teapot to slake our thirst. This was followed by *okroshka*, a cold cucumber, cream and *kvass* soup, *shashlik*, salads and, naturally, vodka. Golden evening sun poured into the courtyard.

Their neighbour, Ivan Petrovich, a man in his sixties, invited us to spend the night in his house. His wife pulled out mattresses for us and prepared more tea while Ivan stoked the fire for us to have a sauna. While it heated we sat down with him round the kitchen table. Ivan was a large man but he had a look of suffering on his face, as though he had seen things he could neither bear to talk of, nor forget. It was a sad, haunting face that held my attention. He asked us what we thought of the Soviet Union. After we had spoken of our impressions of the crushed spirit, the palpable sense of hopelessness, he said:

'I know the system. If anyone understands Communism, I do. I spent ten years in the Gulags . . .' We stared at him, horrified. A silence in the little whitewashed room seemed to ring.

'*Ten years!*' I said. 'For what?'

'Nothing,' he said in a calm, tired voice, devoid of emotion.

'But . . . what do you mean, "nothing" . . . ? I don't understand. Where?'

'On the Kolomna Peninsula. I spent ten years there, in different camps, mining for gold. I saw it all.'

'But why?' I pressed.

'I joined the navy in the war and served on a battleship on the Caspian Sea. The second mate mutinied and tried to steer the ship to Iran but we were caught in neutral waters. I knew nothing about it at the time. I worked in the engine room. But everybody on board was arrested and sent to the labour camps. Everybody. I had done nothing. In the camps there were normally 6–800 people but on Kolomna Peninsula itself, we were eight million. Yes, eight million.'

'What were you forced to do?' we asked, fumblingly, feeling the inadequacy of our questions.

'I was sent to Susuman to mine gold,' he began slowly. 'Some of the work was done with machinery – American machinery – but mostly by hand, in temperatures that fell to −50° Centigrade. Each man was set a target. We had to shift five cubic metres of rock every day. If we hadn't finished during the day we continued all night, we continued until it was finished. Sometimes we worked twenty-four hours straight without stopping . . .' He paused and drew in breath, sighed and continued slowly. 'We were split into small groups. If a group failed to complete their set target they had three days to put it right – in addition to the next day's work, of course. If a group failed to do their set work for three days they were taken away and never seen again. We heard a lot about German fascism but this was Russian fascism and it was worse.'

It was difficult to know how to respond. We were all, for the first time in our lives, genuinely speechless. What could we say? Any remark would sound inadequate. We were in contact with something hardly credible, far removed from anything we could imagine. And yet here, two feet away, sat a man who had actually gone through it all, and survived.

Or had he? Looking at him I felt that actually only part of him had survived; some of him had been crushed out of existence, emptied out with such brutality and force that what was left was a shell, a body that continued to function but in which the spirit had almost given up. It was not so much that he had survived the Gulags as that he had been half-killed by it. When he went in he was eighteen: young, enthusiastic, full of life. When he came out ten years later, at the age of twenty-eight, he was a physical and mental wreck, embittered, disillusioned, his career in pieces. The best years of his life had been spent in unremitting toil in the grimmest of conditions for a crime he had not played a part in. Even now, forty years on, he looked used up, withdrawn, spent. Although still living, it had destroyed him.

'I survived only because physically I was very strong. Tens of thousands died because they couldn't keep going. We had very little food: 320 grams of beef, 300 grams of sugar and two kilos of porridge per person per week – and nothing more. It was American food – bought with the gold that we mined. We were given just enough food to keep us going, so that we could dig the gold. When I came back I worked on a collective farm; it was all I could do.' His nephew broke into the conversation:

'But that was a long time ago and now we live well.'

'I do not talk about these things much. It is better not to. I do not know that my conversation with you will not land me in the camps again.' Later, we asked Ivan what he felt about Gorbachev and *perestroika*. 'Do not trust him. Do not believe what he says. Things will only change here when the system changes, only when we have many parties and not just the Communist Party. Stalinism has paralysed our society. We need a revolution now. People may tell you that Communism is finished in the Soviet Union, that it is no longer important here. Do not believe them.'

'And do you think the army will continue to put down the unrest, to crush the protests?'

'My son and my grandson are in the army. What can they do? Everybody needs to reach the same position at the same moment, to rebel together. At the moment there are not enough such people. Now it is time for us to live in peace.' Igor rose and showed us to the *banya*, handing us fresh branches of silver birch with which to slap ourselves.

'There are many such people in our country,' Vitale told us. After the *banya* Ivan's wife had glasses of strong Russian tea waiting for us and no sooner had we sunk onto the mattresses than we fell into the deepest sleep imaginable.

9

KAZAKHSTAN I

AFTER THE URALS we swung south to Kazakhstan, the second largest republic in the USSR, a vast area of plateau, steppe and semi-desert.

The Kazakhs are a Muslim people originating from the Kypchacs and other Turkic, Mongol and Iranian groups which broke away from the Golden Horde in the middle of the sixteenth century and migrated to present-day Kazakhstan. It was not until the nineteenth century that three nomadic Kazakh states, the *zhouzes*, were incorporated into the Russian Empire as it extended south and east.

Our first and abiding impression of Kazakhstan was of winds bowling over endless steppes. From Moscow to the Urals the winds had generally been favourable; across Kazakhstan it was the reverse. In less than a week the wind had swung nearly 180 degrees. Battling against it, one close behind the other, we made it to Troitsk, a dreary windswept town whose shops had nothing to sell but bread and plum juice. Dusty three-litre jars stretched down the shelves at every level.

In the afternoon the winds were even stronger, buffeting us left and right. An hour after leaving we had ridden five kilometres and Troitsk was still in view. The wind brought us to a halt.

'This is murder!' Howard said. 'We've covered thirty kilometres in five hours, an average of six kph!'

'Let's call it off,' Gilles suggested. 'It may have lessened tomorrow.'

'And if it hasn't?'

'Then we go on!'

We abandoned the idea of cycling further and pitched camp in a small copse of trees, the only trees we had seen all day.

Mosquitoes had taken refuge from the winds in the same wood. We cursed, hopped around and retreated into the tents. When we set off the next morning the winds were just the same.

Fifty slow kilometres brought us to Komsomolskye where we met an English teacher. As we talked in the street a crowd began to form, listening curiously.

'Are people in Britain frightened of the USSR?' the teacher asked.

'No,' I said. 'Why?'

'We have a powerful army.'

'Well, people used to be apprehensive but with *glasnost* they are less so now.'

'It is only the governments that want war. The little people are the same everywhere. They only want to live in peace. You must tell your government we don't want war.'

'Britain has a tiny army for defence but the Soviet Union has an army of four million men. Why?'

'We are a big country. We were invaded by the fascists. We don't want to be invaded again.'

'And who might invade you now?'

'The capitalist countries . . . Germany . . . maybe. We are against the reunification of Germany. This is a great danger for us, of fascism beginning again in Germany.'

'Why? It's more likely to break out in Britain or here in the Soviet Union than it is in Germany. You have far more to fear within your own country than from the West.'

'We must learn to live in peace,' she replied, unconvinced.

She then tried to dissuade us from crossing Kazakhstan, implying there was nothing to see, and recommended a road to the north through the Russian Republic. She was keen for us to see the huge industrial cities of Omsk and Novosibirsk in Russia.

'They are bigger than Ufa and Magnitogorsk!' she told us proudly. She couldn't have chosen a surer method of keeping us south.

Northern Kazakhstan is flat, as flat as the whole world was once supposed to be. Not a ripple, not a swell of land interrupted a vast expanse of grass-covered plain. Trees petered out, leaving nothing but short, dry grass that stretched to the horizon, a horizon that evaporated into a heat haze and merged with the sky. It was early June and the temperature rose to the low thirties and then climbed steadily to 36°, 37°, 38° Centigrade, over 100° Fahrenheit. Occasionally a herd of cattle could be seen far out on the plains, minute specks, dwarfed by the horizontal band of yellow grass and a huge towering sky. There were no fences, no woods, nothing to interrupt the unending sea of grass. The land was like infinity, without beginning and without end, the same one day as the next. Would infinity itself, I wondered, be so deadening, so unutterably boring? The eye roved round looking for some anchor, something to take hold of, to give a sense of proportion, to give one hope. It was a weird, hallucinatory landscape that could easily drive one mad. Even among friends I felt terribly alone.

How can one convey the endlessness of the plains, day after day of yellowed grass blowing in the wind? Buzzards and crows appeared to be the only wild animals that lived on them, the only company for us and the distant herds of cattle that drifted across the landscape like bisons once had on the North American plains. For 1,600 kilometres, grassland stopped and wheat began; wheat stopped and grassland began again. Transferred to Europe, it was as if a grass steppe stretched without interruption from London to Rome, punctuated by a handful of small towns and villages, set down abruptly at wide intervals. As in European Russia there were no isolated buildings in the landscape; it was either steppe or town with nothing in between.

In this landscape we came to recognise the approach of a town by the appearance of a grey rectangle that floated fuzzily on the horizon. These rectangles were massive grain silos, so vast that they could be seen fifty kilometres away or more. We looked out for them as eagerly as the lookout would have done from the crow's nest of Captain Cook's *Endeavour*. With the wind against us day after day progress was slow and it was only with Herculean effort and by consistently cycling ten hours a day that we managed to keep up a daily average of 100 kilometres. The grain silos appeared to float like a magician's trick until we were very close upon them. But the wind drained us of energy and if we made it to a *stolovaya* for lunch we fell asleep at the table, as though drugged.

In the village of Federovka we cycled to the house of a Russian we had met on the road who had invited us to stay. There was no bath or shower, so we stripped off to wash in the back garden while Vladimir kept a ferocious pig at bay with a stick. He invited a Kazakh friend, an architect, to join us and we sat down to *bishbarmak*, a mouthwatering dish of layers of beef and pasta cooked with onions and chives.

'You must be prepared for one Kazakh custom now that you have entered our republic,' his Kazakh friend told us. 'When as a guest you are invited in for a meal, it is our tradition for the guest to carve and present a part of the animal to the host, wishing him good health for the part of the animal that the guest has chosen. If you wish him good eyesight, you present the host with the eye, if you wish him strength you present him with the leg, if good hearing with the ear, and so on.' We swallowed hard at this good news and scrutinised our plates for traces of eye and ear.

Howard mysteriously declared himself full but found a new zest for bread and Vitale quickly lost his appetite.

Vladimir's Kazakh friend was planning to set up his own architectural practice in the autumn, the first time that such private businesses had been allowed.

'We have a new President in Kazakhstan who is very dynamic,' he told us. 'He is introducing a market economy, encouraging private business and Western investment. We are moving ahead with this much faster than the Russian Republic. Many things are possible here that are still prohibited in the Russian Republic.'

'Will Kazakhstan eventually secede from the USSR?'

'Maybe. But there are problems. We Kazakhs are no longer a majority in our own country. When the Kazakh virgin-lands scheme began under Khrushchev the steppe was ploughed up and millions of settlers were brought from the European part of Russia to cultivate the land. Also, two million Kazakhs died during collectivisation and many other nations were deported here by Stalin. So Kazakhs only account for thirty per cent of the population. Our relations with the Soviet Union have not been happy.'

The next day, buffeted by wind, we arrived in Kustanai, the first Kazakh town of any size. Clouds of white pollen from the cotton-wool trees that lined the streets fell like snow, creating an illusion of a snowstorm in a temperature of over 100° Fahrenheit. The pollen floated like dandelion spores, brushing one's face and tickling one's skin.

Kustanai struck us all as different from Russian towns. It seemed more prosperous and people were better dressed; it felt livelier. At the post office I found an intelligent, enquiring face at my shoulder.

'Are you a tourist?'

Sergei Ivanovich worked for the town administration and was a member of the Communist Party. He offered to show us the way to the hotel where rooms had supposedly been reserved for us by telephone by the Sports Committee chairman of Komsomolskye.

'How far is the hotel?' I asked Sergei.

'Walking distance. Everything is walking distance in this country. We have problems with our cars. As you can see they are poor quality . . .'

At the hotel Gilles, Howard, Vitale and Sergei disappeared inside. Theoretically the rooms were booked; the only time rooms had been reserved for us in advance. An hour later Howard reappeared with lemonade and cakes.

'This is to keep you going. We're making progress. Rooms may be available,' he said, and dashed back inside. Twenty-five minutes later they all reappeared.

'Our Soviet bureaucracy!' Sergei grinned. 'But you have rooms.'

In the evening Sergei and two teachers joined us for a meal in the restaurant. The restaurant was full, noisy and Soviet rock blared from the loudspeakers. Everybody apart from us looked flushed and drunk; a young man lurched past knocking into our table. We were hungry but above all we wanted to talk. Even before the waitress arrived we proposed that we abandon the thought of a meal and withdraw to our hotel room, a proposal that was greeted with relief.

There followed one of the most candid conversations of the entire journey and it continued well into the night. Sergei was delighted to talk; five years before, he would have had to recount and justify his conversation with us to the KGB. But although people were freer than before, they were still instinctively wary of contacts with foreigners, still influenced by what Sergei called the 'mentality of fear' that had held sway for seventy years. But practical matters also prevented people from talking to us: they were so busy queueing for food and clothes that they had little time to spare.

'It's very boring but it's true,' Sergei said. 'We spend most of our day looking for food.' Sergei was critical of Gorbachev, accusing him of being 'a compromise politician' who was quick to change sides and Gorbachev's latest idea for a 'regulated social market' struck him as absurd. 'Nowhere in the world is there such a thing. There is either a capitalist economy or one that is completely isolated, like ours.' He explained that everything in the Soviet Union was of poor quality because people were not paid for quality but only to turn up at their factory or farm. What they did when they got there was immaterial.

Gorbachev was deeply unpopular according to Sergei, despite greater personal freedoms, because Gorbachev equalled change.

'One of his slogans is "*Perestroika* is a type of Revolution!"' That's just the problem. People don't want change, let alone revolution; Russians are very conservative people by nature.' He thought it would take a long time and be very difficult to change their mentality. This explained why Gorbachev was finding it so difficult to make changes. 'Most of the deputies in the Supreme Soviet are conservative. Why? Because they were elected by the Russian people who *are* conservative.' And although doubtful of the strength of Gorbachev's commitment to change, Sergei felt that he was being blamed unjustly for the economic disasters which were the result of inaction and corruption under Khrushchev and Brezhnev.

Russians, he said, were confused. For seventy years they had heard harrowing tales of poverty, homelessness and unemployment in the capitalist nations and had been told that they had the highest living standards in the world. And suddenly they were being told the reverse was true, and that they had to change once again. The impetus for change came from the Baltic Republics, Georgia and Armenia because, fundamentally, the Balts, the Georgians and the Armenians were more progressive than the Russians.

'For the Baltic Republics, it's easier,' Sergei said. 'They have had Communism only since 1945 and they have different traditions; they are more developed, they have not forgotten what to do. But we can remember no other system.' He felt that Russians were still afraid of the authorities. They were wary of speaking up, of organising demonstrations or pushing for change. He admitted that he too was afraid of the authorities and that he expected change to come only very slowly, over fifty or a hundred years.

Sergei introduced us to a German professor, the son of one of the hundreds of thousands of Germans deported by Stalin to the region in 1941. Invited to Russia by Catherine the Great, Germans had settled along the River Volga but in 1941 Soviet Germans were one of several nations and ethnic groups accused of collaboration with Nazi Germany and deported en masse to Kazakhstan. Even though they had been rehabilitated formally, no public announcement had ever been made, so that in the minds of most Russians, they remained guilty. The few that had been back to visit their homeland on the Volga had encountered bitter hostility and banners reading 'Better Aids than Germans!' and 'No to a second German invasion!' Some had been beaten up. When they had been deported they had left everything; when they went back they had been shocked at the neglected state of the land. But the move to have their autonomous republic on the Volga restored to them was unlikely to succeed. Apart from local opposition, the government was reluctant to allow it as it would mean an exodus of the most productive workers from Siberia and Kazakhstan.

Fearful of the future and taking advantage of more liberal emigration laws and a welcome in Germany, 800,000 Soviet Germans out of two million had left since 1985.

'The cultural identity of Germans in the Soviet Union has been destroyed,' the professor said, 'and there is no going back. Now people want to get out while they can to find a better life. I don't blame them.'

Sergei and the professor were both deeply disappointed by the motivation of their students. Young people had lost the ability to think for themselves, in part because of the intellectual devastation of Stalinism.

'Our intellectuals were killed off and now people don't know what to do or what to think,' Sergei said. 'Young people have no leaders, no one to look up to and they are scared to think for themselves.' Often it appeared that young people had little idea as to how to occupy their time; we often noticed them sitting around idly, looking bored, in towns and cities. And only then did we realise that we hadn't seen sport being played once in the 3,000 kilometres from Leningrad – neither a football field, nor a tennis court, nor a single sailing boat on the great lakes and rivers. Sport was not organised at school nor, it appeared, by anyone else.

I told Sergei about the history teacher we had met who had realised that for forty years he had taught falsehoods to his pupils.

'Such an experience must be soul-destroying,' I said.'

'Yes, that is his personal tragedy,' Sergei remarked.

'But the Soviet Union is full of these personal tragedies!'

'Yes,' Sergie replied. 'Ours is a very cruel country.'

8 June found us still moving across Northern Kazakhstan like ants across a runway. It was my birthday, as I was reminded by Gilles as I crawled out of my tent. It was overcast and soon began to rain. Far, far away on the plain a train was inching its way forward like a tiny mechanical toy. Apart from its passing and Howard's rack breaking, nothing happened to mark the day. Half a dozen vehicles passed us in the 120 kilometres to Uritsky, which we raced to reach before the massive black storm-clouds broke. The town was already a sea of mud, and the hotel bleak and depressing. While Vitale tried to placate the administrator, Howard and I went into the dining room. Rough tables were scattered on the muddy floor. There was nothing on the walls, no indication that the place was still in use, apart from one elderly man dressed in a worn baggy suit and wearing thick, cracked spectacles, sitting alone at a table. He lifted the spoon to his mouth slowly, methodically. He didn't turn to look at us when we entered, nor when we spoke in English. Perhaps he was deaf. He couldn't have been blind as well. But he looked at his bowl or straight ahead.

'Nice place to celebrate my birthday.'

'Sorry, Simon, it's the best place in town.'

We walked to the *banya* through a sea of mud, having secured a room for four against great opposition. It was dirty and musty. The *banya*, a shoddy grey-black building surmounted by a rusting metal chimney, was surrounded by liquid mud. There was no way of getting to it without soaking our feet. A strip of wood thrown down as a gangplank was half-submerged. Inside it was dilapidated and smelly. Even though the tiles were fairly new many were broken. 'They must be put in broken,' I thought, gazing round in astonishment. But the steam was hot and, after a day's cycling in the rain, enough to revive our spirits. On the way back we looked into the cinema. A film, *Googa*, was just beginning.

'Your birthday treat, Simon,' Howard told me. 'I'll pay for the tickets. Twenty kopecks? Sure.' Although streaked and dated, *Googa* was apparently a new film. It featured the Soviet army and centred round two boyhood friends who joined up to find that life as a conscript wasn't so bad after all. Girls seemed to like them in uniform and the work wasn't too onerous. It could have been a recruitment film.

After twenty minutes, I gave Howard a nudge and we stole out, leaving seven other people in the cinema.

In the hotel Gilles and Vitale had pleaded with the kitchen staff for a special birthday meal. The octogenarian in cracked glasses had disappeared, and we were given the VIP room with chairs and tables of orange plastic. It was no less hideous but not so empty. Vitale brought out a bottle of champagne that he had miraculously carried all the way from Magnitogorsk in the Urals. A can of American beer carried 700 kilometres by Howard, a black and white photograph of Madonna bought in a Soviet kiosk and a birthday card of Grandfather Lenin with two children on his knees were placed ceremoniously in front of me on the table. Turning up the walkman with our miniature loudspeaker we listened to Ella Fitzgerald. The whole sound of 'Duke's Place', 'Mack the Knife', 'Sweet Georgia Brown' seemed so full of *life*. God bless America! I thought. I'd rather live in Harlem than Uritsky. A birthday meal was produced – a thin sliver of roast beef, chips soaked in fat and a tomato salad. We asked for more but the cooks insisted there was nothing left.

Once the party was over I went out for a walk in the main square outside the hotel. The storm had passed and the sky was flecked with pink and gold. The square was paved, with a central statue of Lenin, and overgrown with weeds, grass and brambles. Two cows grazed in what might once have been flowerbeds. Propaganda posters listing figures for milk, wheat and meat production were posted up on warped boards. A statue of an unforgiving soldier painted head to toe in silver like a Martian served as a war memorial. What a weird birthday, I thought as I went back into the hotel. I was climbing the stairs when two passports were thrown down the stairwell from the first floor and I looked up to see the red-faced woman administrator shouting vociferously and roughly pushing two middle-aged men.

'Get out, drunkards! I'll have none of your filth in here!'

Day after day our road stretched ahead as straight as a ruler until it disappeared into a mirage and then reappeared as if inverted on itself in the sky. Hardly a vehicle passed us. Occasionally a line of trees could be discerned far off, seemingly truncated by a shimmering heat haze, floating above the surface of the land. Cycling in temperatures of over 100° we tried to find shade in which to stop at lunchtime. The roads melted and glossy black tar began to form in pools.

In Lomonosovka a row of new propaganda posters were stuck up in the centre of the village; inexplicably one was in English, portraying a crowd with fists raised in anger, a nuclear explosion in the background and the caption 'No to world holocaust!' Another portrayed a grain silo with the words 'Our politics are the politics of Peace!', a third a dove superimposed against the globe and the words 'For peace in space and our world!' the fourth a red cross against a nuclear bomb hitting the world and the word 'No!' Another portrayed a defenceless, naked girl clutching the world in her arms and the call 'Defend Peace!', and the last, ironically, a grim-faced Soviet soldier brandishing a sword and surrounded by missiles and fighter jets with the words 'We must defend the achievements of October!'

The money and effort involved might have been put to improving the bleak *stolovaya* or building a public *banya* or even to installing a public water supply, there being nothing other than pumps in the street. But constant propaganda keeps alive memories of the Second World War.

After several months I couldn't help but feel that the Russians' attitude to peace and war was very different from the European one. Despite two World Wars, Europeans generally view war as an aberration from the normal order but in the Soviet Union it almost felt as if the reverse were true – that peace was the aberration. Only their historical experience can explain why the Russians are prepared to put up with such limitations on their freedom and such poor conditions. Howard, Gilles and I increasingly wondered what it would take to provoke the Russians onto the streets *en masse* demanding change. As it was there was little in the shops: very little meat, fresh vegetables or tinned food, not much in the way of clothes or shoes, and everything of poor quality. What else could happen or disappear from the shops before people had had enough? Bread perhaps? We asked Vitale.

'No, I don't think so. No, not even if bread disappears. We are used to suffering.'

As we cycled up a bank in the village Howard's back wheel collapsed. We took it apart carefully. The kevlar strings had slipped off the hub and several had broken. It was irreparable. That meant we needed a new wheel: we would have to build one. We had spare spokes and a spare hub for just such an emergency but none of us had built a wheel before. We found shelter in a dilapidated pavilion under 'restoration' at the edge of the village. We swept out a room and, with a roof over our heads, a nearby well and a wood-burning stove we had everything we needed. Constantly checking against a front wheel we slowly began to piece it together. We took it in turns to work on the wheel, while the others scoured Lomono-sovka, looking for food. Ten hours later we had a wheel we could feel proud of.

10
KAZAKHSTAN II

With its faded wood cabins, dust-filled windows and dreary, empty streets, Ruzayevka appeared to be yet another nondescript village identical to hundreds we had passed through. And then, round a corner swept a fast-moving crowd, whistling, shouting and singing. As they drew closer we realised they were students in grotesque fancy dress, hideously made up and half in drag. They crowded round any car they could find, bouncing it up and down until the embattled driver handed over some roubles, in return for which he was handed a liberal glass of vodka and sent on his way with shouts and cries. They advanced down the street, whooping and pirouetting in the dust, wearing masks, kerchiefs or turbans. One clutched an axe, another a loaf of bread impaled on a toasting fork, a third vodka, a fourth a large jar of gherkins. At the back came an accordionist, unsteady on his feet. Inevitably we were spotted and the crowd swooped over with blood-curdling shrieks and plied us with vodka to delighted shouts and cries. Then, as suddenly as they had arrived, they moved on, leaving us each holding a gherkin.

Beyond Ruzayevka grassland stretched for fifty kilometres, over which ranged huge herds of horses. Forty kilometres on, we came to a small town. The hotel was next to the Communist Party headquarters and a gold statue of Lenin. There were no showers, no hot water. We were told to eat immediately if we wanted any supper as the staff were closing the restaurant early to go to a film. We were lucky to get some scrawny chicken, rice, a few slices of cucumber and sour cream. None of us bothered to look round the town. We knew what it would look like.

The next day we cycled 130 kilometres to Kotchetav, known in the Soviet Union as 'the Switzerland of Kazakhstan'. We approached it over a gentle hill, the first for weeks. Factories belched smoke; chimney stacks, warehouses and buildings were strewn out along the grey lakeside. It looked more like Windy City set amidst dun-coloured hills of dried grass than Geneva. We cycled to the hotel and sank down wearily on the steps while Vitale negotiated rooms, one each. We felt the need of having the luxury of our own rooms, but the hotel was full of schoolchildren who waited patiently outside our rooms for autographs.

In Kotchetav, we ate well. A matronly waitress seemed to magic everything that we wanted out of the kitchen and her service was impeccable, the first and last such service in six months. The woman was a goddess. We decided to have a rest day; we were exhausted and had not had a day off since Magnitogorsk in the Urals. We needed a break.

We went to the market, passing a huge queue of women waiting to buy a recent delivery of clothes. The government had announced price rises and people were desperate to buy anything that could be found. The market building was massive, almost Arabic in style, built of concrete outside with marble-topped tables within. Inside it was deserted. In the huge hall, big enough to accommodate several hundred market sellers, there were two women, one with five trays of meat, the other with a jar of red roses. Neither had any customers.

Another market was taking place outside. Kazakh and Russian women sat in state behind volcanoes of black sunflower seeds, cross-legged, like Eastern potentates. Privately grown tomatoes, aubergines, onions and parsley were on sale at high prices but a long queue had formed at the only stall selling state produce which had only two vegetables – cucumber and cabbage. Two Uzbeks fondly piled up huge mounds of burgundy cherries: otherwise there was no fruit. When we returned to the hotel the queue of women had hardly moved.

'What would the Swiss make of this "Switzerland"?' I asked Gilles.

'Obviously no one knows what Switzerland looks like. Why would anyone in Kotchetav go to Switzerland? And if they did why would they come back?'

The few rounded hills dropped away and the flat steppe flooded back. We were in wheatfields again – just when we thought we had seen the back of them. Crows cackled noisily from nests beside the road; it was as though we were reliving the experience of a month ago, as though some invisible hand had picked us up and set us back 3,000 kilometres.

'I hate those birds!' Gilles rasped.

In Kotchetav Vitale had telephoned home. His father's illness had taken a turn for the worse and Vitale said he would have to fly home from the next city, Barnaul, and he thought it unlikely he would be back. It was desperately bad luck. His mother was so arthritic that she could only walk a few metres, and it was Vitale's father who had looked after her and done the shopping and the housework. But if he was in hospital, Vitale would be the only one who could look after her. We had cycled nearly 6,000 kilometres and were nearly half-way. To have to stop now, having accomplished so much and with Siberia ahead, was a real blow.

Vitale had proved to be good company, humorous, patient with our foibles, our endless questions and criticisms of his country, and easy going. We told him we would wait a week in Barnaul for him if he wanted to try and rejoin us. 'I knew there was a chance of this happening,' he said, with sadness in his voice. 'But that's life!'

Each day's cycling seemed to demand greater and greater effort. The winds were against us again and the heat turned the road to sticky, wet tar that slowed us down terribly. The cycling was dull and our spirits fell steadily lower, headwinds being a hundred times more demoralising to a cyclist than the steepest mountain.

At Kziltu, to compensate, we received a wonderfully warm welcome from the hotel administrator. Kziltu was an oasis of trees in the grass desert of Kazakhstan. Our arrival coincided with a yearly event – Kazakh dances in the Cultural House. The hall was packed with Kazakhs and Russians, the former predominating. The dances were performed by a professional troupe from Alma-Ata, the capital of Kazakhstan, and they danced rhythmically, in magnificent traditional costume, with elegance and grace. Apart from hideously distorted music, played at full pitch, it was fun to watch. Yet it was also sad to see these Kazakhs turn up in their shapeless Russian clothes to witness what, until a short time ago, had been their own dances, their own culture now reduced to folkloric spectacle. As I left, I turned to say goodbye to someone in the dark, fell down the steps and sprained my ankle. I hobbled back and the next morning my ankle looked like a football.

I could hardly walk, which delighted the administrator, who wanted us to stay. She insisted that a doctor take a look at it and the next thing I knew a green, military-looking ambulance had drawn up at the hotel.

'Whose idea was that?' I asked, annoyed. 'I'm hardly a hospital case.' But apparently I was. I hobbled to the ambulance on the arm of a nurse while Gilles and Howard grinned, and took photographs like paparazzi. At the hospital I was propelled directly to a doctor, a Soviet German, being given precedence over a dozen patients. An X-ray was suggested, something I regretted agreeing to the moment my body started being strapped into a coat-of-armour made of lead and leather. It was as if I were being prepared for the guillotine. There must be a lot of radioactive particles flying around, I thought, if I had to wear a lead flak-jacket for an X-ray of an ankle. But nothing was broken. I was bandaged up, shook hands with the doctor and asked if I could pay.

'No, nothing to pay,' he said. 'Good luck on your travels.'

Back at the hotel, the Communist Party boss arrived to escort us to the collective-farm games. Two hundred farmworkers drawn up in ragged lines listened to a long speech from the Party boss and then a beautiful Kazakh girl in red and white costume stepped forward and presented us with bread and salt – the traditional Kazakh gesture of welcome. Howard replied suitably on our behalf, an overweight farmhand ran round the sports ground with a flaming torch and the games were declared open. Small children dressed in brilliant outfits went through pre-rehearsed, American-style dance numbers waving coloured balloons to the tunes of Elvis Presley and Buddy Holly. It was a most unlikely scenario.

'What are your impressions of Kazakhstan?' a journalist asked us, while a crowd gathered, listening intently. We said that we felt that the Kazakh people appeared more curious, more open and livelier than people in Russia, and the economic situation did not seem so bad. There was more food in the shops and better clothes.

'That is why we want our own economy,' she said. 'You have seen a lot of our Soviet life. What do you think of our problems and why we live as we do?'

'Lack of incentive, lack of motivation is the main problem,' Gilles said. 'If you give people an incentive to work for themselves and start their own businesses, then people will work more and be happy to do so. But at the moment no one has any incentive to work.' Once the crowd started putting their own questions, the Communist Party chief pulled at my sleeve.

'We must go. Come! Come!'

'What do you think of Gorbachev?' a farmworker asked.

'Gorbachev is popular in America,' Howard replied, 'because of *glasnost* and *perestroika*. The problem is he is more popular in America than in the Soviet Union.' The crowd laughed appreciatively. 'But your problems existed before *perestroika*. *Perestroika* is not responsible for them.' The journalist agreed.

'What is your opinion of Eisenhower?'

'Very good as a general and no good as a politician, especially over foreign policy.' The crowd cheered and applauded.

'What is your opinion of war veterans?'

'In the US,' Howard said, 'war veterans from the Second World War and Korean War are respected and well treated, but less so the Vietnam

War veterans. Like here, with Afghanistan.' Murmurs of approval rose from the crowd. The Party boss tugged at my arm again.

'We go now,' he said. 'Tell Howard,' and he walked a distance from the crowd and waited impatiently.

'What do you think of a reunited Germany?'

'Germany is the most prosperous, stable and democratic country in Europe. What happened in Germany fifty years ago is history. You must look to the future, not to the past. People do not need to be afraid of a reunified Germany.'

'This is good,' the journalist replied. 'I will put this in my article . . . We wish you a good journey and good memories of Kazakhstan. You are now part of our history. From now on everything in our village will be dated from your arrival here. People will say "that was five years before or five years after the foreign cyclists came to the village".' And then, under a blazing Kazakh sun, she broke out into a rendering of 'Auld Lang Syne'.

We left the sports stadium to the obvious relief of the Communist Party chief. As at many *stolovaya*s, there was a VIP room into which, for once, we were ushered. Only padded chairs and wooden walls with rough wooden sculptures marked it off from the main dining room, but the food was better. We asked the Communist Party boss what he felt about the proposal to sell land to those peasants who wished to leave the collective farms.

'Land is not like a whore. It cannot be sold to the highest bidder,' he said dismissively.

He soon lost interest in us and excused himself from the table. Back at the hotel we found a young Kazakh policeman in the foyer.

'I've been sent by the Party chief to look after your things, to prevent any problems,' he told us.

'Great,' I said. 'I didn't know we were in danger, did you, Gilles?'

'Only from sunstroke and speeches.'

And whether it was intentional or not, his presence probably deterred anyone who might have wanted to talk further with us at the hotel.

The next day we crossed the River Irtish, which runs 3,000 kilometres north before emptying into the Arctic, and arrived at Pavlodar.

'We do not have permission to be here,' Vitale told us. 'Pavlodar is a closed city. I think we will have problems.' But no one seemed to notice. Nevertheless we left very early the next morning, and followed a terrible road of loose rock and scree. Howard was suffering from diarrhoea – or dysentery – Vitale was quiet and withdrawn, and Gilles began to feel weak.

Ninety-five kilometres under a blistering sun brought us to Shcherbatki where we were served something inedible in the *stolovaya*. Although no effort had gone into the food a great deal of time, and presumably money, had gone into the weirdest interior decor we had yet seen – the walls were covered with red and black interlocking plastic triangles that alternated with protruding maroon squares and knobs and panels of coloured glass lit by a single light bulb. As with most Soviet cafés, there were no windows. However, by some twist of fate, there was an espresso coffee and ice-cream machine, but alas, coffee and ice cream were *defitsit* items.

As we cycled into Kulunda we stopped to buy tomatoes and asked two little girls, aged ten or eleven, where the hotel was.

'*Pozhálaysta, skazhite mnye, gdye góstinitsa?*' They looked at us in astonishment and began to giggle. Why could they not understand? I asked again and so did Gilles. They looked alternately perplexed and amused, repeating the word '*góstinitsa*' aloud to each other. Surely they must know what a hotel is, I thought. We cycled over to ask some older people who understood straightaway and gave us directions but the moment the two girls heard the word pronounced correctly they collapsed with laughter.

'*Ah! Gostínitsa!*' they shrieked, hysterically. And from that moment they followed us, riding together on a bicycle far too big for them, shaming us all the way through the town, crying out at the top of their voices '*Góstinitsa! . . . Gostínitsa! . . . Góstinitsa! . . . Gostínitsa!*'

Every time a tomato fell from our racks they picked it up with glee and peals of laughter, holding it up to us impishly while keeping just out of distance. For an afternoon we were the Pied Pipers of Kulunda.

Gilles fell asleep with exhaustion at a wooden table outside the hotel until rooms were secured. Howard was used up, drained of energy by dysentery and the side-effects of the anti-dysentery medication, Flagyl. To send telegrams, Gilles and I dragged ourselves off on foot to find the post office and asked a passer-by for directions. He happened to be an off-duty policeman and, in response, he flagged down a passing motorist and commandeered the car, ordering the driver to take us all to the post office.

The post office refused point blank to send telegrams in English, something we had done from other Russian towns. Sending telegrams in Russian to people back home seemed somewhat pointless, so we commandeered another car, believing we would arrange the matter from our friend's office. The drivers seemed to take it in remarkably good spirit. However, instead of going to his office, we found ourselves in his flat drinking small cups of black coffee. He looked round wondering what he could give us as presents, and then pulled two of the biggest and heaviest books off his shelves and inscribed them. Gilles's bedtime reading was a history of the Soviet police force, mine a handsome quarto on Soviet gems. We tried to decline them in vain; he seemed sorry he could not give us anything better. After an hour and a half we gave up trying to send a telegram. We were too tired to wait any longer; we were both asleep on our feet. We arrived back at the hotel in a police jeep to the horror of Howard and Vitale, who thought at first we were under arrest.

'That was our roughest ride of the trip,' I said, climbing down with a grin.

'They're opening the *banya* specially for us,' Howard told us. 'Grab your towel.' And it was true; the administrator of the hotel had arranged for the baths to be opened just for us. Later in the evening I went off with a fuel bottle in search of petrol. Outside the police station were eight policeman, two sitting on old, heavy motorcycle combinations, brilliant yellow and blue.

'How much do you need?' one asked. When I showed him the bottle, he unplugged his feeder pipe and filled it from the tank on his motorcycle.

The next four days were the longest days in history. The roads were white pebbles and rock, raw hardcore making every inch a battle to cycle. When it was possible we cycled in the fields, following the smooth tracks worn by tractors and cars that had also found the road too rough. Grassland or sparse wheat stretched away, unrelieved. There were no trees, no shade and the temperature hovered at 38–9°. And then there were the headwinds which blew steadily at us from dawn till dusk.

There was very little on the road. At one point a police jeep stopped beside us. It was the policeman who had given me the petrol from his motorcycle the day before. He jumped out, shook us all by the hand, topped up our waterbottles and disappeared in a cloud of white dust.

Our road lay beside a railway which ran straight to the horizon. When the earth track looked smoother on the other side, Gilles and I carried our bikes over the railway tracks and continued on the far side, out of sight of Vitale and Howard. We sped along for a long time, protected from the wind by the embankment, until we had a nasty feeling that we had not heard anything on the other side for an awfully long time. We climbed the embankment, the only vantage point on the plains, and looked around. The road was nowhere to be seen. Our track and the railway had continued in a perfect straight line while the road must have turned off at an angle a long way back. On the far side was a salt flat, brilliant white and crystalline. Unable to bear the prospect of retracing our route, we carried the bikes over and struck off at a diagonal, hoping to meet up with the road, but got stuck in the huge expanse of white salt. Most of it was too soft to cycle on. We began to push.

'How much water have you got?' I asked Gilles.

'Quarter of a bottle.'

'So have I. We'd better start rationing it.'

'Yes, this would be a sad place to die,' he replied.

Eventually we made it to Blagoveshchensk, our lips chapped, our throats dry and croaky, and collapsed beside a shop. Howard and Vitale were already there, sprawled in the shade. Not only did the shop have watermelons, the first we had seen, but it was half-blocked with them, stacked up from the floor to the ceiling. We ate two straight off in silence at a rickety table outside. We were too tired to talk. We found a hotel, dragged the bikes upstairs to our rooms and, white with dust, walked to the *banya*. Turning the taps to fill our tin bowls with water we jumped back with a terrible shock, hearts thumping. The pipes and taps were picking up an electric current and we had nearly been electrocuted.

A Russian in the *banya* also tried the taps, winced and jumped in the air with shock, and went out to complain. Two minutes later a woman came in and tossed us industrial rubber gloves.

'Here, use these. It sometimes happens.'

'These people are mad,' Gilles said. 'Electric currents in the *public baths*. Perhaps they *do* want to kill us.'

'What a country!' Howard said.

Barnaul was an elusive destination. In the morning we passed a sign marking it 326 kilometres ahead. In the evening, after ten hours in the saddle, we came across another, marked 325. Two days later we passed an encouraging '180 km'; two hours later it was back up to 200.

It was monotonous cycling, dry, hot and dusty. Rusty combine-harvesters were out in the fields but the crop was thin, short and sparse. In Kazakhstan, we were told, they only had a good harvest once every ten years. The roads melted, pools of oily black tar covering the road and sometimes flowing like treacle at the side. It was like glue, slowing us down, covering the bikes, our shoes and legs. When the occasional car or lorry passed us their tyres made a strange suction sound as they pulled up the tar. Again we were forced to take the bikes to the fields and cycle in the tracks. Gilles felt weaker and weaker, and began to fall behind. Howard was still suffering from dysentery. Vitale became more and more morose. I alone felt well, if tired, but I was increasingly depressed by everything I saw and heard.

'If I was doing this on my own I'd have stopped long ago,' I told Howard.

'Yes, the only thing that's keeping me going is the cycling.'

For two days the roads were covered with crickets, tens of thousands of them. At first I thought they were locusts and tried to avoid them but they soon became too thick on the ground. For two days the only sound was that of the wind and a horrible crunching of crickets beneath the wheels. When we stopped at a *stolovaya* crickets hopped down off our clothes and heads onto the table throughout the meal.

For a week Gilles had grown steadily weaker, until barely able to cycle at ten kph. We made an emergency stop at Pavlovsk. There was no hotel but an Azerbaijani invited us to stay with him and his friends. The four of them had arrived that very same day to spend the summer doing construction work for a *sovkhoz*, a state farm, as wages were higher than in Azerbaijan and they had been given a house by the *sovkhoz* to live in. We followed him down a sandy lane past wooden cabins, duck, geese and silver birches. A small girl was playing amidst a vast pile of white bricks that had been dumped, pell-mell, over a vast area in such a way that most of them were broken or chipped. I stopped to get water from the pump.

'It doesn't work,' a tiny *babushka* shouted. 'Go to the pump at the other end of the village.'

The house given by the state farm for the Azerbaijanis to live in for the summer was a typical Russian village house built of wood. There were four whitewashed rooms, empty apart from unassembled metal beds and a brick, wood-burning oven. But the house had been left in a filthy state. The Azerbaijanis had had time to put up a strip of white sheet to keep the flies out of the room they intended to sleep in and to sweep it out; that was all. The other rooms were thick with flies. We assembled a bed for Gilles and he lay down, shattered. Flies settled on the bed, on his hands and face. He took some homoeopathic medicine and fell asleep. It was stiflingly hot but impossible to open the windows. We tried beating at the flies without success; they rose in their thousands like bees swarming.

The Azerbaijanis appeared to have no possessions. All they had brought with them for the entire summer was a small attaché case each, as yet unpacked. They had no cooking pans, no utensils, nothing other than a single mug, plate and spoon. The temperature indoors was unbearable, so the Azerbaijanis built a fire outside to cook on while Vitale and I negotiated for food in the village, coming back with eggs, onions and potatoes. We prepared a meal and tea and took it inside to Gilles.

'Leave it there,' he said feebly, indicating the windowsill.

'Flies are too bad,' I said, 'you'd better eat it now.'

'Can't eat it now, just leave it there.' We did and immediately a cloud of black flies descended to cover it. Outside Howard and Vitale and I conferred, agreeing that Gilles stood little hope of recovering with the flies and the heat. We tried to persuade him to take a lift to Barnaul. In a decent hotel with a clean bed he stood a chance of recovering and we could call a doctor; but he was adamant that he was going to cycle every single kilometre. On top of everything else he was suffering from diarrhoea and occasionally had to rush from the room. When we went in to see him, he looked as though he were on his deathbed.

Maybe in the morning he would feel recovered enough to cycle to Barnaul, only 80 km away. The flies were so bad that we could not sit down to eat, even outside. We wandered around, eating on the move. It was like a furnace inside the house. To the hilarity of the Azerbaijanis and the bemusement of Russians passing on their horse-drawn carts, Howard and I laid our sleeping bags down outside and went to sleep. The sun only set after 11.15 pm, slowly revealing myriad stars as midnight blue eclipsed the last traces of the evening sky.

Howard and I woke at five o'clock after a perfect sleep to see the dawn. Everything was utterly motionless, the branches of the birch trees drooping gently, weighed down with the night dew. A wave of pink spread across the sky, blotting out the stars, before fading into the faintest blue. We rose, lit a fire, prepared breakfast and filtered water before going in to see Gilles, who felt no better and said he was too weak to move. But with no running water, no chance of a shower, no decent food, no clean bed, nothing in Pavlovsk other than stifling heat and flies, we insisted that he took a lift. We flagged down a truck and loaded Vitale's and Gilles's bikes on board, Vitale accompanying Gilles to get him safely checked into a hotel.

At 6.30 am Howard and I set off, cycling fast to cover as much ground before the wind blew up but by 7.30 we were already fighting a strong headwind. At 8.00 we found a shop selling fruit cakes, the only ones we had seen in 6,000 kilometres. We bought four, devoured two on the spot and stowed two away for later. At 11.00 we cycled through grim suburbs – churned earth, bleak apartment blocks and grey factories under a grey sky.

Of that day, Gilles wrote later: 'In the Azerbaijani fly-house I felt tired; my stomach ached. The flies bothered me. I could feel them on my skin and hear them buzzing. They wouldn't land and stay put. They had to keep landing and taking off. I covered my arms and legs with the blanket but I was too hot to cover my face. The smell, the sweat and the temperature attracted the flies. They went into my ears, my eyes and between my lips when I opened my mouth to breathe. Their noise was amazing. I saw them on my food bowl, my cup, my water-bottle, my medicine – dozens of them. I couldn't sleep, and I got up once and went outside with diarrhoea. I felt very weak. On the way, I passed a dead goat's head lit up by the moonlight. And the night was beautiful, peaceful and warm, and I remembered how much I usually enjoyed such nights . . .'

11
INTO SIBERIA

W E HAD FINISHED the third leg of our journey. We were back in the Russian Republic and, beyond Barnaul, Siberia stretched east to the Pacific.

It had taken us exactly a month to reach Barnaul from Ufa in the Urals, a distance of 2,600 kilometres against consistent headwinds, and we needed a break. We were exhausted. We needed to rest but our equipment sent from Moscow had to be collected, the bikes stripped down and serviced, telegrams sent and food supplies bought for the next stretch.

On paper it all sounds easy and simple; in the Soviet Union, not so. Everything involved the usual complications, queues, time-wasting, disorganisation and muddle. And there were uncertainties: Vitale was leaving for Moscow; we did not know whether we had to have a replacement or whether we could cycle alone; and Gilles was ill.

The novelty of our journey had worn off. We were tired of the conditions, the shambolic towns and villages, the overpowering ugliness wherever we looked, the fact that to have a meal, to get into a restaurant, or to check into a hotel at the end of the day, we had to plead, beg, argue and wait endlessly. We were worn down by dreadful food, and fed up with drunks and shabbily dressed people. In Asia people were poorer but managed nevertheless to look wonderful in their clothes, even a sarong tied at the waist. The simplest people carried themselves with pride. Nothing could make a greater contrast than the Russians, ambling along in their shapeless clothes like prisoners-of-war on the move. Only the Kazakhs seemed to know how to make something of their apparel.

Gilles and I had noticed that Howard's attitude to the journey had changed radically after the Urals. Up to the Urals we all believed that the journey would improve, that we would come across interesting communities with their own traditions and culture, that people would become more open, that we might meet people with hope. Once we got to the Urals it dawned on us that what we saw was what there was. There *was* nothing else to look forward to. Howard's infectious enthusiasm for the journey deserted him. He had one goal from this point, and one goal only: Vladivostok. It became increasingly apparent that he wanted to get there as fast as possible and to get out. He had commitments to twenty-five sponsors whom he would not disappoint; he would accomplish what he had set out to do. But after the Urals, we felt that Howard had abandoned hope that the trip would live up to expectations.

'I think Howard is pretty low,' I said to Gilles.

'Who wouldn't be?' Gilles replied.

'I don't think the trip is what he expected.'

'It's pretty *brutal*, I must say,' he said. He shook his head slowly, with a tired smile. 'Extremely *brutal*.' The disappointment was bad enough for Gilles and me, but Howard had spent two years planning and organising the journey, negotiating with the Soviet authorities and conferring with sponsors.

We hoped that Vitale would be able to rejoin us but had told him that if he was unable to do so we would rather cycle alone than have another Russian. Over two and a half months we had settled down to a routine; we knew what had to be done and how to do it; we had evolved a pattern and a pace that suited us; we knew how each other worked and responded in different circumstances. We dreaded the prospect of a new arrival to whom everything would have to be explained and who would take a few weeks to fit in. We were therefore taken aback when we came face to face with Sasha in the hotel. He spoke virtually no English and we thought, mistakenly as it turned out, that he would be too timid to be an asset in meeting people along the route. No one had consulted us about a replacement, but we were too tired to react. Gilles and I raised our eyebrows. It was a *fait accompli*. While Gilles recuperated we set about our tasks. It took seven hours alone to collect our box of spare parts at the airport. From it we extracted new tyres, inner tubes, oil, grease, bearings, mosquito repellent, derailleurs and dried mountaineering food. At the post office we collected a box sent from Moscow with Syrian chocolate, porridge oats, dried meat, walnuts and sugar, all of which were unobtainable in the shops. We took the bikes to pieces, cleaned and regreased every part on the balcony of our hotel room on the twelfth floor and put them back together again. At the post office we met two Russian girls, Anna and Tatiana, who showed us to a new cooperative restaurant, the best in Barnaul. We reckoned we were due for a celebratory drink but neither wine, nor champagne, nor beer were available.

'It's a great advance on the others,' Howard said wearily.

'I guess we'll just have to cycle another 2,000 kilometres to Irkutsk for our beer,' I said. 'That'll make it 4,000 between beers.'

'We don't like the new cooperatives,' Tatiana said. 'The quality of their goods is no better than those in the state shops and their prices are terribly high.'

In the evening I walked with Tatiana to a friend's flat.

'Does Olga live with her parents?'

'Yes, she's too young to have her own flat in the Soviet Union.'

'How old is she?'

'Twenty-eight.'

Anna was still a student but Olga and Tatiana had graduated from the Language School and were working as translators. Olga lived with her parents in one of the greying and pockmarked apartment blocks that had become synonymous for us with Soviet Russia. Inside it was comfortably furnished and neatly ordered. With student grants of fifty roubles a month it had only been possible for them to study in their home town, 'Besides which most people only get into University through their connections,' Anna said, 'so that too obviously limits you to your area. Our passports also have our residential address in them and it is very difficult to get this changed.' I asked Olga what she thought of the law that had been proposed, which would enable Russians to travel abroad freely for the first time.

'It will not be possible,' she said dismissively. 'They only talk about such matters. Maybe it will be possible in Moscow but not here. Here the authorities will want to know why you want to go abroad and then turn you away.' She laughed. 'How do you like our *perestroika*?' I had to admit that we had been disappointed. We had, I told her, expected change, enthusiasm and debate, and we had basically found young people indifferent and older people hostile or disillusioned.

'*Perestroika* started in 1985,' Olga said. 'Now it is 1990. What have they done? You see those factory chimneys over there?' she said, pointing to half a dozen brick chimneys smoking on the horizon. 'At night I cannot sleep when the wind blows this way. I cannot open the windows. You can smell it now, can't you?' There was an acrid smell in the air. 'They have done nothing about pollution from those factories.'

'But you now have the freedom to do something about it, to protest, to organise a petition, a demonstration.'

'No, we don't,' Olga said vehemently, 'it is still not possible here.' Anna disagreed with this but both were agreed that a demonstration would be a complete waste of time.

'Why?'

'No one would pay any notice.'

'Why not?'

'The men who run the factory are also senior members of the Communist Party in this town, so if you complain to the Communist Party you are complaining to the very same men.'

'Isn't there anyone else you can protest to?'

'No. No one else has any power,' Olga said angrily. 'But in any case they probably have filters, bought at great expense from abroad, but they just lie there in the rain and rust. No one knows what to do with them.'

'Why not?' I asked, surprised.

'They don't know how to fix them. They don't have any specialists to fit them. And they think everything will be alright. They don't believe they're really necessary. The factory can get by without them, that's what they think.'

'We have an expression,' Anna said, 'that is difficult to translate. It's very Russian. It means "perhaps everything will be alright", or "it'll work out somehow". So no one is too concerned as people know that everything will "work out alright" in the end.'

The television was on, showing a Soviet film about the United States, made before the advent of *glasnost*. It portrayed family life in small-town America as selfish, violent and vindictive, children and parents alike caught up in a materialistic, uncaring society. It was preceded by and interspersed with documentary film of Broadway, war atrocities in Korea, menacing American troops marching past filmed from boot level, fleeing and dead Vietnamese civilians, and US warships firing – all cobbled together to create a vivid photomontage of the callousness of American society. Or was it nothing more than a valid personal interpretation on the part of some film director? How was it that we had seen so many in a similar vein on hotel televisions?

'Yes, it is propaganda,' Anna said. 'At least, that is what I think but my father would not. He believes implicitly in the Motherland and he hates the United States. But what does the concept "the Motherland" mean to you?'

'A narrow-minded and partisan attitude to one's own country and the rest of the world.'

'For him the Motherland is everything, justifies everything. He hates Gorbachev, whom he thinks is ruining and humiliating the country; for him Stalin was the best ruler the USSR has ever had.'

'What about the millions that were killed or sent to the labour camps?'

'He thinks that if there is a global aim, people don't matter. It is the state, the Motherland, that matters.'

'The "state" is only an abstraction; in reality it's made up of people. Is it not *for* the people that the state is created in the first place?'

'I tell him also that it's an abstraction but he won't listen. And if I ever say anything positive about the USA he becomes very angry.'

'I still cannot understand how he can admire Stalin,' I said, 'if he *knows* that millions were killed. I could understand if he didn't know. Just recently Gorbachev himself said publicly that Soviet war losses were far higher than they need have been, directly because of Stalin's acts. What would your father think of that?'

'He would not accept it. He *believes* in Stalin. Under him the Motherland was feared. We were a great country.'

'Let me tell you a story about the time of Peter the Great,' Olga interrupted her, 'and maybe you will understand. It was at the time of our war with Sweden. He had some foreign military advisers, Austrian and German I think, in his army and they held senior positions, I forget their names. In one of the wars they had to attack and take a certain town. The foreign advisers assessed the situation, went to Peter the Great and said, "We can take it in three months", and they put forward their proposals for besieging the town. "No," Peter replied. "We can take it in three days." And they did. The town was taken. The cost in lives was not material. People have never mattered in this country.'

At the hotel we studied the map to see how we could salvage the expedition by injecting some excitement. The original plan had been to strike east through small mountains to Abakan, north to Krasnoyarsk and south-east to Lake Baikal, in effect a huge semicircle to the North through unspectacular Taiga. But if we could get through the Zapadnyy and Vostochnyy Mountains to Irkutsk, keeping close to the Mongolian border, the route would be much shorter and we would pass through wild, unvisited country.

'For 200 kilometres there are no roads, no tracks, nothing,' Gilles said. 'We may have to push the bikes, we may have to carry them, but we'd have to average twenty kilometres a day. There's a track as far as Kizil and beyond that we would have to follow the Kham-Sira or the Ka-Kem Rivers upstream and cross over to Orlik. It would be tough, but the landscape would be awesome.'

'We might come across Mongol nomads there. We would be only fifty kilometres from the Mongolian border,' I said. 'We would have to take the absolute minimum: one tent, sleeping bags, a few tools, two panniers each, a water-filter and enough dried mountaineering food to keep us going for two weeks.'

'You're crazy,' Howard told us. 'You'd never make it. You need to have pack frames made and four people to carry the bikes while four others carry food, cameras and medicines. You can't just carry your bikes. You need frames. It takes time to make them. We've got very detailed aerial maps and if they show no trail, that means there is no trail. When we trekked in Himachel in Pakistan there was a trail marked on our map and we could walk it but not bike it. You'd need yaks or horses to carry your gear, you'd need porters, you'd need ropes and petons to set protection on the pass, you'd need cold-weather gear because you would have to cross a 6,000-foot-high pass. To cross 200 kilometres of rough terrain will take two weeks minimum of walking and six days of climbing. It may take three days to cross the pass: one to the summit, one to rest and one to repel. You're going to need food for three weeks and then food for the porters.'

'I think there's a lightweight alternative,' Gilles said carefully, 'with two panniers. We use the bike itself as the frame and the panniers to cushion the weight. We take the minimum and with little weight we can move fast.'

'How fast?' Howard was angry.

'Twenty kilometres a day.'

'No way! Maybe you'd do five! This is a twenty-five-day trip, not a ten-day one. Sure, it would be exciting but it could delay our arrival in Vladivostok. We've got a real obstacle ahead of us – the swamp. We've got to be rested for that and we won't be if we try and carry our bikes through mountains for two weeks.'

Gilles and I disagreed with Howard on whether it were feasible and how long it would take. Howard saw it in terms of a major expedition, complete with yaks, base camps and teams of porters toiling up the mountain side. He envisaged us belaying off cliff faces, setting protection and reaching a summit. We envisaged it as a quick push up one river valley, over a pass, and down a valley on the far side, but we weighed the difficulties carefully.

Neither side could accept the other's reading of the map, disagreeing over the interpretation of the gradients and nature of the terrain. In truth there was no way of knowing for sure without going to investigate – a round trip of 1,000 kilometres. Howard thought of every possible way to dissuade us and implied that we were jeopardising the success of the expedition itself. We had different philosophies of travel. For the first time on the journey tempers were frayed and no consensus was reached.

The following day Anna and Tatiana came with me to the post office to help me send two boxes and two telegrams. There was a queue of five people waiting to send boxes, served by one woman. She worked laboriously, slowly; she gathered up sheaves of papers, arranged paper clips and began to fill out forms in triplicate. There appeared to be no carbon paper. Boxes had to be carefully inspected, wrapped in official brown paper, stuck down using pots of ancient glue; string had to be measured, precisely cut and tied. Then they had to be covered with cloth, sewn up and addressed before red sealing wax was dribbled carefully onto each string intersection and impressed with a heavy wooden-handled stamp. Each action was treated as a separate operation of infinite gravitas.

The clock ticked noisily in the small room. Once the box was sealed, official forms had to be filled out and counterchecked, the cost and change calculated on the abacus. It took fifteen minutes just for the woman at the front of the queue to send her first parcel.

I needed two cardboard boxes to put my gear in. Only one size was available – small. Anna asked very politely if she could buy one so that I could start to pack it.

'I'm working,' the woman said testily, without looking up, as if stretched to breaking point. And yet three post office girls were leaning against a wall slightly further round the counter, talking and doing nothing.

'Can't they sell me a box?'

'No, it's not their job!' Tatiana whispered.

So we queued for thirty minutes to secure boxes and another twenty to have them tied with string and weighed. Then we were handed a cotton sack, thread and needle to sew them up ourselves. And then we had to wait until the woman was free again. She scrutinised the boxes minutely, sealed each one seven times with sealing wax, checked the forms and stamped the parcels. By the time we left after an hour I was seething with frustration.

'There's no point trying to rush,' Anna said laughing. 'You cannot beat the system. If you rush, only one person will suffer – you. You must go the same speed as everybody else.'

Soviet bureaucracy, it appeared, had changed little: 'There are, it seems,' Dostoevsky wrote in *The Idiot*, 'so many government offices that one's imagination boggles at the mere thought of it; everyone has been in the civil service, everyone is in the civil service, everyone intends to be in the civil service . . . but the trouble is that our civil servants are the most impractical men in the world and things have come to such a pass that abstraction and lack of practical knowledge were, till quite recently, considered even by the civil servants themselves as the highest virtues and qualifications.'

Sending telegrams was no more straightforward. In principle they could be sent in English, but mine were rejected on the basis that they used Qs, Vs and Xs. As the telegram-telex machine lacked those three characters they would have to be replaced with alternative Roman ones. It was proposed therefore that 'request' should be replaced with 'reoest', 'axle' with 'akle' and so on. That the message should be reduced to gibberish in the process appeared to be of no concern. But that would be someone else's problem. Half an hour's debate ensued as to how to resolve the issue, until the woman went off to consult the director of the post office, who agreed that Cyrillic characters could also be used. Why a Roman-alphabet telex machine should be made with three characters missing remained a mystery.

On the way back we dropped in at the student café/bar. Holidays had begun but there were still students around. As usual in Soviet cafés, the interior was dark and gloomy, without any windows. There was no music, no beer or alcohol of any sort and we sat in the gloom with coffee, fruit juice and ice cream.

'Do you like the coffee?' Anna asked.

'Yes . . . it's . . . it's good,' I said.

'You are too polite,' she said. 'It's very bad.'

For the fourth evening in a row I went round to Olga's flat. Howard was busy and Gilles still recuperating. I took with me two bottles of champagne. I had been in the USSR long enough to know it was pointless to look for them in shops and had bought them from a waiter in the restaurant, at five times the official price. On the way two drunks, having spotted the bottles, waylaid me, blocking my path, but were too unsteady to be a threat.

We had gradually begun to realise that it was only in the security of private apartments that Russians felt comfortable enough to talk openly. In public places, in cafés and restaurants, conversation was still circumscribed. I joined Olga and Anna in the kitchen sorting and destemming strawberries, grown in their *dacha* garden.

'We grow as much of our own vegetables as we can now,' Olga said. 'There is so much pollution and we don't know where the products in the shops come from. Some probably come from the areas of the Ukraine and Byelorussia affected by Chernobyl. There is no way of telling, as nothing is marked. So now we grow our own.'

Later in the evening Anna picked up a guitar and began to sing. She sang melodiously, naturally, completely at ease. At first she sang John Denver's country-and-western songs, then Simon and Garfunkel, and then turned to Russian and Ukrainian songs that were lyrical and intensely beautiful. When she put the guitar down, it was picked up by

Natasha, a tall girl with a hauntingly lovely face, marble-white skin and deep brown eyes. Shy though she looked, she played the guitar and sang unselfconsciously. Olga and Tatiana joined in as if I were not there. It was heartening to be with them and it seemed completely natural, as if I were an old friend.

'You know, it is very difficult for young people in our country – I mean the ones that think,' Anna said. 'We want change and we dislike our system. But older people, of my parents' age, consider our generation to be mindless, stupid, cruel, without an aim. I can't agree. We are cruel because we are kinder, we are stupid because we study life better, we hate our life because we love it in general. You don't understand me? I'll explain. Many generations before us lived without trying to think what they were doing, how they were living. They broke records in construction, in culture and so on. They were sure that our country had always been, was and always would be the best in the world. They *believed* that. They never thought about a person as he is, as an individual, unique and special. Their words were different from their deeds. But they didn't want to notice that they were lying, lying to the people and to themselves. My generation says now "There is no future for us!" Because we have noticed all the injustice of our system and we don't want to live so but, being dependent on this system, we can only do a little: survive. All the vices of our society we keep in our hearts. Look at us and you can find the history of several generations. Yes, we are dirty and unlucky, but our dirty life is much purer than the life of our parents. I say again: they are guilty because, living in an imagined world, they *didn't want* to notice that they were not right.'

'Society, not the individual, was what mattered?'

'Yes,' Anna said. 'Anything personal or individual didn't count. Individuals didn't count. The heart didn't count. Beauty didn't count. Production was the only thing that mattered. Only tangible things. I often wonder why people in my country are so wicked. They all know that. And I think it is because people can't be beautiful if they don't see beauty around them. We live in such conditions that spiritual life is moved aside. You have just witnessed that on your journey.'

'What can you do to change things?'

'I try and do little things to help my friends. I think that is best.'

'But will that change the system?'

'No, not the system, at least not for a long time.'

Much later I asked Anna if she had ever thought of leaving the USSR and living abroad.

'No,' she replied. 'I love my country, with all its problems.'

'Will you do something for us?' Olga asked hesitantly. 'Will you read aloud a passage of our favourite books so that we can record you?' So I recorded passages of *The Picture of Dorian Gray* and *Doctor Jekyll and Mr Hyde*. What better proof of fame, I thought, for Oscar Wilde and R. L. Stevenson than that they were being read with pleasure in a Siberian city on the River Ob!

After five days Gilles had recovered enough for us to move on. It was a sad moment when we saw Vitale onto a plane for Moscow but we set off from Barnaul in higher spirits than for a long time, refreshed by rest and delightful company. We crossed the wide River Ob and soon found ourselves in quite different country – hilly and thick with pine trees. After uninterrupted plains from dawn till dusk for two and half months, it was a sight for sore eyes and we drank it in, headily.

East of the eighty-eighth degree of longitude only a single road is marked as running east–west through the Soviet Union in the 3,000 kilometres that stretch between the Mongolian border and the Arctic Ocean. But our satellite maps, produced by US Intelligence, marked a secondary road leading from Novokuznetsk to Abakan through the Kuznetsky Mountains, the foothills of the Altais. It was this road we intended to take, although there appeared to be some confusion about its very existence. With temperatures consistently over 100°, the roads continued to melt. Rivers of black tar glistened and sucked at the wheels. Some stretches looked entirely normal but brought the bicycles up sharp, as though some invisible hand had applied the brakes.

Sasha kept up with us out of sheer willpower, Howard giving no quarter as to the number of kilometres we had to cover, determined not to be slowed down. Sasha had to cycle 130 kilometres on his first day on rough roads while the temperature hovered around 100°! Late afternoon we turned off into a miserable village of rutted roads of baked mud, pitiful wooden cabins and concrete apartment blocks. Both the *stolovaya* and shop were closed, but Sasha cycled up to a wood cabin, dismounted and called out to the owner. Two women wearing white kerchiefs stuck their heads round the corner. Conversation ensued, Sasha bantering cheerfully and provoking a great deal of mirth from the two women. The next thing we knew, Sasha was entering the picket gate, giving us a wink and a wave to follow.

A teapot and a glistening silver samovar were soon on the table, followed by bowls of *borscht*, brown bread, butter and homemade blueberry jam. The two sisters bustled in and out bringing more and more food as if we were their own sons, and when we came to leave they absolutely refused any payment whatsoever.

In the evening we stopped in a tiny village full of wooden cabins where Sasha persuaded the local Communist Party boss to open up the Party VIP *dacha* for us, an attractive wood cabin with three rooms, a simple kitchen and primitive bathroom. I settled down to remove wet, black tar that covered my bicycle, panniers, shoes and legs. An hour later I looked up to find Sasha returning loaded with provisions, followed by two Azerbaijanis bearing watermelons.

'You've just won your first Order of Lenin,' I told him.

Another 100 kilometres brought us to Novokuznetsk, a sprawling industrial city at the heart of the Kuzbass coal-mining basin, a forest of concrete and blackened giant factories spilling forth acrid smoke. We cycled past the Kuznetsky Metallurgical Kombinat steelworks, a gigantic Babylonian complex of furnaces and factories, and a symbol of Soviet might, built by men using shovels and wheelbarrows in the 1930s under one of Stalin's forced industrialisation programmes. Novokuznetsk is not a healthy place to live. Industrial dust and sulphur dioxide emissions have produced lung-cancer rates thirty per cent higher than the average for Soviet industrial cities, and respiratory infections and eye inflammations among children are higher. Two coking ovens that released sulphur and nitrogen compounds had been closed, but fourteen furnaces continued unabated. In summer the pollutants were mostly blown away to settle on the suburbs and agricultural land but in winter the fumes and dust we learnt could be choking.

Under *perestroika*, many heavy industries are supposed to move over to 'self-financing' which would mean that new equipment, including pollution-control devices, would have to be bought from profits. Prices for Soviet steel, however, are so low that this would effectively rule out any anti-pollution measures at Novokuznetsk.

Obsession with quantity rather than quality means that much of Soviet steel has to be sold abroad at knock-down prices to Third World countries. The Soviet Union produces far too much steel, but to shift from producing vast quantities of poor steel to small quanties of high-quality steel is fraught with difficulties. The whole economic system has been geared to maximising production for so long that piecemeal changes sabotage it all down the line.

For decades the production of Soviet cars was measured in terms of weight. A particular factory producing Ladas might have to turn out cars to the tune of 100,000 tons. The unintentional and unforeseen effect was to make Soviet cars exceptionally heavy. Factory directors soon found that it was less effort to produce half the number of cars at double the weight than double the number of cars at half the weight.

Grotesque Soviet statuary and wasteland sprouting weeds between drifts of greying apartment blocks accompanied us to a hotel where we waited an hour for a room. We were amazed to find Turks staying in the hotel.

'We're here to build a new hospital for the city,' one told us.

'Why aren't the Russians building it themselves?'

'They don't know how to do it. Not only has a Turkish firm been given the contract, but all the builders are from Turkey and all the materials too!'

'How do they get here?'

'They're flown from Izmir.'

'Surely the steel girders come from the steelworks here?'

'No. Everything comes from Turkey. We're not the only ones here. There are Yugoslavs building too.'

Shortly after we left, 300,000 miners in the region went on strike, demanding the government's resignation, the end to Party cells in work places and the depoliticisation of the army, police, KGB and judiciary, angry that the government had fulfilled only a handful of promises made the year before to improve declining living standards. They also demanded that the government give them more control over their own pits. By striking they openly defied legislation passed a year earlier outlawing political strikes and temporarily banning stoppages in key economic sectors. And at their congress, the miners passed a resolution declaring that the Communist Party could no longer be considered the champion of the workers' rights and called for a mass exit of members from the Party.

There was a great deal of confusion as to whether we could get to Abakan through the Kuznetsky Mountains. A long way off everyone assured us there was a tarmacked road that went all the way. But the closer we got, the more varied had been the replies and in Mezdurshchensk itself we were told categorically that the road stopped three kilometres beyond the city.

'Just stops?'

'Yes.'

'And beyond that point?'

'Only the railway.'

As our satellite map marked a secondary road we figured there must at least be a track of some description. Beyond Mezdurshchensk we entered a valley flanked by high hills, the first real hills in 6,000 kilometres. First the tarmac road ended, then after four kilometres the dirt road came to a halt and we followed a footpath between the railway and the River Tomé.

Two kilometres further on and the footpath itself came to an end. We left the bikes and walked down to the river to see if a track existed further down. None did. It was, literally, the end of the road. We dragged the bikes up onto the railway line and began to push them, walking between the tracks where the chippings were nearly flush with the sleepers. Long before they appeared we could hear trains approaching but with a cliff on one side and a steep embankment on the other there was little room to wait while they hurtled by, crashing and cranking.

After a while we spotted a track below us and scrambled down the enbankment to follow it. It ran along beside the River Tomé, half-overgrown with willow and rowan. Branches brushed against us as we rode through pool after pool of water. Soon the track disappeared into the river, 200 yards wide, sparkling and fast-flowing with pine-covered forests climbing steeply up the far side. Three hundred yards ahead we could see the track rise up again out of the water. Half pushing, half carrying the bikes we waded upstream and rejoined the track. It soon became impassable and we took to the railway line again, arriving at a tiny settlement of eight houses. We were greeted by a large and cheery woman station mistress.

'Where does the track begin again?' we asked her.

'Not till Tieba station, in eight kilometres.'

'Can we buy potatoes and onions here?'

'No, there's no shop,' she said. 'But I can give them to you. Wait here.' She came back with potatoes, onions and milk.

'Are you Estonian?' she asked, curiously.

'French, American, British and Russian.'

'Foreigners! Here! And you're one of ours?' she said turning to Sasha. Many times over I had noticed in conversation the same turn of phrase addressed to Vitale. 'But you're one of ours?' said with reassurance and relief. It was as if only two groups existed in the world, us and them. Either you were a Russian or you were not. People often relaxed once they knew we had a Russian with us. And instead of referring to 'Western' countries, Russians used the single word '*Kapstrana*' – capitalist countries. The divide was always there.

We stopped beside the river that ran pure and fast over white stone. Far across the water a thin beach of gold sand caught the evening sun. Above it lay a narrow rock ledge and then untouched pines, Prussian blue, rising vertically. Colours were intensified and the air was remarkably crisp and light. Not a sound reached us except the quiet gurgling of the water. We set the tents on a bed of wild thyme, opening onto the ice-cold water, swam, collected dry wood and built ourselves a fire.

The track, where it existed, was rough and overgrown. Cycling over roots, fallen branches and tree stumps, Howard's derailleur got caught and snapped in two. We had a replacement but took to the railway line again, temporarily, to avoid further damage. Progress was slow, advancing three kilometres in one and a half hours. We dragged the bikes up to the embankment of loose gravel and then off the track when a sixty-wagon load of wood hurtled past.

We picked up thorns and had to stop to mend punctures. Eventually we arrived in Tieba station, a cluster of half-collapsed wooden houses with roofs of wood or tar, chaotic railway sidings and a sawmill. As we paused in the dusty street a drunk hailed us, staggered up and tried to put his arm around us. Apart from dust, heat and chickens the place was deserted. No sound came from the sawmill or the sidings.

We found the *stolovaya*, a log cabin unchanged since the Revolution. It was empty and we sat down to our usual gruel, but soon another man appeared, dishevelled, purple in the face, and paralytically drunk. He staggered over to the canteen, shouting, and barely managed to carry his food to the table. He sat alone, talking aloud in a slurred voice, and then got up, knocking into the table and sending everything flying.

When we came out, we talked to a group of young boys and girls and were about to set off when we noticed that all four Avocet speedometers were missing and the boys had vanished. The speedometers were crucial; apart from our speed they told us the daily distance we had covered, the total distance from Leningrad, our fastest speeds, and served as watches and time-clocks. Without the cables and electronic sensors that had been left on the bikes they were useless to anybody. The girls were upset and said they thought they knew who the culprits were.

Six weary hours were spent tracking them down. Howard and Sasha trooped off with an escort of small girls while Gilles guarded our bikes and I roamed the village in search of food for our evening meal. There was no policeman in the village; the Communist Party chief was away and everyone else in the village appeared to be drunk. No one was working. No one was capable of working. As Howard and Sasha went through the village, boys ran like scared rabbits. Led by the girls to the house of one of the culprits Howard and Sasha knocked at the door and entered. A boy jumped up and ran through the house with Howard and Sasha in pursuit and was pinned down in the attic. Trembling with fear he promised to get two of them back for us. On their way back through the house, Howard and Sasha came face to face with the boy's father. Reeking of vodka, he stumbled past them without saying a word or even noticing the two strangers walking around in his own home. After two hours one speedometer had been retrieved, after another hour a second.

'They're all boxed in this town,' Howard said. 'We've talked to lots of people and no one cares a damn!' Eventually, however, we found a sober woman who was distressed at the news and promised to help. She was very overweight and when she reappeared an hour later she was red in the face with exertion. She was upset; she had had no luck. Much against our principles we offered a reward of five dollars, twenty-five roubles and some adhesive stickers in return for the last two speedometers. The news spread like wildfire and in an hour we got them back.

We met only one man who was sober in Tieba. He came and sat down beside us for a few minutes.

'*Perestroika?*' he said with loathing in his voice. 'Look around you!' And he cast an eye over the wooden shacks, the rutted earth streets, pot-holed and corrugated, the dilapidation, the pigs nosing around in the garbage lying close to the houses or half-buried in mud and dirt to cool off.

'What has *perestroika* done here?' he said and spat on the ground.

By this time it was pointless to move on as the sun was setting. We sought somewhere to spend the night and were led to the fire station by a motorcycle combination. To get the keys the alarm bell was set off and little by little a handful of men appeared, angry at first at the false alarm. It was difficult to imagine how these drunks could have coped with a fire with any effectiveness; one still clutched a bottle of vodka and it was only with combined efforts that they got the key into the padlock.

We were given a room with a portrait of Lenin and Politburo figures on the wall (most disgraced and some dead), including Gorbachev, painted in the early days of *glasnost* when the birthmark was omitted. A woman arrived out of the blue with spring onions, bread, potatoes and eggs. She had heard what had happened and had come to make up for it.

12
ABAKAN

W E SET OFF early from Tieba station as mist rose from the valley, crossing the River Tomé on a bridge made of massive pine logs strapped together. Downstream lay the twisted remains of the old metal bridge that had been washed away by floodwater. For six kilometres there was no path or trail whatsoever and we pushed along the railway track at the side of or over the sleepers, the wheels crashing against them. In Tieba we had learnt that there was no road for 170 kilometres and only a foot-trail after twenty-five. Progressing at one and a half kph, we estimated it would take us sixteen hours alone to reach the trail and we eyed the occasional fisherman drifting in his boat down the broad river with envy.

The day after Tieba was a day of disasters. Eventually we found and took to a rough trail over rocks and branches, wading or cycling through pools of stagnant water covered with green slime or oozing rust-coloured scum. Gilles fell in, immersing himself in bright green algae. A little later he hit a log, his cycle crumpling sideways as he fell, so that his entire weight was thrown onto the front wheel. Although barely cycling at ten kph the wheel buckled into a twisted figure of eight; it looked as if it had been run over by a truck. It seemed irreparable but Sasha positioned it with great precision against a rock and exerted all his force on it in a short, sharp blow. As if by magic it snapped back, almost to true.

We experimented cycling along the railway track between the sleepers. Intermittently, where the gravel lay level with the sleepers, it was feasible but rarely for more than one or two hundred metres, after which the bikes had to be carried or pushed to the next rideable stretch. Trains could be heard approaching long before they were visible but there were few places to take refuge except by hauling the bikes down the steep embankment of loose scree until sixty or seventy wagons had thundered past, and then pushing them up again.

Keen not to be slowed down, Howard rode ahead over the sleepers while the rest of us pushed. When we caught up with him, we found him inspecting his rack, which had broken; we held it together with jubilee clips and moved on. Six kilometres further on, it collapsed on the other side, necessitating further repairs. And then, after riding across a stretch of broken rock, Gilles's wheel buckled again. This time when Sasha tried to snap it back, the rim cracked right down the middle all the way round, creating two gaping holes. Our luck had run out.

As we surveyed the wreckage, black clouds and forked lightning played around us in the steep valley, and large drops of rain began to fall heavily. We had been warned that the River Tomé swelled dangerously after storms, so we ferried our bikes and equipment to a spot well above the water level and set up camp. One thing was sure – we were not going to get any further that day.

It seemed highly unlikely that the wheel would be able to take any weight. Perhaps cycling gently on an excellent road it might just have stood the strain but we had 160 kilometres ahead of us on the roughest trails imaginable and then another 150 of dirt road to Abakan. There was not a hope in hell of it holding. Undaunted, Sasha began to cut a metal strip from a tin of Chinese pork that we had eaten for supper, doubling it over for strength, piercing holes for the spokes and inserting the metal strip within the rim to reinforce it.

'When we travel in the Soviet Union and this happens,' he said, 'we take metal and put it so.'

'I've seen wheels less bent than this thrown away before now,' Gilles said, impressed by Sasha's ingenuity. We found we had lost our file, however, making it nigh impossible to file down the new spokes. Sasha was still at work when it grew too dark to see.

We were up at 6 am working on the wheel. Thick fog lay over the water, deadening the sound of the river and the trains upstream. After four hours' work, however, the wheel still wobbled alarmingly.

The accident could not have happened in a worse place. We were in the remotest spot of the entire journey; we had progressed only forty kilometres in three days, hardly a good average. We assessed our food supplies: four packets of dried food, one kilo of floury Russian pasta, two small tins of fish and half a kilo of biscuits to last us the next stretch unless we could buy anything from the locals.

We watched while Gilles tried to cycle on the repaired wheel. It collapsed after ten yards. Further attempts to mend it were clearly pointless. Leaving Gilles behind, we cycled, waded and pushed our way to the next station, a forlorn, abandoned settlement, with half a dozen collapsing houses, and overgrown with weeds. We explained our predicament to a fat, red-faced man with a prominent Adam's apple who was sitting in the sunshine on the wooden steps of his house. We begged for a wheel and from a dilapidated shack he dragged out a rusty child's bike from which we were invited to take any parts we needed. Removing a wheel from Sasha's bike and strapping it onto my rack, I set off back downstream to where we had left Gilles. We set up a relay system, shuttling to and fro using seven wheels between the four bikes. Meanwhile Sasha worked on the child's bicycle wheel until it turned tolerably, even if wobbily.

In Moscow we had spare wheels and rims but the dilemma was how to get hold of them. They could be sent to the nearest town, Abakan, but that was 320 kilometres away and Aeroflot, we had been warned, was wholly unreliable as far as delivery dates were concerned. To cap it all, there was nowhere for hundreds of kilometres from which to telephone Moscow, even if we had wanted to. The only option was for Gilles to use the small wheel off the child's bike; pitching forward, he looked as if he was part of a travelling circus.

What the few inhabitants of this half-abandoned settlement did for a living it was hard to tell. Evening fell and we were invited in. The men were drunk and sat round a table telling stories noisily over a bottle of vodka. One woman, rough but friendly, invited us to eat.

'We haven't got much. We live badly but no one leaves hungry,' she said, bringing out soup, loaf after loaf of bread, tea and pots of blood-red *glubnika* jam. Noticing that Gilles had cut his leg badly crossing a river, she set about cleaning, iodinising and bandaging the wound.

To be in hills again after 6,000 kilometres of wheatfields and steppe was a great relief, even if the midges and mosquitoes were bad. But after two days' pushing along railway lines I began to wonder just what it had all been for. When I saw the odd fisherman drifting downstream in a rowing boat with the current, I began to think that if we'd been sensible, we'd be doing the trip by boat instead.

Although the hills were beautiful, the colours were disappointing. Across Russia and Northern Kazakhstan the skies were never the spectacular deep blue of Asia, Australia or South America. Even the colour of woods and fields was washed out and weak. The landscape lacked vibrancy and intensity as if the Northern latitudes had bleached out all strong dyes; the insipidity of the light seemed to correspond well to the monotony of the landscape and the omnipresent listlessness. It was hard to imagine a passionate, dynamic race inhabiting such a land.

In order to minimise the weight on Gilles's wheel, we carried his front panniers, adding further to our own loads. By ten o'clock it was already 30° in the shade, by midday in the high 30s. As we cycled and pushed forward along the railway tracks, conversation became curtailed and jokes fewer. We spoke only when we needed to, each of us living with our own thoughts, husbanding our energy.

At dusk we arrived at the tiny lumber village of Balyksa. In the twilight we found the village leader and explained our need to find a bigger wheel. Quick and alert, he disappeared into a shed and came back with his old bicycle but the wheel proved too large to be of any use. A crowd of boys had gathered round but the moment the village leader started to take an interest in the wheels of their bikes they fled and watched the proceedings from the safety of a street corner. Climbing onto his motorcycle he disappeared, returning after thirty minutes clutching two wheels, one of solid rubber and the other with the axle locked solid.

The village leader, also the local Party boss, unlocked the Communist Party building for us to spend the night in. At the front was a verandah shielded by a wide, overhanging roof. We must have made a curious sight, cooking our supper and working on the wheel by torchlight well into the small hours on the steps of the new Communist Party building, protected from the rain that deluged down in the mud street. A rustling sound close by in the dark made us start but it turned out to be a solitary cow, nosing around. The storm continued through the night and even though the building was the newest and most impressive in the village, Howard woke to find water cascading through the ceiling onto his sleeping bag.

As we left in the morning, on the replacement wheel, we passed twin brothers lurching along the dirt track, hardly able to walk. Their heads bowed, their arms hanging down beside their bodies, they zigzagged wildly across the road, continually tripping and stumbling but somehow just managing to remain on their feet. We greeted them cheerily and encouraged them on their way but they did not even see us. As we glanced back we saw the first stumble and fall, then get up and stagger on, and then the second fell: pure Laurel and Hardy, Soviet-style.

We climbed steeply on dirt tracks, the hillsides covered with dense green pine trees, except for a few near vertical pastures high on the hillsides that had been cleared and scythed. Most of the time we had to wade through the rivers: as there was no road, there were obviously no bridges. But from time to time we came across a rough bridge of pine trees lashed together, under which flowed streams of pure sparkling water.

'Don't you wish you had your fly-rod now?' I asked Howard.

'Don't even mention it!' he replied tetchily.

It seemed absurd that every day we struggled to find food and yet every evening we camped at a river's edge; we resolved to buy a fishing-rod once we reached Abakan. All we would then have to do would be to stop an hour earlier than usual and fish from the riverbank; it seemed the ideal way to end the day.

The only sound that reached us was the wind sighing in the pine trees, the gurgle of fresh water and the occasional mechanical clatter of a train. Once or twice, far from any habitation, we came across Russians scything grass in the narrow valley. With their flat white caps, baggy cotton jackets and long scythes, it was a scene unchanged since time immemorial. As we approached they stopped their work and watched us silently, immobile, until we were out of sight.

In a tiny village inhabited by Khavkass people, striking, high-cheek-boned and almost Mongolian in appearance, we were warned to look out for bears if we camped. Although we were only 400 kilometres from the Mongolian border, the landscape of dense pine forest, low blue-black hills and fast-flowing rivers bore no resemblance to our idea of Mongolia. One evening, well after the sun had set, we crept into a tiny village by moonshine, following a river that steamed as if heated by lava. We had, we realised, finally met up with the track that led up the eastern side of the mountains. Smoke from log cabins rose languidly in the still evening air and one or two naked light bulbs pierced the dark. Pausing to consult the map, we found that we had still not reached the village we had hoped to make that day.

We looked up from the map to see a well-built man approaching, a scythe over his shoulder. As he drew level with us he said simply, 'Do you want tea?' as if it were the most natural thing in the world.

'Maybe we spend the night here,' Sasha whispered as we went in. 'It's much better than the hotel. There are only bad hotels in the next town: no water, bad food. Here we have a *banya* and we will sleep well.'

Sasha seemed to have made the decision for us, for two minutes later we found ourselves seated on a wooden bench peeling a bucketful of potatoes. After a *banya* that relaxed aching muscles, our host, Dmitri, helped us re-weld Howard's back rack. Exhausted by twelve hours' cycling – pushing along railway lines and wading rivers – I fell asleep with a pen in my hand writing up my journal.

The next day we emerged into a quite different landscape; it bore no resemblance to the western slopes of the Zapadnyy Mountains. It was drier and wilder, and the forests abruptly vanished, leaving bare, rounded mountainsides the colour of bleached bones. Bare-footed Khavkass horsemen tended flocks of black goats that watched us pass scornfully.

Scattered across the open landscape lay innumerable burial mounds, thirty to forty feet in diameter, circular and gently rounded, and surrounded by standing stones four to six feet high. Before Genghis Khan invaded from Mongolia, the Khavkass had had a developed civilisation of their own. Their kingdom, however, came to an abrupt end in the twelfth century when eighty per cent of the Khavkass people were reputedly put to the sword at the order of Genghis Khan.

Despite strong headwinds by evening we had left the foothills of the Zapadnyy range, an offshoot of the mighty Altai Mountains. Coal-black clouds hung over the foothills we had left behind us. High on the bare hillsides stones had been arranged in massive letters. *'Lenin s'nami'*, the message read: 'Lenin is with us'.

The next day we rejoined an asphalted road after more than 300 kilometres of dirt trails. We cycled fast to Abakan, relishing the new-found speed, Gilles coping manfully on his heavy, wobbly wheel. Yellow wildflowers and cobalt-blue flowering mint lined the road in huge clumps, like desert flowers after rain. The land was as soft as velvet, a few bluff escarpments eroded smooth by age. Weasels, the only animals to inhabit this wild and desolate landscape, popped up and stood up on their hind legs to watch us with puzzled expressions. At one point a man jumped down from his truck and ran across to us with a loaf of bread.

'Molodtsy! Molodtsy!' ('Fine fellows! Fine fellows!') he said, shaking his head in wonder. Thanking him, we raced on, determined to reach Abakan by nightfall, elated by the desolate feel of the landscape.

'We'll get you to Abakan in time for crumpets and tea in the club,' Howard said to me with a grin as the city hove into view. I cannot remember now why we had such high hopes of Abakan; perhaps because it lay so close to Mongolia and the Altai Mountains. There was a vast military barracks behind a ragged concrete wall at the edge of the city, Abakan being the last town of any size before the Mongolian border. We found the hotel in the city centre but although the doors were open, we were told that the place was closed for *remont* (repairs).

'Remont' is quintessentially Russian in spirit; nothing quite captures the feel of the country as well as this word which implies renovation, refurbishment, reconstruction and takes the place of 'maintenance', a word that does, but would appear to have little reason to, exist in the Russian language. From the moment it is finished, no Russian building, it appears, receives any care or attention. Eventually a day comes when nothing works and *'remont'* then becomes unavoidable.

We were directed instead to the Friendship Hotel in Factory Street. A huge red banner hung over the entrance with the English words, 'You Are Welcome'. It was too good to be true.

'You have no permission to be here,' the receptionist told us coldly. 'Abakan is not on your visa. Abakan is a closed city.'

'*Every* city we pass through cannot be listed,' Sasha explained. 'There isn't room on our visa, as you can see. There are only three short lines, space for only nine cities to be listed.'

'You have no authorisation to be here,' she replied brusquely, ignoring Sasha's logic. 'SovIntersport should have sent a telegram. You will have to request them to send us a telegram authorising your stay.'

'But can we stay tonight?'

'I will request authorisation from the Foreigners' Registration Bureau for tonight but you must leave tomorrow. Where do you go next?'

'To Krasnoyarsk.'

No. That will not be possible. Krasnoyarsk is also a closed city. And the road to Krasnoyarsk is closed too.'

'It's blocked?'

'No, the road is not authorised for you.'

'Why not?'

'Because the lake beside it is closed,' she replied without the least flicker of humour.

'Did you hear that?' I asked Howard. 'The lake is "closed".'

'That's a first!' he replied, grinning.

We asked why there was a welcoming banner in English if foreigners were prohibited from visiting Abakan.

'It was erected for a foreign rugby team,' the receptionist told us icily and the next morning the banner had gone. Rugby teams were welcome, it appeared. Cycling teams were not. Irony was not high on the agenda at the Friendship Hotel.

'She works for the organisation that deals with registration and visas,' Sasha told us when we reached our rooms, 'it's connected to the KGB.'

Sasha and I then set off to buy a fishing-rod in the large sports shop, the only one in Abakan, but there were none available. Nor was there a bicycle wheel to be had for love or money, nor rims, nor spokes.

'We have no bicycles,' the assistant told us in a bored voice.

'What spare parts *do* you have?' I asked, curious.

'Saddles.'

'Nothing else? No pumps, chains, pedals, brake blocks?'

'Only saddles,' she said.

'To buy a bicycle is a big problem,' Sasha told me, laughing, as we walked back. 'There are only five bicycle factories in the Soviet Union and they make 300,000 bicycles a year; it's not so many for 280 million people.' Sasha was surprised to learn there were bicycle shops in Britain; specialised bicycle shops do not exist in the Soviet Union; one sports shop theoretically deals with everything. 'Don't rub salt into the wound,' Sasha begged me.

We found a café in the central tree-lined street. Coffee was unavailable and we queued for ice cream. In Britain I would not queue for ice cream if it meant waiting more than a few minutes, but in Abakan, I realised, I was quite prepared to wait twenty minutes or more. Our perceptions were beginning to alter. To buy ice cream, shoes that fitted or a bicycle wheel began to take on a new significance. They were not things that one did as a matter of course, without thinking. They were achievements in themselves.

Gorbachev had remarked on his visit to the US that it took three Russians to do the same work as one American. The longer we spent in the Soviet Union, the kinder Gorbachev's assessment seemed to be. Howard, Gilles and I put it closer to 10:1.

'Would you say you worked hard?' I asked Sasha, over our ice-cream.

'No,' he replied, with a laugh.

'And your colleagues. What about them?'

'No,' he said, after a pause, 'I don't think so.'

'But would they be prepared to work harder if they were paid twice as much as they are now?' Sasha was pensive for a while.

'No, I don't think so,' he repeated, grinning.

Admittedly there was little point in having money when there was nothing to spend it on, but the Russians appeared to be unmaterialistic both by nature and force of circumstance.

'Russian people used to work out of fear,' Sasha said. 'Now that fear is gone and we need something else. But at the moment there is nothing.'

Sasha and I explored the city. Like Vitale, Sasha took advantage of being in a distant city to look for products unavailable in Moscow. For there may be no electric kettles and a surfeit of toasters in Moscow, while in Novosibirsk the reverse holds true. The police we learnt are usually the first to realise when a *defitsit* of goods is biting deep; the theft of carpets began in Moscow not long after the supply of carpets dried up in the shops.

We entered a jeweller's shop with a wide shop-face. Half the velvet-lined cases were empty, while others had one or two items spaced far apart. Any jewellery that could hold its value had been bought and, as there was nothing for the assistants to sell, they sat in the corner, talking, knowing that they were unneeded.

The telegram we requested from SovIntersport never arrived. We studied the map to see if there was an alternative route to the 'closed' road leading north but apart from walking along a railway track for 300 kilometres there was none. Gilles and I had abandoned our idea of pushing east through the Vostochnyy Mountains close to Mongolia. Gilles had not recovered his strength and we realised that if we split up with Howard and Sasha, it was unlikely we would see them again.

Instead we cycled north for 350 kilometres skirting the edge of Lake Krasnoyarsk, a valley flooded by a massive HEP dam. Why the lake was 'closed' remained a mystery but perhaps military barracks surmounted by radio aerials and receiving discs at the southern end gave a clue. After Abakan the mountains fell away and we entered undulating arable land, stopping to camp amongst birch trees in golden evening light.

Each day as we battled against headwinds, Gilles grew weaker, feeling increasingly drained of energy. Even when we carried all his panniers he could hardly manage to cycle faster than ten kph.

As Krasnoyarsk was another closed city we approached carefully, keeping eyes open for the police post found at the edge of every road leading into Soviet cities. The police, however, had stopped a bus which blocked the passing traffic from view and we sailed by unnoticed.

Later, as I turned round in the saddle to look for Howard and Gilles, my wheel disappeared into a deep hole in the tarmac, two feet square. I somersaulted in the air and then on the road, conscious of what was happening as if I were a bystander, seeing myself turn in slow motion through the air, the bicycle upside down above me.

The bicycle appeared to have come off worse than I had. The front wheel had buckled exactly as Gilles's had done in the mountains; a pannier mounting had broken; and the pannier containing my camera and lenses had been tossed across the road. We straightened the wheel as best we could by some judicious bending and jumping, and hobbled on. Only one spare wheel had been sent to Krasnoyarsk, to replace the heavy, ragged Russian wheel that Gilles had been using for over 600 kilometres. Now we needed a second.

We had been given an address where we could stay in Krasnoyarsk. Sasha had only been able to join us for three weeks and at the apartment we were supposed to meet Sergei, his replacement. But at the address we had been given, no one had heard of the man we had hoped to stay with and there was no sign of Sergei. For an hour we searched for a workers' hostel that was meant to be close at hand, being directed forward and back through a bleak group of windswept grey apartment blocks set in a wasteland of beaten earth and weeds.

But Gilles was too weak to go any further so I stayed with him while Howard and Sasha went in search of a hotel.

We found a spot out of the wind at the foot of a shabby apartment block and Gilles lay down outstretched on the ground, his head resting on his helmet. Little by little a crowd began to form, those at the back pushing forward to see what was the matter. In a 'closed' city it was not encouraging to find we were the centre of attention and my repeated reassurances that Gilles was only tired did nothing to dispel the crowd. Gilles ignored the throng and his silence, combined with his haggard face and motionless body, only served to confirm the crowd's worst fears.

A middle-aged man pushed his way through, and handed me a plastic container and a little bottle of brown seeds.

'Kvass,' he said. 'It's good when you are tired and these limonik seeds have restorative powers. Your friend must take them.' But Gilles refused to touch them. 'They are good, I promise! It's natural medicine,' he told us, kneeling at Gilles's side. 'Here, watch!' and he swallowed two seeds himself. Gilles remained motionless, eyes closed, beyond caring about the commotion. The man seemed so upset at Gilles's refusal to take his medicine that I took it instead to keep him happy. 'It's not good to lie on the concrete like that,' he continued, shaking his head. 'It's cold.' And ten minutes later he was back, clutching a huge roll of foam and a blanket. He uncut the string, rolled it out and Gilles was lifted, protesting, onto the foam mattress. By the time he was lying motionless and covered with a blanket, Gilles looked as if he genuinely was at death's door.

Ten minutes later a bottle-green ambulance came bouncing across the hard-packed earth to the thick crowd that had grown too large to disperse. Voices buzzed as newcomers enquired as to the nature of the commotion and the crowd parted to let through a white-coated doctor, complete with stethoscope and bag.

'I don't want a doctor,' Gilles said, allowing his blood pressure and temperature to be taken with great reluctance. The doctor recommended rest and gave him aspirin while an unseen hand in the crowd stretched forward with a tin of Pepsi Cola, a rare luxury which we had not seen since Moscow.

'Does he want tea?' Valery, the man who had brought the foam mattress, the kvass and the limonik seeds, asked, with a concerned expression. I knelt down and passed on the message.

Five minutes later Valery was back with a flask of tea and a cup and saucer. The crowd parted and then fell back as Valery held up tea for Gilles to drink. In all the confusion, with Gilles on his mattress, the crowd surging forward and the doctor taking his pulse, a figure loomed over me.

'Hello,' a voice said in English. 'I'm Sergei, your Soviet cyclist.' A pale, overweight and flabby man in his late thirties with a colourless face as round as a soup-plate hovered above me. With the ambulance nearby, the huge crowd, the police standing around and drab grey apartment blocks with broken metal railings and dusty trodden earth, it was all shaping up to the stuff nightmares are made of. Someone tugged at my shirt, telling me there were empty rooms on the fourth floor where we could stay.

'Bed . . . for him,' a man said. 'Come!' But Gilles refused to move and I was reluctant to leave him. Eventually, telling Sergei to watch over our bikes, I went to have a look. There were four rooms, furnished only with beds, and a communal kitchen and bathroom which the young man, Maksim, said we could use. Shortly afterwards Howard and Sasha reappeared; they had been away two and a half hours.

'Nothing,' Howard said. 'No one wants to know.'

Just as we decided to take up Maksim's offer to stay in the rooms upstairs a militia jeep with a flashing blue light bounced across to the crowd.

Not waiting for the police to start asking questions we began to move inside and as we did so the crowd surged forward to help. Gilles was lifted up and carried upstairs with a man on either side, like a war-wounded; hands came forward to carry up the bikes, the panniers, the *kvass*, the tea, the mattress, the blanket. The narrow concrete stairs were crowded with heaving, shuffling figures under the dim light bulb going up to the fourth floor, the heads on the stairs sprinkled with policemen's peaked caps.

Every room was suddenly crowded with people as if an impromptu surrealist party was being given. Eventually the crowd retreated, Sasha and Sergei being taken off in the jeep to the police station to explain what we were doing. The following day a KGB couple arrived to investigate further. They were bland-looking, in their thirties, dressed in casual clothes. They noted down every detail from our passports and documents, offered to move us from the shabby apartment to accommodation more fitting for international guests, which we declined, and eventually departed.

Then, the next morning as we were having breakfast, we looked up to find a policeman wandering around the apartment. No one had heard any knock at the door.

'What time are you leaving?' he asked us.

'Not for two or three days,' we told him. He wandered around, gazed at our gear and left.

'Booby!' Valery said with a grimace and a dismissive wave of his hand. Valery lived in an apartment block a hundred yards away and came back frequently to see how Gilles was recovering and to bring him presents. First he brought an orange, as rare as gold-dust, then Tibetan medicine, *Mutiyo Brakshen*, made from musk, that looked like yak droppings. On our second day he arrived with a yellow canary in a wooden birdcage.

'The bird will help him recover,' he said. 'Songbirds always do.' The same evening he returned with a frozen chicken and tins of fish. On the third day he brought a beautiful embossed leather gourd, took our axe away and sharpened it for us and then tried to present us with an even finer one.

I was later reading the Soviet newspaper *Moscow News* when Valery came over. On the cover were two very different photographs, placed side by side. On the left was a photograph of a wooden Russian church and a *babushka* peering over a stack of empty vodka-bottle crates; on the right a photograph of delegates wearing grey suits walking past a concrete sign proclaiming the 27th Party Congress.

'*That* is Russia!' Valery said, passionately, pointing at the left-hand photograph. 'And that is rubbish!' he added, waving in disgust at the delegates to the Party Congress.

Maksim, our host, was a lecturer at the Siberian Technological Institute in Krasnoyarsk, a biochemist, aged twenty-six, earnest and absorbed. He had lived alone for three years in a small room in the hostel of which he appeared to be the sole resident, where he had the use of a tiny kitchen and a dilapidated bathroom. On the second evening in his apartment, I asked him what life was like in Krasnoyarsk.

'Bad,' he replied. 'There is terrible pollution here from chemical factories and radiation from missile testing nearby. Even the River Yenisey is polluted with radiation. This area has many military factories and military cities. My parents live in a military city.'

'A *military* city?'

'Yes, it's called "Krasnoyarsk No 26", but it's a separate city in its own right. Only those who work there are allowed in; it's secret and surrounded by high wire fences. But many Russian people now want demilitarisation as the army has too many *apparatchiki*.'

We talked about our journey. Maksim had made a cycle journey in the Ukraine with a friend.

'Those are my fondest memories!' he said. And when I told him about a journey I had made from England to Australia he replied, 'For me that is just a dream.'

Before Sasha left we sat round maps discussing the route with Maksim and Sergei. Sergei had four weeks' holiday and could only come as far as Chita. Beyond Chita lay 1,200 kilometres of swamp, the toughest part of the journey. In that section there were no roads or trails marked on any of our maps. We had little idea what the swamp would be like but knew it would be gruelling; we expected to push our bikes some of the time and to be plagued by mosquitoes.

'Why don't you come and join us when Sergei leaves in Chita?' we asked Maksim. He studied the map with a furrowed expression in silence for a long time and then suddenly roared with laughter.

'It will be very difficult,' he said, 'but I don't like comfort.'

Despite four days' rest Gilles had not regained strength; he decided to fly back to Moscow to consult a French doctor.

'I want to cycle the whole way,' Gilles said, 'you know that. If I fly to Moscow and then back here it'll set me back a week at least. Maybe with light panniers I could average 130 kilometres a day but if you're averaging a hundred a day, I won't be able to catch up with you until Irkutsk. And I might have problems getting back here at all, as it's a closed city.' Sasha and Sergei looked worried.

'You cannot cycle alone,' Sasha said, 'first there's the language . . .'

'That's no problem,' Gilles said. 'The real problem is that it's not allowed by the authorities.'

Gilles and Sasha flew to Moscow, Gilles taking his bike, hoping to return to Krasnoyarsk and catch us up. We shared out the communal items that Gilles had carried – the axe, pots and pans, seasoning, sugar, coffee, tea, spare chain, ball bearings and derailleur, adding extra kilograms to our heavily laden bikes. We serviced the bikes, replacing worn axles and ball bearings, and put the new wheel intended for Gilles's bike onto mine. He was to pick up another in Moscow.

The following morning we left Krasnoyarsk.

'So we see you in Chita maybe?' we said to Maksim.

'I hope so!' he said, grinning.

Our departure from Krasnoyarsk took place against mounting political change. In July the 28th Congress of the Communist Party took place. Gorbachev's speech to the 4,680 delegates was greeted with five seconds of perfunctory applause that contrasted sharply with the thunderous standing ovations usually accorded to party leaders at previous congresses. Gorbachev declared that 'the Stalinist model of socialism' was being replaced by a civil society and that the over-centralised Soviet state was being encouraged towards greater self-determination. It was 'simply rubbish', he said, to blame *perestroika* for all the country's troubles. *Perestroika*, he claimed, was still in its 'transitional period', and he criticised conservatives who refused to accept the reform processes either politically or psychologically.

Ryzhkov, the Prime Minister, gave a report to the Party Congress which was heard in an atmosphere of chilly disdain, while Schevardnadze declared that 'by squandering one quarter of our national budget on military expenditure, we have ruined our country'. But the trenchant criticism of Gorbachev from the conservatives was strikingly at odds with their docility when it came to challenging his will outright and he was re-elected, the Party old guard realising that there was no alternative if the Party was to avoid disintegration.

Boris Yeltsin, the most prominent radical, stunned the Congress with the announcement that he was resigning his Party membership. He was followed by the radical mayors of Moscow and Leningrad, Popov and Anatoly Sobchak – and other reformist Communist Party figures subscribing to the Democratic Platform announced that they too were leaving the Communist Party to set up on their own.

13
ON SIBERIAN ROADS

HALF AN HOUR after leaving Krasnoyarsk an explosion rent the air as Sergei's back tyre blew up. Removing the remaining fragments of shredded inner tube, we found Sergei had forgotten to insert the thin strip of rubber that protects the inner tube from the spokes. Of the two spare tyres and inner tubes we each carried, Sergei had used up half his spares for the next thousand kilometres in the first thirty minutes.

After fifteen kilometres we rounded a corner to find four motorcyclists and a film crew waiting at the side of the road. 'What happened to you?' an American voice said, somewhat irritated. 'We've been waiting for half an hour.'

Tabitha and Jim were motorcycling across the Soviet Union with two Soviet motorcyclists, a professional, English-speaking, guide and an American film crew. Tabitha and Jim were hot and dusty, dressed in black leather, and uncommunicative.

'How did you know we were even on the road?'

'The police told us you were coming,' Jim said, to our surprise, as we had not seen either a police post or vehicle.

Although Tabitha and Jim were travelling by motorcycle they looked more exhausted than we did. We opened up maps and discussed their route from Vladivostok but as they had transported their motorcycles by rail through the swamp we learnt little that was useful. But their Russian guide told us to stick close to the railway at all times.

'Don't be tempted to think there's a better route elsewhere,' he said. 'There isn't.' He warned us that unusually prolonged summer rain had burst the banks of the Shilka, Amur and Zeya rivers, that five metres of flood water had engulfed Khabarovsk and that certain sections of the

Trans-Siberian railway track had been inundated with water, marooning trains for days. It was, he said, one of the worst years on record. 'You may not be able to cross the rivers at all but in some respects the dirt tracks will be easier for you on your bicycles than it was for us.' When Tabitha and Jim were out of earshot the guide confided that he would prefer to be travelling by bike, like us. They did not seem a happy team.

'Jim and Tabitha aren't easy people to travel with,' the sound recordist said. 'Everything has to be done their way.' Jim was blasé about his journey but not interested in ours. They did not want to talk. After fifteen minutes they said they had to press on and roared off, Tabitha and Jim in front, communicating via microphones attached to their helmets, followed by the two Soviet motorcyclists, the guide in a jeep and the film crew in their van. There was something in the nature of a cavalcade about their progress. When the dust had settled, we pedalled away.

After thirty kilometres Sergei was sweating profusely and bright red in the face; after forty his clothes were soaked through and a pained expression spread across his face.

'Did you do any training, Sergei?'

'No. No training,' he said.

'You've got to drink water!' Howard told him. But when Sergei started to pour water from his water bottle onto his head and shirt we had to stop him. With forty kilometres to the next village we could not afford to waste it. After fifty kilometres he had slowed to a snail's pace and we waited at the top of every hill for him to appear. At one point we saw him pushing his bike uphill.

'We'll never get to Vladivostok,' I said, 'if Sergei's going to push up hills.'

'This is a tarmac road,' Howard said, alarmed. 'It hasn't even begun to deteriorate.' We watched the figure of Sergei inch its way towards us through the heat haze that rose in shimmering lines from the melting road. 'We're not slowing down every time Este foists a new cyclist on us,' Howard continued. After sixty kilometres, when Sergei began to cramp up, we called it a day and found a semi-abandoned restaurant, built of wood, off the road.

The proprietor was a Georgian, Grennadi, with a sister in Florida. He welcomed us like old friends, offered us rooms in his house and prepared a meal while we went for a *banya*. Once again we had fallen on our feet. When we returned from the *banya* the table was spread with champagne, cheese, tinned Dutch ham, potatoes and watermelon – a feast.

Grennadi's restaurant had been the first private cooperative enterprise in Siberia.

'It was opened in 1986,' he said, 'the beginning of our wonderful *perestroika*.' The opening celebrations had been attended by the press, the local mayors and the Communist Party chiefs of the district and region. Grennadi's restaurant had been in all the newspapers and had been the talk of Siberia, a portent of a brighter future. He showed us his scrapbook with the photographs and cuttings from a dozen different newspapers. Despite the auspicious beginning, Grennadi had closed the restaurant down six months earlier. 'The authorities don't want these businesses to succeed,' he said. 'The taxes are impossible. They rob me of everything. It's not worth having the restaurant open, I only lose money. In your countries if you buy a shirt for one rouble, Howard buys one for two and I buy one for three, that's business, isn't it?'

'Sounds like it to me.'

'Here it's speculation, a crime. Profit still equals capitalism here. It was impossible for me to buy meat, fish and other ingredients. I had the money but the state wholesalers would not supply private cooperatives with the things they needed to buy. So you have to bribe them. Half of your profits disappear in bribes. The rest goes to the state.'

After five years Grennadi had given up. He planned to abandon the Soviet Union for good and join his sister in Florida. He wanted to know if there were any Soviet products he could take to sell in the US. It was hard to think of any Soviet-made goods that Americans might want. We suggested precious stones, antique carpets from Uzbekistan and Kirghizistan and Soviet watches.

The following day we had covered sixty-five kilometres by midday. Sergei was shattered, cycling only six-eight kph uphill.

'Look,' Howard told him at lunchtime, 'it's not your fault but you're not fit, are you? Just for the first few days, until you're feeling fit, why don't you take a lift in a truck to the next town and we'll catch you there?' He looked unhappy. He was not keen on the idea but he had little choice. We flagged down a truck and loaded him on board. 'So long, Sergei!' we said as the truck pulled away, leaving us without a Soviet escort for the first time in 7,000 kilometres.

Sergei was thirty-six and lived at home. He was an engineer working for Tupolev, the Soviet aircraft company, and Howard and I pulled his leg mercilessly about Tupolev safety records, to which he responded angrily.

For fourteen years he had been waiting for his own accommodation but as his fortieth birthday approached there was still no sign of it materialising. As a bachelor Sergei took low priority on the housing lists. His parent's flat had three rooms excluding a small kitchen and bathroom. His parents slept in one, his brother, sister-in-law and their ten-year-old child in the second, while Sergei had the third which doubled up as the communal drawing and dining room. To get to their room his brother, sister-in-law and child had to walk through Sergei's room. That was the way it had been since his brother had married ten years ago. Between them they had forty square metres, an average of 6.6 square metres each, a fraction below the Moscow norm.

The second and third day we again loaded Sergei onto a truck, much against his will, and met him in the evening.

'You haven't cycled much recently?' I asked Sergei as we sat round a camp-fire in a silver-birch grove.

'Not this year. I usually go, at weekends, to our *dacha* outside Moscow.'

'With friends?'

'With my parents.'

'What do you do at the *dacha*? Put your feet up and relax?'

'No,' Sergei said, in a resigned voice. 'I work, I dig potatoes. Soviet people always work.'

Gilles and I had admired the massive Soviet Ural motorcycle combinations, with their rounded 1950s modelling, that appeared to cope with even the roughest Soviet road surfaces. At the end of the journey we planned to buy one each and motorcycle home from Moscow with our bicycles and panniers in the sidecar. When we asked Sergei how we could buy one, he laughed out loud.

'You cannot have everything that you want in this country. I have wanted a new bicycle for years but I cannot get one. There aren't any bikes in the shops; there haven't been for years. If there is a delivery they are sold out within a day or two, or even a few hours. I ride the bicycle my mother bought twenty years ago.'

Sergei was amused by our suggestion that he could, as an engineer, set up his own bicycle business. He liked the idea but said it was impossible. Factories would never sell him the parts he could not make himself. We suggested he could advertise for the parts he needed in a cycling magazine.

'We don't have cycling magazines as we don't have bicycles,' he replied wearily.

Sergei was painfully slow and disorganised, and soon began to drive us mad. At Kansk, after rising at 6.30 am, Howard and I were packed by 7.00, having eaten a breakfast of cold, fried fish, boiled eggs, bread and tea. We were outside ready to go by 7.30. Of Sergei, however, there was no sign. We went back into the hotel, fetched his bike out of the store room for him and went to his room. He had not even finished packing.

'Time to go, Sergei!' Howard told him. But fifteen minutes later there was still no sign of him.

'What's the man *doing*?' Howard asked impatiently. He stormed back in again. At last Sergei appeared. We climbed on our bikes and were setting off when Sergei disappeared inside again. 'Christ! What's he doing *now*?' Howard said, jumping off his bike and racing inside after him, furious. Eventually we left. 'Not exactly busting his ass to get off, is he?' Howard said angrily as we left town. By the time we had cycled for an hour Sergei was long out of sight. Fifteen minutes later he appeared painfully.

'We simply can't cycle at his speed or we'll never get to Irkutsk; and we can't let him fall behind – if something happens to him we'll have no idea where he is!'

At lunch we explained the position to Sergei.

'Sergei, we need to cycle today to Nizhnaya Poyna which is over 100 kilometres and we need to average 100 kilometres every day in order to get to Chita and the swamp before it starts to get too cold. Now, it's difficult for you to cycle at the same speed as us because we've already cycled 7,000 kilometres and we're fit, while you've hardly cycled this summer. We need to stick together but in the morning we're used to cycling fast whereas in the afternoon, when we're tired, we cycle slower. So why don't you take a truck half-way and cycle the afternoon only? I'm sure we would find it as difficult as you if we came to join others as you have. What do you think?'

He looked miserable.

'I don't want to slow you down,' he said. 'Let me sit on your tail.'

'OK. You want to slipstream. Fine. Let's see how it goes, but otherwise you take the truck, alright?'

In Nizhny Ingash we stopped to draw water from a well. Two *babushka*s and a singularly beautiful woman greeted us from a nearby bench. When they heard we were British and American, one *babushka* gave a big sigh.

'Ah! I cannot forget the war,' she said, shaking her head tearfully.

'You must watch out for escaped prisoners in the forest,' the young woman warned us earnestly. 'They are desperate men and will stop at nothing. God help you if you meet one. There are many here. Be careful.'

Soviet prison camps, the Gulags, were not only to be found in Siberia; there were hundreds in European Russia but in Siberia they were thicker on the ground and conditions were harsher. Much of the Trans-Siberian railway had been built using forced labour between 1928 and 1953, and most of the minerals, natural gas and oil found in Siberia were exploited initially by prison labour. The numbers involved defy belief: it is estimated that between seventeen and twenty-five million people were sent to labour camps between 1928 and 1953, the date of Stalin's death, many on the flimsiest of pretexts. Old scores were settled as people informed on those against whom they held a grudge. German soldiers captured during the Second World War were sent automatically to the camps for ten years. So too, after the war, were Soviet soldiers who had surrendered, so that tens of thousands of men freed from German concentration camps found themselves sentenced to ten or twenty years' hard labour close to the Arctic Circle. Hundreds of thousands died of cold, disease and malnutrition; hundreds of thousands were shot out of hand.

No section of society was spared: the Communist Party, government officials, armed forces, engineers, scientists, managers, artists and intellectuals were all decimated, but even together these comprised the minority. Millions of ordinary workers and peasants too found themselves in the camps on trumped-up charges. Fooled by propaganda and paralysed by fear, people applauded the elimination of 'enemies of the people' and 'wreckers' of the Five Year Plans. In the words of the Soviet historian, Roy Medvedev, the terror spread to 'anyone Stalin didn't like'. Medvedev estimates that ten per cent of the Gulag prisoners died each year of malnutrition, tuberculosis and execution, and thirty per cent in the first years of the War when rations were cut and workdays were as long as fourteen hours. Robert Conquest, an authority on Stalin's terror, estimates deaths in the Gulags at seven to ten million, with another ten million dying from mass dislocation and deliberate famine as Stalin crushed the peasantry in the 1930s.

Gone was the Mongolian-like grass steppe we had crossed south-west of Krasnoyarsk; for days we cycled through dense pine forest, the road bordered with banks of cascading, pink rose-bay willow herb. The tarmac was soon replaced by concrete slabs that shook limb from socket at every intersection. But slabs disappeared in their turn and we continued over loose hardcore to Nizhnaya Poyna, a rough settlers' village of log cabins hacked out of the forest. We found a two-storey wooden hotel and dragged the bikes up the broad wood steps.

'There are fifteen prisons within an hour of Nizhnaya Poyna,' the hotel administrator told us.

'There still are?'

'Yes. There are a lot of ex-prisoners in the village – about thirty per cent of the population is from the camps. Many prisoners decide to stay in Siberia when they come out: it's a better life here than in European Russia and many have nothing to go home to anyway – no home, no wife, no family.'

We left at seven in the morning. The roads were terrible, made of large stones, loose rock, gravel and occasionally liquid tar that reflected a van Gogh blue. Villages were few and far between. Wood-smoke rose from log cabins and red geraniums nestled in the windows. Massive wood stacks and large patches of potatoes surrounded the cabins; it felt like pioneer country. *Babushka*s sat in the shade under cool, white kerchiefs, cows wandered lazily in the road, chickens scratched at the dry earth and a hobbled horse nosed amongst the grass. There was rarely a sound to be heard, only a few vehicles passing in the course of a day.

Inexplicably, in the middle of nowhere, we came across a newly asphalted road, smoother than any road we had seen, and raced along, relishing our new-found speed. Four kilometres later it ended as abruptly and mysteriously as it had begun and we returned to stones and hardcore, on which our wheels spinned and twisted. If the wheel was not kept rigidly aligned straight ahead it would jerk sideways and throw us over the handlebars. Averaging no more than ten kph it took us ten hours of solid cycling to cover a hundred kilometres, in effect thirteen or fourteen hours a day with breaks for lunch, filtering water and brief rests.

We left at seven in the morning and stopped at nine or ten at night, too tired to think, to write our journals, and sometimes even to talk. At lunchtimes we saw Sergei onto a truck and set out to do another fifty or sixty kilometres in the afternoons.

One afternoon, Howard and I pulled into a strung-out village of silvery-grey log cabins and drew up at a well. We asked a man if he had any juice we could buy and he came back from his house with a bowl full of tiny scarlet berries, *brusnika*, collected from the Taiga. Pulling ice-cold water from the well, he poured it onto the berries which immediately stained the water blood red. We should have filtered the water first but we drank the juice straight from the bucket. To our parched lips and throats it tasted like nectar.

Leaving the village we passed a cortège on its way to the cemetery. The coffin was placed on the back of an old, open truck which was being driven slowly along the rough road. On the back sat half a dozen men and women, dressed in their best suits, who clutched onto the truck's side as it lurched over the rocks, while one man knelt supporting a crucifix. The cemetery lay at the edge of the village in the shade of a pine forest, the graves surrounded by thin blue railings, half of the tombstones surmounted by a cross, the others by a red star. It was a sad sight. At dusk we arrived at the village of Uk and found Sergei at the roadside in the twilight. He rose to greet us with welcome words.

'Your dinner is waiting!' he told us. 'We stay in someone's house.' It was the first, and last, occasion in six months that food and accommodation was arranged for us.

We had now turned south-east and were heading towards Lake Baikal. For day after day pine forests and rose-bay willow herb was all we could see. Not a single wild animal appeared to inhabit the forest.

Sergei was desperately vague. Having cycled for two days wearing no more than a pair of shorts he had third-degree burns, despite our repeated warnings. Then, to protect himself, belatedly, from the sun, he put on thermal clothes instead of cool cotton ones. When he had a puncture he put in an inner tube with an unpatched hole; he left our expedition funds behind lying on a *stolovaya* table; he had a worrying proclivity to cycle in the middle of the road; and on day one he fell off his bike.

We cycled to Tulun, enveloped in clouds of dust, sunlight filtering through the pine trees. The post office, a magnificent log cabin of two floors, cream and blue, peeling and weathered, looked unchanged since the Revolution. Motorcycle combinations pulled up in rows in the dusty street and 1950s-style buses with oval windows passed, crammed with peasants going home after the market.

While Sergei and Howard disappeared inside, I took my wheel to pieces and reassembled it in the street. A stout woman in a big floral dress kept order, haranguing any small boy who dared to touch the bike.

'Look at this,' an old man said to me, holding up a bag of onions. 'Three roubles a kilo! *Three* roubles! Tell me, where is life better, here or England?'

'Life is good in England. And what's life like here?' I asked in return.

'Bad. We need coupons for meat, soap, sausage and sugar. Do you need coupons in your shops? No? Not for anything?' The small crowd began to put questions, wanting to know what the aim of our journey was, whether we liked Soviet people, whether we were tired, what our professions were, how much tax we paid, whether we were married. 'There are many divorces here,' someone explained, 'many unhappy marriages. People marry too young, to get away from their parents. They have a child and then life gets too hard for them. Yes, our hard life destroys us.'

We followed atrocious roads to Sheragul and Zima, arriving after twelve long hours in the saddle. Zima appeared to have no centre, nothing other than parallel streets of wooden cabins with one area of apartment blocks connected by worn tracks reminiscent of rabbit trails. While Howard and

Sergei washed and began to prepare supper, I went out in search of food. Combing the streets I came across two men attempting to repair a water pipe which ran beneath the road. Water shot high into the air until they plugged the pipe with a home-made wooden peg driven home with a sledge-hammer. Assuring me that the town's two shops were closed, the younger man led me to his house where his mother gave me milk, bread, gherkins and a large hunk of sausage for which she refused any payment.

She was the first Russian we had met in 7,000 kilometres who appeared to have faith in Gorbachev.

'We need more *perestroika*, not less,' she said, before asking the question we were asked more frequently than any other: 'Is it true that you can buy anything in your shops?'

'Yes,' I replied, 'if you have the money.'

'There, I told you!' she said, triumphantly, to her son.

'How long do you have to wait for a car?' he asked, perplexed.

'Five minutes – *if* you've got the money.' He shook his head in amazement, pursed his lips and went back to the leaking pipe.

The following day, we made huge efforts to reach Cheremkhovo, in the hope of having a shower and finding food. Cheremkhovo was marked on our satellite map and Sergei's Soviet road atlas as being located on the road but we found it was seven kilometres down a side track. Too exhausted after 100 kilometres on punishing roads to go any further we camped in the woods and went hungry. From our campsite we could see an enormous open-cast coal mine worked by a ninety-metre-high crane operating a scoop big enough to pick up a small suburban house. All night long the scoop moved to and fro under the glare of spotlights.

Cycling in the rain the following morning redoubled our appetite and as soon as we pulled into the first bedraggled village we asked directions to the *stolovaya*.

'There is no *stolovaya* here, I'm sorry,' an old man told us, spreading his hands wide. It was a poor village. But he could give us hot water, he told us, if we had tea leaves. Happily we could do a favour on this occasion; we left him our entire supply of tea.

Near the hideous industrial city of Angarsk we came across a whitewashed church on a hill above a muddy pond. It was Sunday, the service had just finished and the congregation of about two dozen, young and old, were leaving. As it was the first church we had seen for 1,000 kilometres we went inside. The priest was tall and bearded with an open, intelligent face. The church, he told us, had been closed in 1923 and only allowed to reopen in 1945. The previous priest had been imprisoned for nineteen years and had been frequently led out of his cell by the KGB for mock execution. Eventually, after nineteen years, he had been released and had recently died in Irkutsk.

'And do you still have problems?' I asked.

'Yes, we have what you might call technical problems. There are no religious service books, no Bibles, no New Testaments. They are printed in tiny numbers and impossible to get hold of. We cannot get anything for the church – paint, candles – all these are problems. In order to get a car I had to go to the Communist authorities and request one – I don't mean a car for myself but for the church, and they said "No, never!" Also there are not enough priests; many of us were shot.' He smiled. 'Yes, we still have problems.' I realised that his was the first truly wise face I had seen for a long time – I collected all the roubles I had and gave them to him.

'No, thank you!' he said, embarrassed. 'We have money.'

'To buy paint for the church or candles. It must be useful . . . for something.' He joined us outside, told us to wait and came back with two gigantic tomatoes, each as big as a melon.

'Holy Christ!' escaped Howard's lips before he realised what he was saying. The priest gave a start at Howard's remark and then smiled forgivingly. A *babushka* led him away to point out the damage to the church wall which a truck had reversed into during the night. With his long black cassock, black hat and golden cross he cut an impressive figure inspecting his broken wall. He picked up a loose brick and walked off giving us a smile.

The last 200 kilometres to Irkutsk were back on tarmac roads and we cycled hard to get there. As we entered the city a Russian cyclist joined us and escorted us to the Intourist hotel. Este was meant to have reserved rooms for us but no one had heard of us. With James Baker, the US Secretary of State, and Edward Schevardnadze, the Soviet Foreign Minister, due to meet in Irkutsk four days later, the hotel was bristling with US Embassy staff and the world's press corps. For three hours we tried to secure rooms; in the end we gave up and went elsewhere.

14
IRKUTSK AND LAKE BAIKAL

AFTER 1,100 KILOMETRES of rough roads we had hoped to rest in Irkutsk but, as usual, there was little time to do so. We dismantled, cleaned and serviced the bikes, washed clothes, repaired racks and reinforced broken panniers, collected and despatched parcels, dried out wet equipment, and hunted for supplies to take with us and send ahead. To be certain we would have some food in the swamp we bought apples, pasta, biscuits and honey and sent them ahead in wooden boxes to Mogocha, Skovorodino and Magdagachi. Each process took an age.

Gilles turned up with a Russian girlfriend, fully recovered, the French doctor in Moscow having diagnosed him as suffering from sheer exhaustion. Ten days of rest in Moscow, potassium, Vitamin C – to say nothing of a girlfriend – had set him back on his feet.

Irkutsk is an old city on the edge of the wide Angara River, the capital city of Irkutsk region, an area equal in size to Germany, Austria, Switzerland and Italy combined. In the centre old wooden houses stood cheek-by-jowl, unchanged since the day they were built, their residents fetching water in buckets from pumps in the street. The painted houses, yellow ochre, raw umber and lichen green, with their ornate wood fretwork and heavy shutters, the churches close to the water's edge and the tree-lined streets gave the place a pleasant, old-world flavour. Leningrad and Moscow excepted, it was the only city we had seen of any beauty. In 1890 Chekhov visited it and commented that 'of all the towns of Siberia, the best is Irkutsk', a judgement that appears still to hold true.

Perhaps its civilised feel owes something to the 18,000 Poles who were exiled to Irkutsk after the Polish uprising of 1863. The influx of Polish scientists, teachers, doctors and artists turned the city into something of a

European cultural centre. The Poles gave lessons in music, dancing and foreign languages, organised a theatre and transformed the provincial town into the cultural capital of Siberia, with an unusually high percentage of intellectuals.

During the Civil War, Irkutsk was the headquarters of the White Army under Admiral Kolchak who was eventually captured by the Bolsheviks, shot and pushed under the ice of the Angara River. It was at Irkutsk that the Bolsheviks recaptured most of the Russian state's gold reserves from Czech ex-prisoners-of-war during the Civil War: twenty-nine railway truckloads of gold in 1,678 sacks and 5,143 boxes, and seven truckloads of platinum and silver.

Down by the river, peering through the windows of the locked Church of Our Saviour I found myself face to face with exotic fish and strip lights. The second window revealed silhouettes of deer and antelope antlers, the third a stuffed bear, the fourth, where the iconostasis should have been, concrete steps. The Church of Our Saviour is now the ethnographic museum. Close by, four children in military uniforms and white berets, holding rifles and standing to attention, guarded the war memorial. Only those with good marks at school, we learnt, are allowed the privilege of guarding the Eternal Flame.

The liveliest part of the city lay around the market where hundreds of tiny kiosks sold the produce of the new cooperatives, highly priced and of poor quality, factors that did little to deter large crowds from pressing round in interest. The market in Irkutsk was the largest and most abundant of any we had seen. Tanned, leathery Uzbeks sat behind vast piles of yellow cantaloupe and green watermelons; Kirghizis sat in state behind mountains of black sunflower seeds, Russians behind overflowing tables of red-black Zabaikal tomatoes. Azerbaijanis sold fresh peaches and apricots, apples and pears from Southern Kazakhstan, and grapes from Georgia. Russian *babushka*s sat at tables loaded with red and white gladioli. After the paucity of markets and shops elsewhere, Irkutsk seemed a fabled land.

The Intourist hotel was being quickly spruced up for Baker and Schevardnadze. Windows, uncleaned for years, were scrubbed and polished. Lightbulbs suddenly became available; pot plants and cut flowers materialised out of thin air.

'I don't think this is going to fool Baker,' Howard said, shaking his head.

The Intourist hotel is the best that Irkutsk has to offer. We were used to menus that listed dozens of unobtainable dishes and agonisingly slow service but even we were surprised when there was no sign of our meal an hour after ordering it. Accompanied by a *Time* magazine and Reuters correspondent, I entered the kitchen, waitresses having all but vanished.

The kitchen was vast and virtually deserted but for five women cooks eating at a table in the corner who ignored us altogether. Only one cook was in the kitchen itself and she sat with her chin resting on her upturned hand, half asleep. Fifty plates with a jaded scattering of peas, half an egg and half a tomato lay gathering dust. There was no sign of cooking, no steam and no encouraging smells and yet on the other side of the swing doors, 150 people were sitting, waiting for meals they had ordered, most of them correspondents from some of the world's most important news-papers and television stations, along with US foreign service staff. We appealed to the restaurant administrator, who waved us away imperiously.

'Take your seats, the waitress will come!' But when she did she did not wait for the reiteration of our order but walked away muttering '*Nieto, nye nada!*' ('There isn't anything!'). Ten minutes later she tossed a few plates indiscriminately onto the table as though casting fodder to swine.

'They must be keeping the food for Baker and Schevardnadze,' the *Time* correspondent said. Others suffered more, particularly the Japanese who are at the opposite cultural pole to the Russians. Being extremely polite and never raising their voices, they were ignored completely and therefore got nothing to eat.

The price differential between what Soviet citizens and foreigners paid to stay in the hotel was staggering. Soviets paid five roubles a night ($0.30), while foreigners were hit for $80 to 120 – $270 to 400 times the local rate.

Irkutsk was the only place I met an English tourist in six months. She was on her way through the USSR on the Trans-Siberian to teach English in Japan.

'I think the Russians are the most miserable people I've ever met,' she said, bluntly. 'In Moscow I smiled and smiled at people until my jaws ached but I never once got a smile back.'

At Irkutsk airport there was no sign of the parcel we had sent ahead from Krasnoyarsk and protracted investigation indicated it had never left Krasnoyarsk airport. As it contained valuable bicycle spares we were reluctant to lose, the only certain way of recovering it was to fly back to Krasnoyarsk and find it. At Krasnoyarsk airport we found it exactly where we had left it a month before. Aeroflot officials had not sent it, not believing that a letter of credit guaranteed that they would be paid.

From Irkutsk we rode down to the little village of Listvianka on the edge of Lake Baikal and negotiated with fishermen to take us across the lake to Babushkin, a four-hour journey. As it was overcast and windy, the captain was reluctant to cross immediately, Lake Baikal being renowned for the violence of the storms that blow up on it. Instead we followed the coast north for a while, beached the boat on a stretch of sand and brewed tea, building a fire on the beach from driftwood, until the winds had eased. After three hours the storm clouds had cleared away, leaving golden evening sunshine bathing the wild and forested eastern shore. Strain though we might, we could not detect a single road or village along the eastern shore, except for the tiny settlement we were heading for.

Night had fallen by the time we were put ashore and in the dusk it took us a while to realise we had been landed at Tankhoy rather than Babushkin. Still, Tankhoy had a hotel, from which two loudspeakers, incongrously fixed to the outside of the building, blasted Soviet rock to the night stars. The administrator was a Buryat, a race of Mongolian origin, quick, alert and enthusiastic.

'I try your machine!' were his first words, as he grasped Gilles's bicycle and disappeared in the dark, the unfamiliar weight of the panniers threatening to throw him to the ground. 'There's no room in the hotel,' he said, on his return, indicating the vast and seemingly deserted hotel, 'but I have room for you there,' he added, pointing into the darkness. While we washed he cooked twenty fried eggs which he served with black Zabaikal tomatoes, bread, homemade blueberry jam and tea. 'Follow me,' our host shouted as he set off at a brisk run in the pitch black down the earth track. There was no moon and we cycled blindly for a kilometre until we reached a chaotic engineering works where we were shown a room.

In the morning, he waved us off, warning us not to visit the church beyond Babushkin as it was now a mental asylum. For a day we followed the shores of Lake Baikal with the Trans-Siberian railway track beside us. There was virtually no traffic, nor any sign of life on the lake – not even a boat. Dense pine forest, bordered by large white daisies, descended to the water's edge but there was no visible wildlife apart from buzzards that circled lazily in the warm air.

'In the US we'd have seen elk, deer and moose by now in this kind of country,' Howard said. 'I wonder what's happened to them here.'

Lake Baikal is well known in the West, having received wide publicity on account of its pollution; curiously, the amount of attention it has received is neither in proportion to the actual degree of pollution, nor to worse ecological disasters elsewhere. It is perhaps the beauty of the lake and its size that has gained it such worldwide attention. For Lake Baikal is the deepest lake in the world, is 636 kilometres long and contains one fifth of the entire world's fresh water. And of the 1,700 different types of animal to which it is host, more than 1,000 are not to be found anywhere else in the world.

When we checked into a decrepit hotel without water or bathrooms at Babushkin, the administrator told us there were two Americans in the hotel already.

'*Americans?* Here?' Howard said, flabbergasted. 'I don't believe it!'

It was hard to know who was more surprised at the meeting – us or Don Belt and Barbara Skinner who were researching an article on Baikal for *National Geographic* magazine. Delight at the encounter was mutual.

In 1987, in winter temperatures well below freezing, there had been a mass demonstration in Irkutsk against the pollution of Lake Baikal, one of the first manifestations of public discontent in the USSR and the first on an environmental issue. The protest had been sparked off when 2,000 seals were washed up onto the beaches dead or paralysed in 1987, dying from canine distemper. The local people claimed it was due to toxins in the water issuing from the pulp factories producing cellulose for aircraft tyres. Unlike some pollutants, the danger with toxins is that they gradually accumulate in all kinds of organisms and get passed on down the food chain. Local scientists claimed, however, that they had died as a result of a natural canine distemper similar to that which had affected seals off the Norfolk coast of England in 1987.

'The pulp plants on the lake itself now put minimal pollution into Baikal,' Don said. 'Both have been fitted with massive filtration systems that would meet the highest US pollution standards.'

Excessive focus on the pollution from the pulp and paper factory on Lake Baikal had distracted attention from a more serious source of pollution – 250 factories situated up the Selenga River between Mongolia and Lake Baikal. Another source of pollution was nitrates and other chemicals from agricultural fertilisers seeping off the land from cultivated valleys on the north-east of the lake. By focussing on the visible aspect of pollution, the factories on the lakeside, the greater danger has been ignored. And by cleaning up the pulp-mills on the lakeside the government has accrued far greater credit for tackling Lake Baikal's pollution than it is due.

Over the last twenty years four decrees have been passed to control the pollution of Baikal but none have been fully implemented, as no single body has been compelled to take responsibility. Instead, the area has seen steady industrial growth, while lip service has been paid to anti-pollution measures. We learnt after our trip that the number of small birds has decreased by thirty per cent over seven years, big birds by fifty per cent, and that zinc, mercury, tungsten, lead and iron had been found in their livers. But, at the time, we were astonished by how little wildlife was to be seen.

The island of Olkhon in Lake Baikal is populated almost exclusively by families exiled under Stalin from the Ukraine and Byelorussia. Barbara had met a man whose family, including four little children, had been deported and set to work in a fish-canning factory on Olkhon in the 1940s. They had been given so little food that they had been forced to eat grass to survive. She had taken a Polaroid photograph and given it to him. It was, he said, the only photograph of himself he had ever had and he had promised to keep it for it to be set on his tombstone.

All too quickly we left Lake Baikal behind, climbing through patchy pine forest, burnt by summer fires, until we emerged on a bleak, wind-swept, grass plateau. We had been looking forward to Ulan-Udé, close to the Mongolian border, where Genghis Khan's hordes had streamed across to spread devastation as far as Moscow and the shores of the Black Sea. Entrepôt and trading station, Ulan-Udé had long been a focus for merchants, trappers, soldiers and explorers, being at the crossroads of routes to the Pacific to the east, Peking and Ulan Bator to the south and Russia to the west. As we drew close Coleridge's lines sprang to mind.

> In Xanadu did Kubla Khan
> A stately pleasure-dome decree:
> Where Alph, the sacred river, ran
> Through caverns measureless to man
>   Down to a sunless sea.
> So twice five miles of fertile ground
> With walls and towers were girdled round:
> And there were gardens bright with sinuous rills
> Where blossom'd many an incense-bearing tree;
> And here were forests ancient as the hills,
> Enfolding sunny spots of greenery.

We were to be cruelly disappointed. Ulan-Udé turned out to be an ugly jumble of concrete and raw brick set in a washed-out landscape of dry grass. Chemical factories sent black smoke into the thin, raw air; bleak buildings sat unpainted; walls of concrete slabs enclosed dilapidated military barracks. In the central square was a gigantic bust of Lenin in black stone sitting on a squat black base, as if his head had been decapitated. Twelve feet high from bald pate to severed neck and weighing fifteen tons it was, the tourist leaflet assured, the largest in the Soviet Union.

Outside the city stood the only Buddhist monastery in the Soviet Union not destroyed since the Revolution, allowed to stand, perhaps, as token evidence that religious freedom, guaranteed by the constitution, exists. In 1985 it was accidentally burnt down and has since been rebuilt, its canary-yellow roofs, green and white temple lions and golden stupas creating a rich blaze of colour. Inside, the magnificence of the multi-coloured trappings, weavings, woven decorations, painted columns and roofs left us spellbound. Ten monks in scarlet and maroon robes sat cross-legged on bright silk cushions chanting in a low, humming drone. On either side of a large yellow statue of Buddha were ranged innumerable identical statues of Buddha in gold, flanked by other deities in green and white. Squares of silk, yellow, red, pink, blue, green and orange, sewn together in patchwork, covered the ceiling, and columns were painted white, red and gold with Buddhist motifs or covered with layers of brocaded silk shaped like tongues. Behind glass cases Buddhist images had been executed in brightly coloured icing sugar. A dozen Buryats sat around the edge of the monastery on low benches following intently in silence. No matter how alien Tantric Buddhism was to our own experience, to see that the traditional faith of these people had not been wholly eradicated was remarkably encouraging.

Leaving Ulan-Udé we passed three Soviet cyclists setting out for Ulan Bator, the capital of Mongolia. Groaning with weight, their old-fashioned bikes were equipped with homemade canvas panniers, a fishing-rod and their own aluminium milk churn. One of them had walked across the USSR on a previous expedition, an undertaking that none of us envied.

Beyond Ulan-Udé trees grew scarcer and the smooth, sculpted hills looked as if they had been mown. Devoid of buildings and people, and scattered with lakes, the landscape was like the Scottish lowlands. At Lake Baikal we had entered the Buryat Autonomous Republic and, for several days, we cycled in steady rain, passing a handful of Russians out collecting mushrooms and berries. Pine trees were lost in mist and low clouds, and damp penetrated everywhere. For a while yellow poppies and wild chives bordered the road.

At night we slept in school buildings or tiny log-cabin hotels. As they had no heating, it was impossible to dry our clothes. In the evening we changed into dry clothes and in the morning climbed back into wet ones; at least that way we had something to look forward to at the end of the day.

In a blaze of red evening light we arrived at Petrovsk-Zabaikalskiy, a classic Siberian village. Low log cabins were strung out on the far side of a fast-running brook, clustered behind a wooden palisade, like a pioneer settlement nestling behind its stockade. Petrovsk-Zabaikalskiy was built at the edge of a massive open-cast coalmine and beside the Trans-Siberian railway line that we were to follow virtually all the way to Vladivostok. A motorist escorted us to what was, perhaps, the most hideous hotel ever conceived, a concrete block-house reminiscent of the Maginot line. It was the first time for days that we had been asked for our passports and, to our horror, we realised they were still at the hotel reception in Ulan-Udé.

Sergei went off to ask the KGB if they could help retrieve them but the KGB, apparently, had better things to do. We were surprised that a settlement as small as Petrovsk-Zabaikalskiy should warrant a KGB office.

'They are everywhere,' Sergei told us.

Sergei took a train back to Ulan-Udé and we continued alone, the first time we had cycled just the three of us. It made a pleasant change. At Novopavlovka workers were waiting in a truck outside a *stolovaya* for it to open. Leaning through the open window, we prevailed on the three huge cooks to let us in an hour early. As the doors were opened everyone surged forward.

'*Nyet! Nyet!* Foreigners only!' the cooks shouted vociferously, pushing the workers back out through the doors. Looking justifiably annoyed, they climbed back into their truck.

'This is just incredible!' Gilles said. 'In France we would do the exact opposite, serve our own people and turn foreigners away. Many restaurants in Paris have an unofficial quota: twenty per cent of the tables only for foreigners.'

At Khilok we found Sergei with our passports. We wound our way down lanes deep in mud, crossing a river on a rough wooden bridge, and found ourselves compelled to carry our bikes over the railway lines through a shunting yard.

Half-way across we came to a gargantuan pile of white bricks a hundred metres in length, three metres high and five wide. Instead of having been removed from the wagons in stacks or on pallets the bricks had been tipped out next to the track, and at least half had been broken in the process. We stopped to watch a crane try to scoop them up but the machine was inadequate to the task. After ten minutes the driver gave up and half a dozen railway workers began to pick up the bricks by hand and throw them into the scoop. Although there must have been millions of bricks in the pile they were evidently going to pick them up one by one. It was probably enough work to keep the six men busy for months. Full employment, it seemed, was not hard to achieve when the work was worthless.

The factories and buildings at Khilok were dismal beyond belief: rusty, bleak and dilapidated. For supper, we went to the railway workers' *stolovaya*. They came in at the end of their shift in grimy overalls, faces black with dirt and coal-dust and queued for food. The younger ones talked and looked strong, but the middle-aged and older ones looked worn out and haggard. The latter sat at tables in silence, eating slowly, like men eating their last meal. In their blackened overalls and worn clothes, they looked like a defeated army on the retreat.

'This is what it must have been like in the Depression.'

'Worse!' Howard said. 'Nothing could be worse than this.'

As in most *stolovaya*s there was no running water or soap with which to wash and the men sat down unwashed to a meal that was hardly fit for humans, let alone for men doing hard physical work. The soup stank, the meat was gristly and full of splintered bone, the macaroni congealed.

As we were eating a woman came up and asked us what we thought of the food. For a change we were bluntly honest; we were tired of being tactful.

'Yes. It's bad,' she said. Five minutes later she came back and said she had telephoned the other *stolovaya*. 'You may eat there after the Koreans have gone. It may be better.'

'Koreans?'

'A fraternal group is presenting a show tonight. It is our cultural evening.' Later we saw the North Koreans clustered together in dark shiny suits, ties and neatly ironed white shirts and socks. They made an extraordinary contrast to the Russians.

On our way into Khilok we had caught sight of an attractive girl who appeared in the second *stolovaya*. Although only twenty, Lyena was the hygiene inspector for the town and had been at Khilok for a month.

'And how long are you here for?'

'Three years.'

'*Three years!*' we gasped in unison. 'You chose to come here for three years?'

'I didn't choose. I studied hygiene in Irkutsk for three years and was sent here. We cannot choose our first posting: the government decides for us.' The prospect did not bear contemplating: Khilok was one of the most depressing places we had been through.

'What is there to do here?'

'Nothing,' she said. 'There isn't even a cinema. And you have seen the other *stolovaya*.'

'So what do you do?'

'I go home to Irkutsk every weekend.'

'Is there a café we can go to?' Gilles asked.

'There was,' she said, 'but I closed it down.'

'That was fast work,' Howard said. 'But what about this place?'

'I can't close everything. People have got to eat somewhere.'

Lyena did not have her own apartment. For the next three years she was to live in a small room in a hostel, sharing a kitchen and bathroom with other families. She said she would have liked to invite us round in the evening but the hostel administrator would not approve. Instead we suggested that she join us, in our hotel, which she did, to the consternation of the hotel administrator. Late in the evening Howard went for a walk with her.

'Did you have good walk?' I asked Howard the next day.

'No,' he said glumly. 'You've seen all there is of Khilok. There was nowhere to go. We walked around until we ended up in a field. That was just great!' he said sarcastically.

At Tanga we spent the night in the 'Cultural House' of the Victory Collective Farm, our sleeping bags laid out on the stage. The collective farm had been through three lives, starting out as the 'Stalin Collective Farm' in 1929, changing into the 'Flame of October Collective Farm' in 1945 and maturing as 'Victory Collective Farm' under Khrushchev. The 'Cultural House' had a mural illustrating a wide range of cultural activites: theatre, folk dancing, cinema, billiards, reading, painting and music. I asked the director which of the activities were actually possible.

'There is a disco every Saturday night,' he said, 'and singing on state holidays – that is, Victory Day, May Day and Revolution Day.'

From Tanga we cycled for two days in rain through low, waterlogged grassland which, too wet to be harvested by machine, was being scythed by hand. We were told that the Amur had risen by five metres and that bridges had been swept away – so much for our hope that the swamp would have dried out by the time we arrived.

Chita was the last town of any size before 'the swamp'. Surrounded by huge textile factories and half dug up it was a nightmare of mud and concrete wasteland, leaking pipes and dreary housing. However, pausing to check directions as we entered the city, a motorist presented us with a bunch of yellow tulips. In the centre was a large and hideous square, the inevitable statue of Lenin in red granite and a domineering Communist Party building of grey stone.

At the post office I spoke at length with a retired teacher, Olga, to whom I suggested that we went for a coffee.

'There is nowhere to go,' she said. 'There are two cafés in our town but both are terrible. And I cannot invite you home because nothing is prepared and I have nothing to give you.'

'I don't want anything,' I assured her.

'I can invite you to my house only if you promise not to look around you. It's very untidy for I have been ill and my husband has left me. I'm very sad.'

'Have the doctors given you medicine?'

'Oh yes!' she said with a faint smile. 'They are very attentive and helpful . . . of course, I am being ironic. After my husband left me I did not have enough money to live on. So now I work again. Me – an old woman!' She walked slowly across the huge square, stopping frequently to recover her breath. 'Excuse me if I walk slowly, I have many illnesses. When I walk across this square I tell myself, "I am going to earn my daily bread!" It's hard at my age.' On the way she stopped to buy *piroshki*, traditional Russian pies.

'Do they have meat in them?' I asked.

'They *say* so,' she said drily. 'But I don't think so. I have a friend who is a teacher and I know she would be interested to meet a foreigner. May I invite her too?' Half an hour later the friend arrived at Olga's apartment, so out of breath that she was hardly able to speak.

'I ran,' she said, 'because the bus was late and I didn't want to miss anything. How long can you talk with us for?'

Olga and Natasha were disillusioned by teaching. Their pupils, they said, preferred to lounge around in the streets rather than study.

'There is no incentive for them to excel as there are no rewards. Even if they get jobs that pay well there is nothing to spend their money on, so what is the point? They have nowhere to go and relax. In September most of them go to the collective farms to harvest the crops and, when they can, they drink.'

'Generally speaking,' Olga said, 'women's life in our country is not so easy and pleasant. Our men are not very kind to their wives. My husband left me one month ago, I don't know why. I'm sorry I cannot talk more about the position of women here but it is not a happy story.'

Sergei was accompanying us only as far as Chita, where we found Maksim waiting for us at the Zabaikal Hotel. He greeted us gruffly and said little. Even allowing for shyness and a limited command of English, he seemed remarkably uncommunicative. He spoke monosyllabically and asked us nothing about the 2,000 kilometres we had covered since we had seen him in Krasnoyarsk. He serviced Sergei's bike in monastic silence. Over dinner in the restaurant Maksim came across strongly as severe and short-tempered.

'I do not like alcohol,' he said in a tone of disgust. 'Nor do I like meat. Too much meat is bad for the body.'

'There's not much chance of suffering on that score,' I assured him. Maksim looked round at the tables of drunk but cheerful Russians.

'Pah!' he spat out. 'I go to my room.'

'Oh, my God!' Gilles said, with a groan, once Maksim had left. 'Now we have a stressball on the trip.'

The restaurant of the Zabaikal Hotel was merry and crowded, there being only two restaurants in town. The neighbouring table plied us with vodka and cognac, and every ten minutes a drunken hockey player requested Beatles songs from the band in our honour, handing over five-rouble tips. I was dancing with a Georgian girl when a fight broke out. For no apparent reason a tall and pugnacious-looking captain in military uniform yanked the baseball cap down over the eyes of a man dancing nearby. Once the young man punched back a general brawl ensued. Tables were upset as the scrum of thirty surged to and fro across the dancefloor, women struggling to haul the parties apart.

'Don't get involved!', Katya whispered, giving advice that was hardly needed. Not long passed before three policemen pushed their way through, wielding truncheons indiscriminately. Without much ado the young fellow was dragged off while the captain, undoubtedly the guilty party, went scot free and rejoined his table. I began to understand why Olga and Natasha, the two teachers, did not relish the prospect of an evening out at their local restaurant.

At closing time those that could not walk unassisted were helped to police vans waiting in the street outside. One man picked up and carried a woman struggling and screaming out of the restaurant. She was so desperate that she grabbed at the doorframe and lost her shoes in a bid to prevent herself from being carried off but the police standing idle nearby did not bat an eyelid or make any move to help her. I felt I was witnessing a Soviet 'Rape of the Sabines'.

Opposite my hotel room a party was in progress. A colonel, a political officer responsible for propaganda in the Soviet army, invited me for a drink. A second colonel with a small moustache and a very red face, whose birthday it was, sat in a chair in the corner playing an accordion and singing. On the table were eight bottles of vodka, half of them empty, and two of cognac.

'I served in Berlin,' the political colonel told me.

'Like it?'

'I worked with British and American officers but the British were no good. They drank very little and they drank very slowly. But the Americans were alright. They drank a lot.'

'Did you enjoy living abroad?'

'Russia is the only place to live,' he said, passionately, and then asked, after a pause: 'Do you love your Motherland?'

'We do not have this concept,' I said. He looked amazed.

'What do you mean, no Motherland?'

'I'm British but I do not believe that Britain is, therefore, inevitably superior to every other country.' He sat in silence for a while, considering my reply, and then turned to me again.

'Do you know *pilmeny*?' (*Pilmeny* is a traditional Russian dish of meat-balls wrapped in pasta.)

'Yes.'

'*Pilmeny* and vodka – *that* is Russia!' he said with immense satisfaction, a dreamy look on his face. And then with a disturbing, almost maniacal, shout he turned and said, 'Russia is *not* for sale!' There was a real viciousness in his voice. 'You see this?' he said, showing me a large clenched fist. And he smashed it against the wall with phenomenal force. Not a flicker or emotion crossed his face.

'So?'

'Watch again,' he said and for the second time he punched the concrete wall with tremendous force without the slightest flinch. 'Russia is not for sale!' he repeated violently. I felt sorely tempted to tell him there was just one thing he had overlooked: there were no buyers.

15
END OF THE ROAD

WE LEFT CHITA in torrential rain that lasted all day. Maksim cycled strongly; there was no question of his fitness. In the evening we arrived in Darasun, a town of grey concrete that appeared to be slipping into a chasm. Our 'hotel' was a tiny log cabin cut off from dry land by a moat of brown floodwater. Forked lightning put paid to the electricity supply and we groped around in the dark, searching for places from which to hang dripping clothes.

The following day we somehow ended up cycling due south, adding two extra days of cycling to the journey that no one felt in need of. The rivers were swollen and fast-moving; some had burst their banks and swamped the fields with muddy floodwater. Grass was knocked flat and yawning chasms appeared in the soft earth. On the road a motorcyclist stopped to offer us a room for the night in Mogoytuy; three hours later he met us outside the village to escort us back to his house, nearly overturning his sidecar on the way.

The moment we saw his bedraggled and dilapidated log cabin we knew we had made a mistake but it was too late to back out without giving offence, and a storm was imminent. The interior was chaotic and squalid; saucepans, wood, cement, dirty crockery and a tin bath-tub were piled up beside a sink with no taps. The house consisted of two rooms, one of which had evidently been hurriedly emptied and washed in our honour, the floor not having quite dried. Valery and his wife were somewhat drunk by the time we arrived but they did their utmost to be hospitable and we could not but be grateful.

When the storm broke over Mogoytuy the electricity failed and we were left in the dark. In order to cook Valery split wood with an axe in the kitchen and fuelled the oven until the house glowed like a horseshoe on a blacksmith's anvil. Then, to cool it down, he went outside into the deluge, chipped away at the putty surrounding the window and removed a pane of glass.

We ate our meal by the light of lightning flashes, to the sound of torrential rain and incessant thunder; every few seconds the room was lit brilliantly as if by fireworks. The meat was inedible and, to avoid embarrassing Valery, we tossed it discreetly through the empty window pane between lightning flashes. As we fell asleep people came to look at us and stood, staring, in the doorway. The last time I opened my eyes I saw five policemen, whispering; too tired to talk, I feigned sleep. Next day, heading north-east, we emerged onto a Mongolian landscape of low, grass-covered mountains, gently sculpted and curved, smooth and velvety. After eighty kilometres, we drew into the Buryat village of Khara-Shibir, drained of energy, and asked where we could find tea.

'Follow me!' a young Buryat said, jumping into a jeep. By a stroke of luck Dimchikou Batu's wife, Dimchikova Tsybigmet, was the village English teacher, and he led us home.

'Come in, come in! Don't take your shoes off,' Dimchikova said, smiling. Dimchikova had a beautiful, high cheek-boned face, almond eyes and a perfect olive skin. She wore a close-fitting skull cap of blue and white striped silk, the only indigenous article of clothing we saw any Buryat wearing. She placed a tea pot and a bright samovar on the table and busied herself in the kitchen, assisted by angelic daughters, who brought us plates of hot *aladdi*, small pancakes, eaten with wild blueberries and cream.

'Until the 1930s we lived in *yurt*s,' Dimchikova told us. 'We were nomadic; we moved across the steppes for pasture. Then we were told to move to collective farms. They were terrible years, our animals were taken from us and we were taken to the collective farm villages. This year is the sixtieth anniversary of our collective farm. Things are a little better for us now. Before we could only have two cows, five sheep and two pigs; now we can have as many as we want.'

'But where do you keep your own cattle – on collective land?'

'Yes, on collective land,' she laughed. 'We are not allowed our own.'

'And are there Buryats on the Mongolian side of the border too?'

'Yes. During collectivisation many Buryats fled to Mongolia, including some of my family. For sixty years we could have no contact with them but we can now visit Mongolia without problems.'

'And you, Dimchikova, have you gone?'

'No. Some people from our village went and they said there are problems in Mongolia too. A Buryat folk group from Angina went to Mongolia but they were not well received, I don't know why. Most of the traditions we had when we were nomadic have died out. There used to be forty-five Buddhist temples in this area but today only one still exists; the others were destroyed. People go there once a year at the beginning of the New Year or maybe twice. We have a folk group in the village which meets to sing and play. We have our own instruments: the *khur*, like a guitar, and the *limbe*, like a flute. In the summer we still have a big music festival, the "Yokhor".'

We were struck by the contrast between this Buryat village and the Russian villages we were used to. Instead of the usual ramshackle houses and listing fences, Khara-Shibir was spruce and clean. Houses were neat and well maintained, wooden fences painted and solid, and instead of the usual sea of mud outside many Russian log cabins, the Buryats had cemented an area before their front doors. Their courteous and graceful manner and lively intelligence was engaging.

We arrived in golden evening light at Pervomaiskiy, a small town overshadowed by a massive open-cast coalmine. Our hotel was ugly even by Soviet standards, a five-floor grey concrete bunker randomly plastered with broken blue and cream tiles.

It was Sunday evening and there were two venues for entertainment open: the cinema and the discotheque. The cinema was screening a new Soviet film, based on life in a labour camp, unthinkable before *glasnost*. Although a large crowd was waiting for the doors to open, there was none of the excitement or laughter one might have expected.

Without Limits concerns two new arrivals at the camp, one of them a puny intellectual who is bullied and intimidated by a group of thuggish inmates. The bullying leads to buggery and the intellectual hangs himself. But the assault and suicide of the vulnerable intellectual provides the moral example needed by the rest of the inmates who, hitherto, have been cowed by the brutality of the camp thugs. The suicide turns the prisoners against them and a vicious fight ensues in which the prison is half destroyed and the thugs are killed.

With devastating openness, the film portrays the fear and brutality of the prison-camp system and the inhumanity and hierarchy of violence that it breeds. In the process, the film touches on a recurring issue of Russian philosophical thought – the relationship of the intellectuals to the people. It brought to mind the description of Soviet civilisation by Andrei Sinyavsky, from his book *Soviet Civilisation: a Cultural History*. Sinyavsky had himself spend seven years in labour camps for publishing fiction abroad under the pen name Abram Tertz. For all *perestroika*'s aims, he wrote, 'Soviet civilisation is built of huge, heavy blocks. It is well suited to crushing human freedom, not to nourishing or stimulating it. Overall it resembles an Egyptian pyramid constructed of mammoth pieces of stone . . . an impressive monumentality dedicated to our once grandiose goals . . . Inside, a mummy: Lenin's. Outside, a windswept desert: sand.'

The small town of Nerchinsk lay at a crucial juncture where we had to decide whether to follow the route of the Trans-Siberian railway north to Mogacha or the River Shilka east along a new road that we had heard was being built. The matter was decided for us in Nerchinsk, however, for no one appeared to have heard of the supposed new road. Nerchinsk was at the end of the last stretch of asphalt road and beyond it lay over 1,000 kilometres of track and swamp. What little there was of forest track was impassable in spring and summer, melted snow-water remaining on the surface. In summer it was a land of waterlogged grass and swamp.

We had stopped to ask directions in a village when a passing woman addressed us in English.

'You are English?'

'English, French, American and Russian,' we explained, introducing ourselves. She stopped and appeared lost for words.

'Are you an English teacher?' we asked for she seemed to have been struck silent.

'Yes,' she said, 'I am,' and she fell silent again and looked at the ground. 'I am so excited,' she said eventually, her voice trembling. 'I have never seen an American, an Englishman or a Frenchman before.' And suddenly she burst into floods of tears, her breast heaving. 'Excuse me!' she said, falteringly, tears flowing down her cheeks, so overcome with emotion she was unable to speak. She sighed heavily, her shoulders shaking. We reassured her and told her what we were doing and where we were from. Slowly she recovered her power of speech. 'I cannot believe I am speaking to an Englishman, an American!' she said before beginning to cry again. 'Please don't scold me!'

Sadly we had to leave her and press on all too quickly but the encounter was another vivid reminder of just how isolated Soviet people are.

Almost invariably the first thing we had to do on arrival in any Soviet town or village was to search for food, no matter how tired we were or how far we had cycled. In Nerchinsk, finding no vegetables in the market or in the shops, I asked for directions.

'Follow me!' a taxidriver said, jumping into his car. Pursuing the taxi round town from shop to restaurant we eventually found a *babushka* selling tomatoes at the exorbitant price of four roubles a kilo in some wasteland outside an apartment block. Accepting his offer to show me his map of the region, we drove to his house.

'It's only small,' he said. 'It's not a good house and it's a mess. But I didn't know you were coming.'

Andrei's house consisted of two rooms, one curtained off to make a bedroom for his two children. The ceiling was stained and patched where leaking water had brought it down. There were a few pieces of furniture, and a calendar and a poster were stuck on the walls. Even in mid-summer it struck us as cold and damp.

We talked of Gorbachev, whom he disliked, and Yeltsin in whom, like most ordinary Russians, he had tremendous faith. He was curious to know if it was really possible to buy anything in English shops and if I thought he could find work there. I was affirmative about the first and expressed doubts over the second. Then he changed the conversation, asking a question that brought me up short.

'Do you have cultured people in your country?'

'Yes, many,' I said. 'Why?'

'Here we have none,' he said, in a tone of quiet despair.

We checked into the only hotel. Our room had a bathroom but no running water. Of the two taps, one was broken; the bath was filthy and neither it nor the sink had a plug. The lavatory did not work, nor did the light in the bathroom. The plumbing was awry, resembling a junkyard, streaming with condensation and the tiles on the wall were at crazy angles, broken, cracked and splattered with paint. Although no water came through the tap, there was plenty of it on the floor. The bath rested on two concrete lumps, two galvanised metal bowls, and a loose piece of wood lay under the sink. I pointed out to Maksim that there was no water.

'Streets flooded outside and no water in the hotel,' he laughed. 'Our country is very special!'

In the bleak and half-abandoned restaurant, a drunk man at the next table wandered across and told us to speak in Russian or not at all, unaware that any of us was Russian until Maksim rose from the table and threatened to throw him into the street.

'We need to buy a rifle,' Maksim announced. 'An air-force officer warned me of many bears. But it's against the law. Maybe further on we can exchange one for vodka. So' – he nodded his head determinedly – 'we need to buy vodka.'

'How much vodka do we need to buy a rifle? Ten litres, twenty?'

'Maybe five,' he said, absorbed. 'Maybe five.'

All night and the next day Howard and Maksim were laid low with food poisoning from our evening meal, so Gilles and I took the opportunity to explore Nerchinsk.

The main square was dominated by a gargantuan hammer and sickle made of tin and painted red. Wooden buildings listed drastically and stucco-covered brick buildings were crumbling and disintegrating. Huge pools of water lay in the muddy streets. In the market people sat with tiny piles of potatoes or onions for sale on the table before them. In the shops there was the usual meagre selection of shoddy goods. A delivery of children's exercise books had arrived and people were buying as many as they could cart away. One item stood out, a portrait in oils of Gorbachev, without his birthmark and only just recognisable. Like other unwanted products no doubt it would lie there for years. In the square, frozen chicken was being sold to a queue off the back of a truck. They came from a box marked 'Produce of America, Frozen Chicken, For Export Only'. Not equipped for transporting frozen chickens, I joined another queue and tried to buy tins of Chinese pork, the only tinned meat available.

'Where are your coupons?' I was asked, impatiently. 'Tinned meat is rationed.' In July the Supreme Soviet had passed a law restricting the sale of food to foreigners and we had joked at the prospect of the expedition grinding to a halt out of hunger. But while Russians have an innate distrust of foreigners in general, there is little they would not do to help an individual foreigner and I returned to the hotel clasping tins of Chinese pork and matches which, theoretically, were also rationed.

At 9.00 pm Gilles and I went out to see if there was any sign of evening activity. We had been told the cinema was showing a film about 'a Spanish emperor'. The streets and square, however, were utterly deserted and the cinema was closed, a sign announcing that *Caligula* would be shown the following day. The confusion was perhaps pardonable; Spain and Italy seemed equally remove from Nerchinsk in the Chitinskaya *oblast* of Siberia.

When Howard and Maksim recovered, we pushed on into a huge panoramic landscape, hay and barley fields stretching as far as the eye could see. Each time we thought we had finished with interminable wheatfields, they seemed to make a comeback. We followed a dirt track for ninety kilometres, passing no one.

'I've just realised who's going to enjoy this trip of ours,' Howard said, as we cycled along.

'That's good news, Howard. You mean, someone *is* going to?'

'The people watching the slide show when we get home,' he said, with a tired laugh.

'Well,' I said. 'Let's hope they do.'

'Yesterday I wondered what I was doing here,' Howard continued. 'I felt terrible: splitting headache and vomiting in a filthy hotel with food poisoning. Back home my uncle's died and my mother's sitting there. I should be with her. I put so much effort into this trip, Simon, and I wonder what it was all for. If I didn't have twenty-five sponsors backing me it would be different. But as it is I'm interested in one thing and one thing only and that's getting to Vladivostok. I don't like to think what I could have done with the time, money and effort I've put into this trip.'

'Believe me, Howard, I feel the same way. It's desperate and there's nothing we can do to change it. But maybe things will cheer up in the swamp.' It reminded me of a conversation I had had with Gilles when we had been concerned that Vitale was not enjoying the journey.

'What can we do to make it better for him?' I had asked Gilles.

'That's the problem,' Gilles had said. 'We can't. It's his own country.'

Cherneyshevsk was hideously ugly. After ten hours without seeing a soul we came round a corner to see before us a sprawling town of prefabricated concrete buildings, surrounded by a wasteland of weeds and rusting metal. From a distance it looked as though a garbage can had been tipped out onto virgin land; from close up it looked little better. We found the hotel, the standard grim brick bunker, surrounded by long grass and overgrown tarmac. The first *stolovaya* was closed for repairs so we went to another, infested with flies, for a bowl of thin soup, sour cream, congealed macaroni and cold fried fish. There was no meat, no tea and the fruit juice was little better than water.

'You've watered this down!' Maksim accused the serving woman vehemently. She denied it angrily. 'It's been watered down twice! First in the factory and then here!'

'If only Gorbachev could come with us for a couple of days . . .' Gilles said.

Back at the hotel the administrator brought tea to our room.

'We live badly here, we can do nothing to improve our lives,' she said. 'Nothing changes – except for the worse.'

'But twenty years ago, ten even,' I said, 'you lived better, didn't you?'

'We have always lived badly. Before it was bad but now it is worse. I earn eighty roubles a month and apples cost five roubles a kilo . . .' She shrugged her shoulders.

Maksim told us there had been a great scandal when a car belonging to a member of the *nomenklatura* had broken down and hard-to-obtain goods, such as ham, sausage and vodka had been discovered in the boot.

'Even the *nomenklatura* can't live well,' Howard said, 'if they have to sneak off to their *dacha* to do it unobserved. Ham! That's just great! Ham's the kind of thing you'd eat on a Saturday watching a baseball match without even noticing it. And here it's transported secretly in the back of a Volga!'

The next morning's cycling from Cherneyshevsk to Zherikan was perhaps the most enchanting of the entire trip. We followed a sparkling and turbulent river along a forest track that was exceptionally smooth. For the very first time there was a feel of autumn, a certain crispness and stillness in the air, and the highest branches of the silver birches had begun to yellow. The steep hillsides of rough rock, short grass, scattered pines and birches seemed the ideal habitat of bears, which we had been warned to look out for.

The previous evening a policeman had knocked at our hotel door; we were accustomed to occasional visits from the police; they rarely had much to say. On the way to Zherikan Captain Turanov overtook us in his militia jeep and stopped to check everything was alright, then trailed along behind us, keeping a respectful distance. At one point Howard and I were far ahead of Gilles and Maksim when Turanov sped up and, grinning widely, said 'Tools!' in English.

'How far back are they?'

'Two kilometres.' I dug the tool bag out of a pannier and handed it to him.

'Thanks,' I said, 'it's very good of you.' He looked at it puzzled for a moment, before realising he had been entrusted with a mission. He grinned, turned his jeep round and sped back to the others. 'Might as well give him something useful to do,' I said to Howard.

At Zherikan Turanov escorted us to the *stolovaya* and hammered on the door until it opened up. We invited him to eat with us but he went to a separate table before escorting us to the police station to discuss the route.

'From here,' the police chief said, 'there is no road to Aksenovo-Zilovskoye. You will have to take the train.'

'We're cyclists,' we said plainly, playing the sportsmen card for all it was worth. 'We never take trains.'

Once they realised we would not even consider taking a train they could not have been more helpful, indicating where forest tracks, railwaymen's huts and tiny settlements existed. Water levels were high and road bridges were non-existent. The larger rivers we would have to cross on the railway bridges.

'There are armed soldiers on the major railway bridges,' we were warned, 'and you must get permission from the barracks to cross. Don't even think of crossing them at night.'

As we rose to leave the police chief showed us a massive club and a flick-knife they had recently confiscated.

'Hooligans!' the police chief said. 'You have them as well in your countries, I think? Here there is nothing to do, that is the problem. And nothing in the shops. Nothing! We live badly here.' He rose from his seat. 'We will escort you to the end of the track. Is there anything you need? There will be nowhere to get food until Aksenovo.' We needed bread so they gave us three loaves fresh from the bakery before escorting us in a yellow militia jeep over deeply corrugated earth tracks to the edge of the village. 'The track ends here. You have a footpath for two kilometres, then nothing. Good luck!' We shook hands and departed.

The track indeed soon disappeared into swamp. Our feet submerged in brackish water, we looked around for the trail and found it below us, deep in water. We pulled the bikes up the railway embankment and then dragged them down onto the trail which, rough and rocky, was just wide enough for a pedestrian or a bicycle. After only three kilometres of rocky trail, a loud crack heralded the end of my kevlar disc wheel.

It was irreparable; we had no choice but to build a new wheel from scratch, so we pulled out a hub and spokes, and began to build a new one. Meanwhile we built a fire and brewed up tea, to the amusement of passing train-drivers, and when a storm threatened to engulf us we moved to a railwayman's hut made from old railway sleepers. By the time it was too dark to see, eight hours later, we had a respectable wheel.

The next day, after a morning following waterlogged ruts, we emerged into a plain of unadulterated swamp. Brackish, peaty water rose to our knees, the trails disappeared and progress was nigh impossible. We pushed for two kilometres until we spotted a small camp where three hobbled horses grazed close to a small wood shack and blue wood-smoke rose in the air. Abandoning our bikes, we waded across to ask directions. The hut, made of railway sleepers, was primitive and dark, a sheet of plastic serving as a window. Close to it four men were bent over a knife-grinder, sharpening the blade of a horse-drawn scythe that dated from before the Revolution. They had come from the collective farm to cut hay in the drier part of the swamp and at night they slept in the hut. We joined them for tea before noticing a vehicle moving fast in the distance. 'Is that the trail we should take?' we asked.

'There's no road there,' they said. As far as we could make out the vehicle was a tank which appeared to be heading directly for us and for a moment we thought we had blundered into a military training area. As it approached, however, we could see it was a tracked armoured personnel carrier, tearing across country, plunging through rivers and creeks. As it pulled up beside us, two men in khaki jumped down. They too were from the collective farm, the APC being an old model handed over by the army for use on the farms. It was being used to drag trees out of the wood for firewood. The antiquated horse-drawn mower and the APC made a curious contrast in the middle of the swamp, symbols of different civilisations.

'The next two kilometres are completely impassable. You'll never get through,' they told us. 'But we'll take you through the worst, if you like.'

We waded back to our bikes, dragged them over and set off, sitting on the top of the APC with our legs through the gun turrets. We raced across the swamp, plunging through rivers and huge stretches of water, the tracks tearing up the reeds and grass, and obliterating every bush and small tree in their path. Liquid mud and water were thrown high into the air, and two black tracks of devastated swamp were left behind. We passed a peasant with a scythe who glared angrily at us as we shot by and then, just as suddenly as our ride had begun, it was over and we were back on foot, pushing again through huge pools of stagnant water.

Even after we saw Aksenovo only six kilometres away, it still took us three hours to arrive. On the way in, Maksim's wheel buckled as mine had done the day before and we arrived exhausted, having covered forty kilometres in twelve hours – an average of three and a half kph.

Like most settlements in the swamp, Aksenovo-Zilovskoye was accessible only by railway. It was the first food-drop that we had arranged in the swamp and all our supplies had arrived: Syrian chocolate, dried fruit, coffee, sugar, tea, porridge, Alpine Aire mountaineering food, apples and biscuits, of which only the last was available in the shops of Aksenovo. When we entered the post office we passed a motionless man spread-eagled in the dirt.

'He looks dead to me,' Howard said. But in the two hours it took us to collect, sort through and send ahead excess supplies, he had advanced four feet. No one took the slightest notice of him apart from a few small children and a goat that nibbled at his trousers.

As Aksenovo had no hotel we took over one of the dormitories for waiting passengers in the railway station. Wet and plastered with mud, the only thing we wanted was hot water but the *banya* opened for men only twice a week.

Aksenovo railway station was run by huge women who appeared to spend most of their day cooking meals at the back of their office. We were soon in and out of their office brewing tea and cooking meals and took it in turns, as usual, to hunt around the town for food. Eggs, butter, bread and meat were available in the shops but for milk and vegetables it was necessary to ask at houses. At one house I was given potatoes, at another jam, at another onions; as usual it was impossible to pay.

From Aksenovo we pushed for a week through swamp, keeping close to the Trans-Siberian railway. As there was no road there were no bridges and rivers had to be forded. The water was freezing and we only just managed to cross before our feet were paralysed with cold. But once the storms cleared, the landscape of pine, fir and alder was magnificent in the crisp, clear air. As we curved north-east to clear the Mongolian border, it became noticeably cooler. Even at the end of August, autumn had arrived. Eventually we rejoined a track and arrived at Urum where we found the first of several goldmines.

The director of the goldmine invited us to stay and escorted us personally to the *banya*. The gold camp at Urum was very different in spirit to anywhere we had been; the miners seemed to share a camaraderie and a sense of purpose that united them. They had come to Siberia for one reason only: to make money. Salaries were high; 10,000 roubles for eight months' work compared with an average in European Russia of 3,000 for an entire year. But the work was hard: every man worked a twelve-hour shift, seven days a week, every week, every month, for eight months. Some men had come from the Ukraine, others from Byelorussia, European Russia and Georgia, and most had left wives behind whom they would not see until the eight-month shift was up. For entertainment they had one communal television and a billiard table, nothing more. They lived two to a cabin and took it in turns to prepare the meals and cook. But the camp was clean, orderly and well run.

One respect in which Soviet goldmining differs from traditional mining is that there is no chance of anyone becoming rich. They are not prospectors at all, being paid a flat wage irrespective of the quantity of gold they find. As a result there is none of the excitement of traditional gold-prospecting.

'If gold is stolen what are the penalties?'

'That depends on the quantity stolen,' the chief said.

When I suggested a kilo, he drew a noose in the air.

The following morning we continued in thick fog along a rough, mud-filled track. We pushed through marsh and bog, losing the track altogether, wading through rivers a hundred yards wide, picking our way from sandbank to sandbank. All day we were engulfed in mud and water until in the late afternoon we came across a new dirt road cut through virgin forest of fir and pine. We followed it until it ended abruptly at the edge of a wide river just before the forest village of

Sbega. Deep and fast-flowing, it was difficult to believe that any vehicle could cross it. But before we had decided on a course of action a gigantic truck with wheels eight feet high emerged from the forest. Loading the bikes into the back, we were ferried across, the truck three-quarters submerged – probably in greater danger than we had been at any point throughout the entire journey.

We rose at 6.00 am and left Sbega in pouring rain. For ten hours we cycled along a rough dirt road, stopping only to mend punctures, passing men out mushrooming with large aluminium containers slung on their backs. A jeep passed while Maksim and I were mending a puncture in heavy rain and reversed back fast. It was full of drunken policemen who implored us to take a lift to the next town. They stood round us in the rain and poured out glasses of vodka. We declined the lift but accepted the vodka, lard, bread and tomatoes wrapped up in quickly sodden and disintegrating newspaper. When we caught up with Gilles and Howard we found the police with them, drinking another round of vodka in heavy rain.

The only policeman not in uniform, and the most sober, demanded to see the document authorising our trip. Maksim, whose handling of people tended to be abrupt and even aggressive, brought the document out reluctantly, his irritation clear. When the policeman tried to take the document in his own hand, Maksim held it back. An absurd tug of war ensued whereupon the policeman flew into a rage. He said something to Maksim we did not understand but there was no mistaking his fury and for a moment we felt certain he was about to knock Maksim to the ground. He brought out an identity card and held it up close to Maksim's face with a thin malicious smile, staring at him unwaveringly in total silence. After what seemed an eternity he asked for Maksim's passport, continuing all the while to stare at him with utter loathing. Maksim handed his passport over and looked at the ground but said nothing. Meanwhile the other policemen, who had climbed into the jeep to escape the rain, came back and tried to tug their colleague away but he shook them off. Eventually, after saying something in a quiet, vicious voice to Maksim, he climbed back into the jeep and it drove off.

Maksim refused to talk about the incident but we had no doubt that had we not been there he would have paid dearly for his behaviour. Forty years before, it might have cost him many years' hard labour. In order to avoid any possible repercussions, we avoided the town the police were heading for and worked our way slowly round it, spending the night at another goldmining camp.

Even before this incident we had had a disastrous day. Sand and water caused blow-outs that destroyed inner tubes and tyres alike. A stone was thrown up into Howard's chain, knocking the derailleur into the wheel, ripping spokes out and holing the rim. Towards the end of the day Maksim's tyre blew out too, making a total of three in a single day. Our tyres were collapsing so fast that we began to doubt we would have enough to get through the swamp, let alone reach Vladivostok.

We spent the night at the Klizny-Kluch goldmining camp, where sixty men dredged gold from the rivers twenty-four hours a day. As at Urum, the camp was well organised and remarkably clean, with raised wooden walkways and gravel instead of the usual sea of mud. The camp even had its own gardens, glasshouses, cows, pigs and bakery.

'We have to be self-sufficient,' the director of the camp told us. 'It's the only way we can survive.'

Over supper he told us he was worried about the pollution of the rivers caused by his own dredging machinery and in general about the ecological damage from mining in Siberia. One now had to travel over 120 kilometres away from the Trans-Siberian railway line to find untouched taiga.

'Perestroika has not reached Siberia yet,' he said. 'It will take another ten years to arrive. Soviet people are used to stability and it's only because things are now actually happening after years of stagnation that everyone thinks the country is collapsing.'

What we had been told was a terrible route to Mogacha turned out to be an excellent dirt track through the mountains. Only one jeep passed us all day and, naturally, the driver stopped to talk. Before leaving he gave us a large smoked fish, a glass of vodka, and an invitation to stay with him when we reached Mogacha. Later in the day Howard and I were consulting the map when a jeep roared up from behind and veered across the road, as if heading straight for us. We flung ourselves out of the way just as the door was thrown open, and fresh lilies and nasturtiums came hurtling through the air. Getting up from the dust, we realised it was the same man with whom we had talked in the morning.

When we arrived in Mogacha we asked the police for directions to his house and were escorted by militia jeep with flashing blue light to the gold camp. What our friend had not told us was that he was the director of Mogacha goldmine.

Valery Gritsakof, the camp cook, was from Leningrad and had only been in Mogacha three months. He prepared gargantuan meals, serving six eggs at a time, and stood over us, beaming with pleasure, as we ate. The more we declined food, the more he piled it onto our plates.

In the morning we saw him emerge from the cook-house, clutching his hands to his head, an agonised expression on his face.

'A bad night! A bad night!' he groaned.

'Too much vodka?' I asked.

'No. All night I thought of my wife and my baby daughter in Leningrad and could not sleep,' he said. 'And I'm here for another five months!'

16

THE SWAMP

W^E LEFT MOGACHA in thick, freezing fog that crept into our very bones. Even wearing every conceivable article of clothing the cold was numbing and we cycled at a snail's pace. If it was so cold on the first day of September, we dreaded to think what it must be like in mid-winter. We cycled first to the railway station and asked the station master to alert the soldiers guarding the bridge that we were coming; we had no desire to be shot in the fog. On the way out we passed miners returning from their night shift huddled under blankets in the back of an open truck, looking cold and hungry.

We waited with an armed escort until a Trans-Siberian train had thundered across the bridge before being led across. At the far end, Uzbek conscripts gazed at us. They were quartered in old railway wagons, lacking their wheels, beside the track. Maksim asked them a question but they appeared not to understand.

'Stupid people,' Maksim said, angrily, as we moved off. 'They can't even speak Russian.'

Only after an hour did we see the sun hovering in a luminous grey sky like a silver disc. All sounds were muffled; even rivers were silent until we were right upon them. In the dense fog the sirens of the goods trains, invisible but close at hand, sounded like fog-horns far out at sea. Howard disappeared into the fog ahead and Maksim fell away into the fog behind. We reached a point where the river and our track coincided for a while. The water was icy and our feet froze. To revive our circulation Gilles and I dismounted and walked until Maksim appeared, his hands swathed in lint bandages, looking like a wounded soldier finding his way out of a gas attack.

'Maksim!' I said 'What happened?'

'For cold!' he said.

'Are you crazy? Where are your gloves?'

'I sent them ahead. They're not necessary.' And although we bought Maksim another pair in the next town, he refused to wear them, determined to toughen himself physically against unseen hardships.

Forests of pine and fir extended over low hills as far as we could see, vast areas eerily dead from a fire that swept hundreds of thousands of hectares of Amurskaya and Chitinskaya *oblast*s four years before. In 130 kilometres of forest track and trail we met only two people, both of whom invited us to stay at Amazar.

'Have you seen anyone today?' the first asked. But we had not seen a soul all day. He seemed disappointed.

'I'm looking for my brother,' he said.

It was already late in the day when we met Dmitri Gregorivich who told us it was yet another thirty kilometres to the tiny forestry village of Amazar. The sun was already low, casting the silent forest into weird and beautiful shades of maroon and purple. As night fell, it grew cold quickly and we raced to reach Amazar under an enormous moon that brushed the black silhouettes of the pine trees. At the crest of the hill in Amazar we met Dmitri who had come to find us. We set off to follow him, the five of us spread across the dirt road, just as a heavy Russian motorcycle loomed out of the blackness over the crest of the hill and ploughed headlong into Maksim, knocking him fifteen feet down the hill with a sickening thud. To our astonishment Maksim got to his feet unaided.

'Are you alright?' I asked, hardly able to make anything out in the pitch black.

'Normal, Simon, normal,' Maksim's voice in the dark replied. We pulled the motorcyclist from under his bike and set him on his feet. Steeped in vodka, he cursed softly in the dark but the sound of foreign voices around him was enough to convince him that he really had drunk too much. Without further ado, he remounted and disappeared into the gloom. Maksim's bike had not survived quite as well as the half-ton steel motorcycle: the front rack had been concertinaed up and crushed against the front forks, the tyre was punctured and the front wheel so bent that it could not turn. Panniers that had been torn off lay in the road. Dmitri waved down a passing motorcyle combination, the wreckage was loaded on board and the sad procession made its way across the shunting yards.

In Dmitri's log cabin we worked for three hours to repair the damage before having a *banya* and sitting down to a Siberian feast: salted bottled mushrooms, black Zabaikal tomatoes, cucumber salads, a vast stack of fried potatoes, fried meat, brown bread, jams made from berries in the Taiga, milk, tea and vodka.

In the morning Dmitri helped us reweld the rack and escorted us out of Amazar to help secure permission to cross the River Chichatka from the soliders guarding the bridge. However, we had not even got as far as the bridge before Maksim's back wheel collapsed, forcing us to stop and build a new one from scratch – the third on the journey. Dmitri forewarned the military barracks of our arrival, dozed in the sun for several hours while we worked away and eventually left after fond farewells. When we saw him reappear an hour later we wondered what had brought him back. We soon found out; he had brought a parcel of smoked elk-meat, a Siberian delicacy, for us to take with us.

As it took seven hours to build a new wheel we covered no more than three kilometres that day. At dusk we arrived at the barracks, a squat, white building surrounded by barbed wire. The second lieutenant, casually dressed in an open-necked shirt, agreed to let us spend the night. He led us into the barracks past a Kirghiz soldier who belatedly snapped to attention and we carried the bikes to a dormitory of thirty beds, where a soldier was detailed to guard them. The barracks were shambolic and squalid but were, supposedly, undergoing repair; the canteen was an open-air shack with the look of a disused chicken-run.

The soldiers, who were not part of the regular army but internal security troops, were largely Kirghiz, conscripted for two years' military service. Frozen with cold in their canteen, they hardly spoke; despite temperatures well below freezing at night there was no heating of any sort in the barracks. We joined the troops for supper and breakfast: a bowl of buckwheat with microscopic traces of meat and a mug of hot brown water that passed for tea. As if conditions were not bad enough, the conscripts, we learnt, spent their entire two years' military service in a single location; morale could hardly have been worse.

'Whom are you guarding the bridge against?' I asked the lieutenant.
'Saboteurs.'
'What saboteurs?' I asked. He shrugged his shoulders.

The next morning, preceded by an armed guard, we were escorted across the bridge, passing more guards at either end. Even with fur hats, massive greatcoats and gloves they looked cold. All morning we pushed along the railway, dragging the bikes off the track for the Trans-Siberian express and goods trains, sixty wagons or more long, carrying coal and timber. Sometimes the chippings were level with the sleepers, enabling us to push or even to ride between or beside the rails, but otherwise progress was infernal. The only smooth course was to push the bikes with both wheels resting on the rail itself, a feat that demanded great concentration but at which Gilles, in particular, became adept. When it was feasible we followed trails close to the railway, invariably half-flooded with water, islands of dry land alternating with water so deep that feet and panniers were submerged much of the time. Often the water was too deep to cycle through and we were forced to dismount and push but most of the time we rode through rivers and pools, creating tidal waves of muddy water. Soaked and covered with mud as we were after the first half hour it made little difference how wet we got, except early in the morning before the sun had any warmth. As rivers had to be forded periodically there was little point trying to keep dry. In European Russia we had been called 'Martians' when we had arrived in villages, wearing immaculate shiny cycling clothes, helmets and glasses. From the swamp we emerged looking more like barbarians.

Yerofey-Pavlovich was a small timber and mining town on the Trans-Siberian railway. At the post office we turned round to find Maksim talking to a huge, powerfully built man with sandy hair and a cheerful face. To our disbelief we learnt that the man, Yakov, had been waiting for us, having brought our spare wheels and rims from Moscow. We had sent a telegram requesting that they should be sent to Yerofey-Pavlovich but what Yakov was doing there none of us could fathom.

'If they weren't brought personally,' Maksim told us, 'we would never have got them. They would have disappeared.' So, to ensure we got them, Yakov had flown to Chita and taken a train for fifteen hours through the swamp to Yerofey-Pavlovich and then waited six days for us to arrive! Each day Yakov had gone to Yerofey station and spoken to the train drivers as they pulled into the station to learn of our progress.

We appreciated receiving the wheels but wondered if it made commercial sense to have an employee sitting around in a Siberian town for a week just to hand over a few wheels. They could easily have been left at the post office, the hotel or with the police. We were hardly likely to leave without the equipment we had requested and yet Yakov had waited to hand them over personally. Apart from the wheels, Yakov had brought us eighteen tins of beef and twelve of condensed milk which it was quite impossible for us to carry. We took what we could, Maksim sending the bulk home where they would be greatly appreciated.

Yakov had the mariner's habit of making himself at home quickly in new surroundings and had established himself comfortably in his six days. He had befriended the woman running Yerofey-Pavlovich's only bar to which he took us immediately for champagne.

'I have arranged for you to have a *banya* with my friends,' Yakov told us with a smile. An hour later we set off on a massive Ural motorcycle combination, driven by Yakov's friend, Dmitri, Howard and Gilles riding pillion while I sat back in the sidecar. Plunging in and out of potholes we drove down a bumpy track, half in and half out of the River Chichatka, until we came to a rest beside a *dacha* where two young women were sunbathing in bikinis on the riverbank. They rose to greet us; Tatiana was Dmitri's daughter and the other, Victoria, a friend. Without doubt they were two of the best-looking girls we had seen since Leningrad. We joined Yakov and Dmitri for a *banya* from which we ran, glowing like coal, into the icy waters of the Chichatka. The *banya* was followed by a veritable feast complete with red caviar, river salmon, huge salads, and champagne and Hungarian Tokai wine cooled in the river. The further we penetrated into the interior of Siberia the better life seemed to be. Yakov agreed. He was working in Moscow after twelve years on the island of Sakhalin and disliked intensely the constricted life and limited opportunities that the capital offered.

After ten hours of cycling and pushing through swamp, the *banya* and a feast, we danced until two in the morning. The following day we decided we deserved a day of rest. As we walked into town Tatiana introduced us to the village history teacher.

'Capitalist?' he asked Gilles.

'No,' Gilles replied, taken aback at the question.

'When?' Gilles laughed aloud. 'How long until you are a millionaire?' he persisted, in earnest.

'Never!' Gilles said. Incomprehension was mutual and the two sides moved on.

The following day Gilles and I went for a walk along the riverbank with Tatiana and Victoria. Autumn had arrived and gold and yellow leaves fell steadily and softly to create a rich tapestry of colour. We walked beside the River Chichatka far upstream into the forest of pine, fir and birch, and sat talking beside the river. Far from the town, no sound greeted us except the gentle gurgle of water as it slipped over the stones. Rounded, moss-covered boulders lay along the riverbank. Both Tatiana and Victoria lived on the Kamchatka peninsula, 2,000 kilometres and three time zones away. They had studied pharmacology together in Khabarovsk and were working in Petropavlovsk-Kamchatskiy, the capital city of Kamchatka.

Victoria could not speak a word of English and I understood only part of what she said. But her description of Kamchatka was enchanting, a region of active snow-clad volcanoes, thermal springs and magnificent mountain scenery. Kamchatka was, she said, a 'closed region', prohibited to foreigners, but she hoped that one day it would open. She was curious about life in Europe, and I tried to convey in stumbling Russian what Paris and London were like, describing the streets, theatres, galleries, restaurants and cafés.

'Every Russian woman dreams of Paris,' Victoria said, as we lazed on the riverbank in hot sunshine.

'Perhaps . . .'

'No. We will never see it,' she said, simply, 'because we were born in the Soviet Union.'

'But maybe soon you will have the chance to travel abroad?'

'No. For the rich everything is possible here – they will be able to travel, but for the ordinary people nothing will change. With or without Gorbachev and *perestroika*.'

Suddenly I felt insensitive and ashamed of describing places that Victoria could never visit and things she could never see. I looked at her again. It was warm, she was intensely beautiful, and her deep brown eyes and exquisite face were close to mine. I leant across and kissed her.

'Simon,' she said quietly, after a long pause, leaning back on her elbow to look at me. 'Why do you kiss me?'

'Because you're wonderful!'

'Do you kiss every wonderful woman?'

I had to admit that I didn't.

'Simon, you are the first foreigner I've ever seen. Are they all like you?'

Golden leaves fell silently, the only sound that of water rushing over cobbles. Victoria was wearing a wedding ring, on the third finger of her left hand.

'I was married before,' she said, 'for one year, but I am not any longer.'

'I'm sorry,' I said.

'Why?'

'It's sad for you.'

'Simon,' she said, 'everyone has happy and sad moments in their life.'

In the evening we met Tatiana, Victoria and Yakov in the bar. When it closed at 10.00 pm we were under the impression that we had been invited back to the apartment of Yakov's friend, the bartender, to continue the evening. She indicated a massive holdall we could carry home for her which Howard and I could hardly lift. As we moved off in the dark, it clinked.

'Vodka?' we asked her.

'Yes,' she said, 'it's my birthday.'

'It's going to be quite a party,' Howard said, as we staggered across town in the pitch black. 'There must be forty bottles here.' It was clear there were certain advantages to running a bar in the Soviet Union.

'How far?' we said, stopping for a rest.

'Not far.' There were no street lights; occasionally figures loomed in dark doorways. Eventually we arrived and heaved the holdall to the fourth floor. She unlocked the door and we were about to follow her in, when she turned round, primly thanking us and wishing us all good night. We looked at each other in astonishment.

'Well, that seems to be it!' Gilles said.

'Some party!' Howard said.

It was ten o'clock and there was nowhere to go: no café, no other bar, no dance-hall, no club, no restaurant. It was impossible for Tatiana and Victoria to join us in our hotel: Soviet *dezhurnaya*s, or 'duty-women', we had found, were eagle-eyed and unrelenting in their opposition to visitors.

With no party, the group dispersed, Tatiana and Victoria seeking shelter in a wooden pavilion with Gilles and me as a storm broke. Rain fell in torrents, sweeping the streets. There was no sign of life apart from a drunk in a crumpled felt hat who passed in the dark. Unsteady on his feet, oblivious of the pouring rain, he skipped in pools of water and strummed at his balalaika, the first and last balalaika we saw in six months. It seemed absurd but there was nowhere we could go to drink or talk, so we stayed in the pavilion as rain fell around us in sheets.

The next morning when Howard, Maksim and I rose to pack at six, Gilles appeared to be suffering from stomach cramps. As the days were rapidly getting cooler and we had stopped in Yerofey for a day and a half already, we felt that we had to press on. We all dreaded the prospect of being caught in the swamp once it turned cold, especially Howard who had experienced Tibet in winter. We agreed to continue without Gilles who would catch us up at Skovorodino by train. As for his recovery he seemed to have *no* objection to being left in Tatiana's hands.

The day that followed was indescribable, the worst of the entire trip. For twelve hours we struggled through mud and clay, often on foot, under continual heavy rain, passing only one lorry and a tiny station. For the first time we encountered 'General Mud', thick, clayey mud that clung to the bicycle frame, the brake blocks and the wheels and clogged them totally – the same mud that had brought both Napoleon and Hitler to a halt.

We were forced to stop frequently to free the wheels, carving mud away with a stick, but within minutes they would be clogged again, making them impossible to push. We dragged them up and down off the railway embankment searching for firmer ground, in vain. When we arrived at a semi-abandoned station in the twilight we had covered fifty kilometres in twelve hours and rain was still falling. Utterly spent, we had trudged for the previous four hours in total silence. Only one family was still living at the abandoned station. They led us to a deserted log cabin, split wood with an axe and built us a roaring fire. Despite twelve hours of uninterrupted rain we did have dry clothes. By this stage on the journey everything we had was wrapped in three layers of plastic bags.

The following day was no better. We continued, forever, along the railway, crossing further bridges guarded by soldiers living in antiquated and rusty railway carriages. As we cycled along overgrown tracks Howards' derailleur got caught in a branch and snapped in two. We removed it and shortened the chain; then the chain jumped a sprocket and became as taut as a metal hawser. Eventually we made it to Magdala in red evening sunshine and found a log cabin where we could spend the night.

Three newly qualified teachers had just arrived in the dreary lumber village where they were to spend the next three years. They had arrived the day before to find, like us, a log cabin with no running water, dim electric lights, a log-fired stove and a communal lavatory outside in a wooden lean-to. We invited them to join us for our evening meal, an offer they accepted gladly. But they had not been with us long when our meal was interrupted by a drunken army officer who barged in to our cabin, keen to provoke a fight. Fearing complications for their three-year stay which had begun only the day before, they left when the officer picked up and began toying with Howard's knife.

We evicted him onto the street without mishap but we felt a pang of pity for the three educated and intelligent teachers who were used to city life in Blagoveshchensk. We had encountered boorish, drunken behaviour often enough, but we were always able to move on. For the girls in Magdala there would be no escape from it.

Just before Skovorodino we came across a prison camp, next to a village, at the side of the forest track we were following. A soldier, rifle slung over his shoulder, watched us approach from a wooden watchtower. We cycled along beside a wooden stockade, twelve feet high, strongly buttressed. Through tiny cracks it was possible to see a six-foot-deep dry moat, and then a second stockade, equally high, topped by an unbroken ring of coiled barbed wire. There was a tall watchtower at every corner manned by armed soldiers; it looked identical to the prison camp portrayed in the Soviet film *Without Limits*. From the four corners the guards had uninterrupted lines of fire down the dry moat between the stockades; at one end railway tracks ran into the prison through massive log doors. I asked Maksim to confirm with the locals that it was a labour camp, something he was reluctant to do. However, he did eventually ask and it was confirmed but it was clear that no one was prepared to say more about it.

We made our way to the *stolovaya* where half a dozen civilians and three camp officers were eating. The atmosphere was depressed, even by Soviet standards. No one apart from the officers talked and everyone else looked suspicious and miserable.

The food was, as ever, abysmal: thin, watery soup, overcooked rice and the same dismal '*kutlets*' of bread, fat and gristle that had accompanied us across the USSR.

'If this is what the prison officers eat,' I said, 'I dread to think what the prisoners must get!'

'After eating here every day, month-in, month-out for years,' Gilles said, 'the guards *must* become vindictive.'

'I become vindictive after eating it for one day,' Howard said.

Skovorodino was indistinguishable from hundreds of other Soviet towns. At the shop there was a meagre selection of bottled and tinned food. Holding up a tin of fish I asked the shop assistant if it was any good.

'No,' she said. 'It's terrible. Wait here. I'll get something good for you.' She disappeared into the store room and reappeared with two tins that proved to be the best tinned fish we had eaten.

From Skovorodino there was no track or trail of any description to Magdagachi, 150 kilometres away. We had heard rumours, however, of a new military road, barred to civilian traffic, that ran close to the Amur River. Faced with the prospect of pushing along railway lines for 150 kilometres we took a chance, hoping not to be intercepted, and set off south in the direction of the Chinese border.

Although the road was only a dirt trail it was smooth and gave us our first chance to cycle without dismounting and pushing for weeks. By this stage of the journey our brake blocks had been worn down to the metal backing, and began to screech demonically, like chalk on a blackboard, compelling us to release the front brakes and rely on the back ones and our feet. The hills, however, were steeper than ever as the road had been cut in a straight line without any regard for contours and we made several descents that miraculously ended safely. When a military jeep waved us down we anticipated trouble but ended up being given bottles of mineral water, apples and an invitation to Leningrad by two officers' wives. One brought out a photograph of a blonde on the beach wearing a bikini.

'This is my daughter, aged twenty-two,' she said, laughing. 'She's good, isn't she? Why don't you come to Leningrad when you've finished your journey?'

'Who's got pen and paper handy?' Howard asked, searching for his notebook.

Howard rode ahead and we caught up with him in a village in the pitch black, having cycled the last ten kilometres in the dark. We found him clutching bread and sausage next to a jeep full of sailors in traditional blue and white uniform.

'What the hell are sailors doing here?' I asked Howard.

'You won't believe it! Guess where we are? This is Dzhalinda. You're standing on the banks of the Amur. And that's China over there,' he said, gesticulating in the dark.

'What's going on?'

'These guys are real friendly. They've given us bread and sausage and they're thinking of where we can spend the night. But we're not meant to be here. We were meant to take a track on the left fifty clicks back. See it?'

'I haven't seen a track on the left all day.'

'Well, we're here now. We can only get arrested.'

A motorcycle combination bumped along the track and I waved it down. It was driven by a young man built like an ox.

'Do you know anywhere we could spend the night?'

'Yes,' he said immediately, 'with me.' We followed him and pulled up at a wooden house surrounded by prolific vegetable gardens and outhouses. It was freezing and we stamped our feet while he disappeared inside. A moment later he was back.

'Come in! Come in!' he told us. As we stepped inside his father appeared, yawning as if from a deep sleep, gazing at us in surprise.

'This is my father, Valery Sergeievich, and I am Igor,' he said. Valery Sergeievich, like his son, had a massive frame, grey wiry hair and an enormous, deeply wrinkled face.

'You're Estonians?' Valery asked, rubbing his eyes.

'No, father,' Igor said. 'They are French, American, British and Russian.'

'Ah!' he said, with great affection, giving us each a huge bear-like hug. 'Well, come in and get warm. It's nice to see you. Yes, this is a real pleasure for me.'

Valery had two sons and a daughter in Vladivostok, two studying engineering and economics, and one in the merchant navy. Igor was at home for a few weeks' holiday from the Polytechnical Institute in Vladivostok.

Valery stood watching us.

'I like people,' he said, beaming with pleasure and shaking his head gently. 'I like people very much!'

While his mother began to prepare a meal Igor pulled back the carpet in the living room and jumped down into a cellar to pass up three litre jars of pickled vegetables and tinned milk stored away for the winter. We declined Valery's offer of cigarettes and vodka on the pretext that we were sportsmen.

'Russians do everything!' Valery said, passionately, 'Drink! Smoke! Everything!'

Valery was a forester and adored Siberia. 'I love it here in the Taiga,' he said. 'It's clean, it's pure and it's beautiful. My wife would like to live in the city, in Vladivostok, now that all the children are there, but I don't think I would survive in a city.'

The Amur, he told us, froze in winter, sometimes to the depth of four feet and then it was possible to walk across to China. Temperatures in winter fell to −40° or lower. A Chinese village lay just out of sight around a corner and China was so close that all he could receive on television was Chinese broadcasts.

'It's rather tiresome,' he said.

Our meal was interrupted by the arrival of an officer of the border-security army. Courteously, he asked for our documentation and passports and told us we had no permission to be in Dzhalinda. The following day, as we prepared to leave, a second officer arrived with whom we discussed the roads and consulted the map. Like all Russians who saw them, he was astonished at the detail marked on our US Intelligence maps of the USSR. He understood completely why we were loath to take the inland trail, which was infinitely longer and petered out in marshy bog, and preferred the military highway along the Amur.

'But for this road you need special permission from the highest authorities,' he said.

'Can we get it here?'

'No,' he laughed. 'You need signed authorisation from the Military Commission in Moscow.'

We had to settle for a dirt track to Taldan and Igor escorted us to the edge of the village before waving goodbye. Steam rose from the Amur, 300 metres wide, on the far side of which rose a forest of thin pine trees on a slight rise. A Chinese watchpost was visible and on the Russian side five patrol boats were moored beside naval barracks. It was peculiar to see sailors in traditional naval uniform 1,700 kilometres from the nearest sea.

Our track ran just inside the Soviet border, beside two high fences topped with barbed wire separated by a zone of ploughed earth. We were challenged by frontier guards and, as we approached a barracks, were given a military escort that accompanied us for ten kilometres away from the border. Further on we passed numerous disused pillboxes, relics of the Chinese-Soviet border skirmishes of the 1960s. Then for two days we cycled through birch forest bathed in gold and yellow leaves. Clear blue skies and autumnal sunshine made up for two weeks of almost continual rain.

Magdagachi was the last town of any size in the swamp. It looked forbidding from a distance, tailings from open-cast mines appearing to merge with grey apartment buildings. We lost our way threading through the chaos, Gilles, Howard and Maksim heading one way, me another. Twenty minutes later I found myself lost in a railway shunting yard, full of antiquated steam-engines, coal-back, complete with snow ploughs. Trying to extricate myself, I came face to face with Gilles, Howard and Maksim, equally lost, heading in the opposite direction.

By the time we arrived in the town centre the *stolovaya*s and shops were closed, and a friendly woman led us to a Soviet air-force canteen. We were ushered into the officers' mess, past hundreds of airmen eating at long tables, looking like Second World War pilots in their wool-lined leather jackets. After special pleading and telephone calls on our behalf we were authorised to eat in the officers' mess on the condition that we ate and left before the officers arrived. The table had been laid for them and we sat down without delay. Exceptionally hungry, we ate everything on the table and cleared out with seconds to spare, just as the officers arrived in their long, grey greatcoats. After using air-force hosepipes to blast the mud off our bikes we continued to Tigda.

The weather was changing fast, each day getting noticeably colder, and we pushed ourselves to the utmost to clear the swamp before snow began to fall. At night the frosts were hard and when we camped, water froze in the bottles. We woke to find everything beautifully white, air-frosts crystallising every branch and leaf.

At Sivaki began our last and worst stretch of swamp: sixty kilometres of waterlogged bog without a trail. All afternoon we followed the railway track looking out over a flooded ethereal landscape. Tall, dead, marsh grasses rose from stagnant water scattered with the forlorn trunks and leafless branches of dead birch trees. Pushing and carrying the bikes along the railway track, however, was such painful progress that occasionally we tried the remnants of a winter track deep in water. Rivers had become icy and difficult, so cold to wade through that feet and legs quickly numbed. We stopped for the night at a tiny train-stop called To. Only two families lived here and both were drunk but railway workers gave us a cabin. We built a massive fire and slept on the floor having barricaded ourselves in against rats that kept us awake nibbling at the door throughout the night.

The following day we continued pushing and cycling across the swamp, train drivers tooting their horns and waving to us in encouragement. A weird, luminous light lasted all day, the sun never more than a diffuse halo of light behind continual mist. At midday we came to two huts and asked for hot water to make tea. We were invited in by a tipsy man, Volodiya, who apologised for the mess. The chaos was unbelievable, his unmade bed in the middle of the room surrounded by a television, piles of old clothes, countless empty wine and vodka bottles, newspapers, tools, cutlery, dishes, bowls and three alarm clocks all telling a different time. The floor was covered with green tomatoes, put out to ripen. On the table amongst the papers, pelts, bottles and string was a dead pigeon.

'I had a wife before, but they don't like life in a small village – it's too hard for them. But I repair the house myself,' he said with a wave at the patched and half-painted walls. 'I do it all myself.'

At Mukhino we emerged from the swamp and in icy northerly winds collected two boxes of supplies from the post office. There was nowhere to eat but a woman visiting her mother in the village invited us to her home. It was a classic old log cabin, entered through a lean-to full of clothes and boots into one large room painted a bright matt blue with a stove standing in the middle. Half the floorspace was occupied by colourful pumpkins that rose to the ceiling; these apparently were to be cooked to feed the pig and cow during the winter months. The room next door appeared to contain little other than a large brass bed and a vast pile of potatoes. We gave virtually all the food supplies we had collected to Lyena and her mother, something that they refused vigorously at first.

After twenty-six days we emerged from the swamp and found ourselves back on roads again, even if they were only dirt. Shimanovsk was the first town beyond the swamp and there we re-encountered all the brutality of Soviet life that had been so conspicuously absent in the swamp.

Outside Shimanovsk we rejoined an asphalted road, the first we had seen since leaving it at Nerchinsk, 1,000 kilometres back. South of the swamp the flora changed dramatically to short, stunted oaks with black trunks and glorious yellow, golden and blood-red leaves. The transition was sudden and startling, the oaks seeming so full of character and individuality in comparison with the silver birches, pine and fir trees we were used to. After Shimanovsk there was not a single village for ninety kilometres and, despite the change in flora, no sign of wildlife other than a single sable that crossed the road. Close to Svobodny we passed military bases covering a vast area connected by railway lines. Kazakh soldiers manned the railway crossings and tended herds of Soviet army cows at the roadside.

Svobodny was an ugly reminder of the first half of the trip: long faces, a bleak hotel on a massive square with no hot water, a gloomy restaurant with no heating, inadequate lighting and morose waiters. Of the twenty lights in the restaurant nine lacked light bulbs altogether and of the remaining eleven only three were still working. It was cold and dismal. The hotel was full of army officers, bored and glum; they hung around with their hands in their pockets, wearing tall black leather jackboots, gold-edged uniforms and black military caps. Some clutched plastic briefcases – the only prop that ever made them look as if they had anything to do. Eventually they were borne off in an old school bus.

From Svobodny we cycled in rain all day heading due south down the floodplain of the River Zeya past a vast HEP barrage. There was nothing to stop for. Away to the east, semi-flooded grassland was lost in mist and rain. We felt deadbeat and after having cycled 130 kilometres the day before there seemed little chance we could get to Blagoveschensk, 160 kilometres from Svobodny. But wet through as we were, and with nothing to stop for, we thought we might as well continue. We wondered if we had taken a wrong turning when we found tanks lurching out of the bushes and tearing across the road both ahead and behind us. We cycled past an officer watching the manoeuvres from a bridge; huddled in his cloak against the sleeting rain he took no interest in the cyclists pedalling through his military exercise. In a state of near exhaustion we arrived in the dark in Blagoveshchensk.

Blagoveshchensk lay on the bank of the Amur and on the far side lay China. We checked into the Chinese-built 'Friendship' hotel, the best in the city and the thirteenth of the journey. Water and mud cascading from us, we pushed our bikes through the lobby. For the first time in weeks there was hot water and we cared little that we each paid 500 per cent more than Maksim for the privilege. In the hotel's restaurant, Maksim was about to sample his first Chinese food. He stared intently at the noodles, bamboo shoots and chop-suey, and savoured them slowly, fascinated.

'Very interesting!' he said and roared with laughter. When he tasted the beer it was as if he was sampling an unknown drink.

'Chinese beer's very good!' he said, and he looked around him in astonishment at the Chinese lanterns with their hanging silk tassels.

As usual our 'rest' day was spent servicing the bikes, which we did in front of the hotel before a crowd of 200 Chinese tourists. We went to the airport to collect spare parts that we needed: eight new tyres, new chains, freewheels, derailleurs, bearings, crank axle, chainset, headset, oil, grease and gear cables, a thousand kilometres of water and sand having taken their toll.

'How much more of this ugliness can we take?' Gilles asked as we tripped through mud, sand and ditches to get to the broken-down baggage office at the airport.

That day in Blagoveshchensk was hot and sunny; the following day, when we left, rain set in again. We had been unlucky in our choice of year; it was, everyone assured us, an unusually wet Siberian summer.

The country was dead flat and entirely cleared of forest. We could have been in Kazakhstan all over again, except it was cool. It was dark when we stopped after eleven hours' cycling and tried to find the director of a workers' hostel in a small village. In the pitch black Maksim and I lost Howard and Gilles, and spent an hour and a half traipsing through liquid mud. Disconsolate and wet, we eventually found that Howard and Gilles had long been in dry clothes, drinking tea in the hostel. Happily, we were invited to stay.

'Davai! Davai!' the hostel's director told us, enthusiastically, when food was put on the table. *'Kushet! Kushet!'* ('Tuck in! Tuck in! Eat! Eat!') As we discussed the state of the roads ahead we noticed that the director's map marked a number of villages left out on ours. Within seconds, before anyone could stop him, he had ripped the pages out of his atlas and handed them to us.

The next day, after fifty kilometres on an asphalted road, we reached the Buryea River, which could be crossed only by ferry. Waiting for it to return from the far bank we learnt that there was no asphalt on the other side of the river for 350 kilometres.

'It was nice while it lasted,' Howard said philosophically.

The river was wide and gently flowing, dappled by shade from oaks along its banks, and looked like an angler's dream.

'You won't find any fish,' a man told us as we peered down into the water. 'It looks beautiful but it's polluted. There haven't been any fish for five years.'

'What happened?'

'They built factories upstream at Zavatinsk,' he said, 'and everything died.'

We returned to tracks of dirt and soft sand through dense oak forests interspersed with cleared stretches of rough grass. The yellow, greens, reds and golds of the oak leaves were as bright as stained glass, creating a wild landscape of intense beauty. We stopped for a snack in the late afternoon and were about to set off when I noticed what for an instant I took to be a dog stepping out onto the sandy track fifty yards away. A fraction of a second later Maksim dropped the apple he had been eating and froze.

'My God! A bear! . . . With young bears!' Gilles was facing the wrong direction and virtually jumped out of his skin with fright as he whipped round.

The black mother bear was magnificent, her fur the most lustrous jet black. Even on all fours, she was well over waist high. Behind walked three baby bears, each one precisely behind the other. We stayed rooted to the ground, hearing nothing but the pumping of our hearts. Apparently not noticing us, the mother crossed the trail with slow, gently swaying steps, the babies trotting at a faster pace to keep up. Long after they had disappeared into the oaks on the far side we remained motionless, our eyes fixed intently on the spot where they had disappeared.

'Maybe the father is close!' Maksim whispered quietly. Several electrically charged minutes passed before we edged forward and photographed the tracks in the soft sand. Needless to say we cycled the rest of the day with renewed energy, fired by pumping adrenalin, wondering what would have happened had we set off a few seconds earlier and been fifty yards ahead as the bears stepped out onto the track.

Intermittent but heavy rain set in yet again, accompanied by a cold head-wind. The smooth dirt road disappeared yet again into knee-deep clayey mud through which we pushed and slipped. From Arkhara the next day we followed another military road, cycling past a group of officers and soldiers waving red flags. For a while Gilles fell behind but suddenly caught up, cycling at a phenomenal pace and out of breath.

'Another bear!' he gasped. 'It crossed the road right behind you and in front of me. I had to stop but I didn't know whether to turn round and go back, or what. Was he awesome! Far bigger than yesterday's, at least four feet high on all fours. You didn't see anything? He was a hundred yards behind you.' Maksim and I had been talking and had seen and heard nothing.

For two days it was wet and cold, mud and water so deep that we put plastic bags on over our socks and tied them round our legs. At least that way the feet kept warm. Sometimes our hands were so swollen and pink that it took five minutes to get on a pair of gloves. We arrived at Ushurl and slept on the floor of a log cabin, and the next morning I awoke with what felt like minor heartburn. It did not go away.

I set off before the others, telling them I did not think I could cycle very fast. Cycling was excruciatingly painful, and the muscles in my back and shoulders began to ache terribly. Breathing became difficult and painful. Every few hundred metres I had to stop. By the time Gilles, Maksim and Howard caught up with me I was hardly able to pedal without violent stabbing pains in the heart.

'Are the muscles in your arm and hand aching as well?' Gilles asked.

'No.'

'That's good', he reassured me. 'Otherwise, I'd say it was a heart attack.'

We rested for thirty minutes but it made no difference.

'I'll take a truck to the next village,' I said. 'You can catch up with me there. It'll probably pass.' We loaded the bike into the back of a collective farm truck and I was dropped in a tiny village, Ivestnikovo, where I walked to the nearest log cabin.

'May I sit here?' I asked an aged *babushka* with a kindly, wrinkled face, indicating the bench outside her house.

'Of course,' she said, with a smile. 'Would you like tea?'

'Of course he would,' her husband replied on my behalf, and soon I was in the summer kitchen, a separate wooden building beside the house.

'We only have *borscht* here. Would you like some?' Bread and *borscht* were followed by tea and honey, and I sat back, half listening, while the ache spread up into the left side of my neck and travelled down my left arm into the palm of my hand. I reckoned that we were exactly midway between Khabarovsk and Blagoveshchensk, 300 kilometres from a town of any size. I had no medical knowledge but the way I felt was exactly the way I imagined a heart attack must be.

'We have our own bees but this summer has been terrible,' the *babushka* was saying. 'Rain, rain, rain and the bees sat in their hives all summer!'

Three hours later when the others arrived, a dull, powerful ache wracked the entire left side of my body from the waist up. We were shown to an empty house and I lay down, while Howard stoked up the oven.

'He must go to hospital,' Maksim said, and as the pain had increased rather than diminished, we decided that I would go ahead to Khabarovsk by train, accompanied by Gilles. Luckily we had kept close to the Trans-Siberian railway and we cycled in the dark to the railway station, for the 1.00 am train. As usual in Soviet stations there was a dormitory for passengers to sleep in but our entry was blocked by a surly woman in uniform.

'Passports!' she snapped. Maksim explained that mine was elsewhere, in a pannier on the bicycle. 'I need his passport,' she repeated, affronted.

'Why?' Maksim shouted, frustrated by yet another attempt to make life difficult. 'Why do you need his passport? Tell me. Why does he need a passport to lie on a bed? He's ill. He needs to lie down. He's going to hospital in Khabarovsk.'

'Why?' she retorted angrily 'What do you mean, "Why"? It's the rules!' But she let me in, after giving me a look and a half.

A policeman told us to take the bikes out of the ticket hall and the station guard refused to put them on the train until they had been washed and he had been given a bribe.

We knew that Tatiana, whom we had met in Yerofey-Pavlovich, was in Khabarovsk and we had been pushing our pace partly to give Gilles the chance to see her again. Maksim telephoned ahead and left a message that we were arriving by train.

It was odd to be travelling by rail, having seen so many trains hurtle past us in the swamp. This one was clean and comfortable, and designed so that every passenger had a berth. When it started, it set off with a powerful yank that must have jolted a few of the lighter pensioners onto the floor and we were woken in the morning by the wagon attendant who went along the corridor, giving every passenger a sharp twist of the leg. The ticket office of Khabarovsk railway station looked like an evacuation scene. Families were sleeping on mattresses on the station floor with clothes hung up on lines around them. Cooking pots, clothes, parcels, boxes and suitcases were piled about them like refugees who have become accustomed to their plight.

Within minutes we found Tatiana, looking radiant in a thick white jumper and gold necklace and carrying a sleek black handbag. She had only arrived at eight o'clock the previous evening after a thirty-hour train ride from Yerofey-Pavlovich. And although she had not received our message until midnight she was there to meet us at 5.30 am.

As Tatiana had studied pharmacology at the Medical Institute in Khabarovsk for five years she knew the city well and we walked to the hospital, a red-brick building on Lenin Square. At the hospital we had a thirty-minute wait, so we sat outside in the appropriately named 'Central Park of Rest and Relaxation'. Inside, there was little sign of patients or nurses. After scanning the electro-cardiogram the doctor and I had a comical conversation, as we took it in turns to thumb through an English-Russian dictionary in search of words.

'First, I can tell you that your heart is normal,' he said. 'You are suffering from sheer over-exhaustion and you need rest. Your blood pressure is high. The muscles around the heart seized up but not the heart itself. Excessive exertion, lack of salt, inadequate food and cold winds were probably the cause.'

For treatment the doctor recommended potassium, ginseng and a visit to the *banya*. Ginseng was only available for hard currency at the Beriozka shop; for ordinary Russians it was unobtainable.

'Now we go to my uncle,' Tatiana said, as we left. 'You must sleep and eat.'

When Tatiana's uncle had separated from his wife, he had had to move to a small one-room apartment with a tiny kitchen and bathroom. He waved us in and folded two armchairs down into beds; Gilles too was dead tired and ready to drop. But if we slept in the living room where, we wondered, were Tatiana and her uncle going to go?

'And this is my grandmother!' Tatiana said. To our astonishment we turned to see an aged *babushka* sitting on the edge of a bed in the corner. She was so small and motionless that we had not noticed her.

'Does she live here too or is she visiting?'

'She lives here with my uncle,' Tatiana said. 'And now you must sleep.'

'But . . . what about your grandmother?' I said, falteringly. It seemed bad enough that Tatiana and her uncle were being forced to retreat into the kitchen while two mud-spattered foreigners hogged the living room, but sleeping in the grandmother's room while she sat there seemed rather too far beyond the bounds of reasonable behaviour.

'She will sleep too,' Tatiana told us. So all three of us slept in the same room. As the first foreigners the grandmother had met, we must have created a strange impression.

17
THE LAST LEG

K HABAROVSK TOOK US by surprise: it was the most attractive and
civilised city we had seen. Despite being located 10,000 kilometres
east of Moscow, it had a cosmopolitan and dignified air with its three
broad, tree-lined avenues. Karl Marx Street, the main thoroughfare, was
shaded by tall, mature trees, and lined with handsome and substantial
nineteenth-century buildings, washed in pastel hues. From a tranquil
square, public gardens stretched down a steep slope to the Amur that was
busy with barges towing timber down-river towards Sakhalin and the Sea
of Okhotsk. Most striking of all was a relaxed atmosphere that we had
been conscious of only once before – in Irkutsk – and the number of
beautiful women. Restaurants were livelier and people appeared to be
better dressed.

At the Intourist hotel we waited two hours for a meal of which only half
eventually arrived. Even after months in the USSR, it was still hard to get
accustomed to Soviet notions of service. Japanese and American tourists
fared no better, even though they were paying in hard currency. While we
paid eight roubles for a bottle of champagne, they paid the equivalent of
240 and commented on how cheap it was.

On our second day in Khabarovsk, Tatiana arranged for Gilles and me
to have a *banya* and a massage. Only later did we realise that in order to
make the reservation and purchase the tickets she had had to go in person
to the *banya*, miles from the centre, the day before. Telephone reserva-
tions, it appeared, were unknown.

Gilles and I were in our hotel room when there was a tap at the door.
We opened it to find Sasha, our second cyclist, on the threshold.

'What on earth are you doing here?' we asked, dumbfounded.

'I have some things for you,' he said, handing us two spare pumps, balaclava helmets, three pairs of snow mittens, two shirts and a jacket which we had asked Alexei to send us a month before and had subsequently forgotten about.

'You've come from Moscow just to bring us these?' we asked, staggered.

'And I wanted to see you, and the bikes,' he said. He had flown 10,000 kilometres to hand over a few inessential odds and ends and would then fly another 10,000 back. It made no sense at all.

Before we left Khabarovsk Sasha and Maksim tried their utmost to help get permission for me to fly to Petropavlovsk-Kamchatskiy on the Kamchatka peninsula, as I hoped to see Victoria again after arriving at Vladivostok. The whole of the Kamchatka peninsula, however, an area larger than Britain, was officially closed. Only with a letter of invitation stamped by the local *ispalkom*, or executive committee, could a visa be given, and all three *ispalkom*s in Petropavlovsk at city, territorial and regional levels refused permission.

'It's impossible!' Maksim said, putting down the phone. 'Even Russians who don't have relatives living on Kamchatka are not allowed to visit. Five years ago it was opened but after one year the military succeeded in closing it again. It's a military region, too close to Alaska.'

It gave an idea of how sensitive the Soviet military was to security: Petropavlovsk-Kamchatskiy was 3,000 kilometres from Alaska even as the crow flew. But with permission refused there was nothing to be done. Such an official refusal would normally have tempted me to make my own way there all the more but in Siberia the geographical impediments were daunting: neither railway nor road led to the Kamchatka peninsula which by air was 2,000, and by ground 6,000 kilometres away.

After five days in Khabarovsk I felt well enough to leave. By Khabarovsk we had cycled around 10,800 kilometres and I was not going to miss the last 750. As we left Khabarovsk, queues at the bus stops cheered and waved as we cycled by. It was an extraordinary contrast to our departures from Leningrad and Moscow.

'The people of Siberia suffered much,' Maksim said, 'but from suffering they came to honesty and strong will. Happiness is always blind but suffering can help people to understand the value of life. The soul is like a rock and the suffering of a human's soul can make it a diamond. This is why Siberian people are different from the rest.'

We left at 7.00 am in the dark and cycled in heavy rain that lasted all day. Rough asphalt roads, water and headwinds slowed us down so that it took us eleven hours to cover 147 kilometres. Dripping water we begged for tea in a village and were invited in by two pensioners, aged seventy-three and seventy-six. 'Gorbachev! Pah!' the man spat out. '*Perestroika* is lies, rubbish! Before there was everything – vodka, sausage, food, clothes – everything! Since Gorbachev we've had nothing! He's ruining the country. He's given away Eastern Europe for nothing!'

'What about Brezhnev?'

'Yes,' he said, bitterly, 'under Brezhnev there was everything.'

As his wife served us tea and boiling water from the glistening samovar, the conversation turned to the Ussiriisk tiger that still exists in the mountains on the Chinese border.

'I saw a tiger once, only once, as far away as that tree,' he said, pointing to an oak 200 metres away. Eighty *pood*s he must have weighed, but it was a hundred kilometres from here and you won't see one here. They like to eat sheep, goats and small cows, but dogs are their favourite.'

We calculated that with sixteen kilos to one *pood*, our host's tiger must have weighed 1,300 kilos; we would rather not stumble across one. Revived by warmth, tea and biscuits we thanked our hosts, and set off again in the rain.

'I'm fed up with having to beg for things all the time,' Howard said, as we cycled away. 'We have to beg for food, beg for tea, beg for every hotel room, beg for every damned little thing. I hate it. I just want to go in and pay!'

Soaked through, we arrived at Bikin, a dreary town set in a forest of small, stunted oaks. Gilles and I set off in the dark determined to find the *banya* that we had been assured was still open. The directions were simple: 300 metres down on the right. We ploughed around through puddles in pouring rain and the pitch black without success; all we could find were factories. There was no one to ask as the streets were deserted except for a single car, driving slowly with its sidelights on. I turned to ask the driver for directions but before I could wave it down, it slowed of its own accord and a back door was held open from inside.

Out of the darkness a voice spoke in heavily accented English: 'Please – sit down!' We peered inside and could just make out the silhouettes of two uniformed policemen. Unable to find the *banya* and fed up with floundering around in puddles in the pitch black, we climbed in and the car turned round and drove back towards the hotel.

'Have we done something wrong?' I asked Gilles, unconcerned.

'Yes. Six months ago we decided to cycle across the Soviet Union,' he replied. The police, it turned out, only wanted to help and, after transferring to a marked militia car, we drove off again in search of the *banya*. The lights of the building, however, were switched off and it was locked with a massive padlock.

'Soviet Union,' one officer said. 'You can't even wash.' Then we drove to the second *banya* which was closed for repairs.

We drove back to the hotel and told Howard the police were waiting outside to take us to the restaurant.

'Have you guys had your *banya*?' Howard asked.

'No.'

'Jeez! Then what have you been doing for the last hour?'

'Driving around in a police car looking for hot water.'

The restaurant was deserted; only one of the twenty-five tables was in use. A four-man band was playing with distinctly limited enthusiasm for the only occupied table and a lone waitress. The policeman showed us to a table, disappeared into the kitchen and came back to ask us when we thought we would finish our meal.

'Ten o'clock?' we suggested.

'I will come to collect you at ten,' he said and departed.

'Are we under mild house arrest?' I asked Howard, 'or are they being exceptionally friendly?'

The policemen gone, we fell into conversation with the neighbouring table of swarthy Georgians, who requested the waitress to bring us half a litre of Armenian cognac.

'What are Georgians doing here of all places?' Howard asked them.

'Internal exile,' one replied, briefly.

'Why?'

'I don't know!' he said laconically, shrugging his shoulders.

'We've been sent here for a year's exile from Georgia,' said a second. 'There's nothing to do. That's why we were sent here, of course. But you're free.'

'You can say what you want in England,' the third Georgian said, in a low voice. 'In the Soviet Union we cannot. No, not even with Gorbachev. You understand that, do you?'

'Yes, I understand,' I told him.

'Tell people in England!' he said. And when our policeman came back the conversation was abruptly dropped.

As we arrived back at the hotel Maksim arrived on his bike in the dark. He had forgotten the crucial document authorising our journey at Khabarovsk, had taken the train back to get it and then tried to catch up with us by bike. Soaked through, and too late for supper, he had ridden for the last two hours in the pitch black, chased by dogs.

'Terrible!' was all he could say. 'I could only see two metres ahead. Terrible!' The hotel administrator had made a big fuss about giving us the 'luxury suite', which consisted of two cold, damp, interconnecting rooms with an old fridge and a sofa, but no heating, no hot water, a broken television, a curtain rail at a crazy angle and a single dim light bulb in each room. She asked us whether we liked it.

'It's just great!' we said, too tired to explain.

It was fortunate that Maksim had gone back for our document; the next day we came to a police post with barriers across the centre of the road with razor-sharp metal thorns laid in rows on the road in case any vehicle tried to ram its way through. It was only the third time in 11,000 kilometres that we had been asked for our documents on the road. The police were friendly, gave us tea and escorted us by jeep to a restaurant in Guberovo, turning on the red flashing light as we entered town.

We cycled through a landscape of bright autumnal colours. From Skovorodino we had dropped a thousand kilometres south and it was noticeably warmer. It was as if we had abruptly reversed back to the beginning of autumn and were now to experience it all over again. Thick mists that hung around in the early morning lifted to reveal a wild landscape of scrub oak, red, gold and purple, rising to low pointed hills.

In Dalnerechensk we shared a table in the restaurant hotel in the evening with two Soviet army officers who were to retire in four months' time. Both had served for several years in Afghanistan where one year's service counted as three in the USSR; as a result both were eligible to retire on a full pension aged thirty-one.

'And what will you do then?' I asked.

'I want to work in America,' one said.

Some unseen slight or insult sparked off a fight in the restaurant. This time the parties had the decency to move outside, followed by half the other diners. We seemed to be one of the few tables that had not taken sides. After ten minutes the victor came in, his shirt spattered with blood, and sat down again at his table. The officers took no notice of the commotion and continued to talk. 'Normally,' one said, 'we drink three or four bottles of vodka between three of us in the evening.'

'So what?' we said, tired of boasts about how much people could drink.

After the swamp Vladivostok took on a new reality and the last 750 kilometres from Khabarovsk seemed a mere bagatelle. The Chinese border was only a few kilometres west and we passed innumerable military posts, radar installations, barracks and airfields with giant helicopters and silver MiG fighters. Close to the road we came across a tank that had lost part of its track; we climbed onto it to take a few photographs. Minutes later a passing car ground to a halt and an angry face appeared.

'Why are you taking photographs?' a man shouted.

'I don't understand Russian!' Howard shouted back in Russian, and we ignored him.

'You wait!' he shouted. 'There'll be trouble!' and he drove a hundred metres on, pulled in and watched us threateningly, before driving on again.

'It looks like a museum piece, in any case,' I said.

'I don't mind what happens when we get to Vladivostok,' Howard said. 'Once we're there they can chuck us out of the country for all I care and they'll be doing us a favour.'

We had anticipated an excellent road from Blagoveshchensk to Vladivostok. On the Soviet road-map it was marked with thick double lines as a motorway but the first third was a dirt track, a playground for black bears, and the rest pot-holed asphalt. Only a hundred kilometres from Vladivostok did a good road begin.

The landscape for the last two days of our journey was not so beautiful, however. Perhaps once it had been, but a scattering of barracks, factories and small towns was enough to dispel the magical beauty of the Taiga we had emerged from. The oak-covered rocky hills opened out into a broader, tamer landscape across which we could see far into China. Even the road bridges here had sentry boxes at either end but the only soldier we saw on duty missed us as we cycled over while he was gazing into the river.

The breadth of the Soviet Union we had come across innumerable police posts beside the roads, half of them now deserted, where the police had previously checked identity documents.

'What do they all do now?' I asked Maksim.

'They sit in offices instead,' he replied.

'But what do they do now they don't have to check documents?'

'They don't *do* anything,' he said. 'They exist.'

In the evening of 2 October a car drew up beside us, driven by a professional cycle trainer, Sergei, who had been in the Soviet cycle team; intrigued by our journey he invited us to stay with him in 'Vladi', as he called it. Before departing he promised to cycle out and escort us into the city the following morning.

We had stopped, by chance, next to a nearly built house in which we were invited to spend the night by the owner, the director of a nearby cement factory. He introduced us to Victor, a sailor in the Soviet Pacific fishing fleet, who had something of the sailor's swagger, born of foreign ports. His terms of employment were handsome by Soviet standards: 560 roubles and $150 per month for a year while aboard ship, and then an entire year off work during which time he continued to receive 560 roubles, twice the national average salary.

'And what do you do during the year when you're not working?' I asked him.

'Work!' he replied, with a grin.

We walked to the cement factory where, to get to the *banya*, we passed through a room with over 150 fridges. Why so many fridges in a cement factory? I peeped inside one to find a pair of boots and dirty work clothes hung up on pegs. When the factory was being built, the director explained, there had been a *defitsit* of cupboards and a surplus of fridges.

The next morning, 3 October, we set out for Vladivostok and met our friend, Sergei, the cycle trainer, on an Italian-made Hygina racing cycle, looking every inch the professional.

As we cycled towards Vladivostok, I asked Maksim how he intended to celebrate our arrival.

'When I arrive in Vladi, he said, laughing, 'I want to throw my bike into the sea. I've had enough of cycling. I want to walk! To run! To read newspapers! To go to the theatre! To the cinema!'

Howard, too, was in characteristic form as we cycled the last forty kilometres down the Vladivostok peninsula.

'Simon,' he said, 'this time, we've nailed this son of a bitch!'

Vladivostok lies at the end of a short peninsula so long before the city came into view we caught sight of a pale grey-blue sea – the Sea of Japan. It was our first glimpse of sea since leaving the Baltic on 21 April, 175 days and virtually 12,000 kilometres earlier; it held the same emotion for us as the first sight of land does to a mariner. As if in recognition that nothing could stop us now from reaching our destination, the last two days were stunningly beautiful with hot summer sunshine.

Vladivostok occupies a dramatic location on steep hills, scrubby and forested, almost volcanic in appearance. New tower blocks were scattered over the hillsides, dwarfing the remaining old, painted, wood houses surrounded by listing grey fences and sheds. Eventually we rounded a corner to a panoramic view of the bay of Vladivostok, alive with white and red merchant shipping, and the blue-grey hulks of naval frigates and destroyers. Within the bay the deep blue water sparkled brightly in the sunshine.

With only one set of worn-out brakes it was a miracle that we descended the precipitous hills into the city without mishap. We cycled down onto the quay where people strolled quietly arm-in-arm; just 200 yards from the water's edge, Gilles had a final puncture and so pushed his bike to the sea. We cycled across a beach of golden sand, stripped and plunged headlong into the sea. The water was warm and the sand hot from the sun. For a long time we did nothing. We felt liberated, victorious, exuberant. As we lay on the beach a woman came over to ask where we were from. When she heard that we had arrived, that very moment, by bicycle from Leningrad, she was close to tears. She fumbled around in her handbag and brought out a simple metal bottle-opener.

'Here,' she said, 'take this as a gift. I'm sorry but I have nothing better. It's all I've got on me.'

'It's the best conceivable present,' I said, accepting it gratefully. 'There's only one thing we want to do – and that's celebrate.'

'Ah! We don't have any beer in the city!' she replied with a sad smile. 'But maybe it will be useful for you one day.'

Beer being absent, we celebrated on the quayside, Soviet fashion, with ice cream.

Behind us, on the steep hillsides, buildings were dotted amongst dense green woodland, autumn only just tinging the leaves with golds and yellows. In the very heart of the city, fishing ships were tied up in the harbour, and seagulls wheeled and cried overhead and fought for scraps. The streets were flooded with naval officers and ratings in traditional blue and white sailor's uniforms, the blue ribbons of their naval caps trailing in the wind. Vladivostok, the headquarters of the Soviet Pacific fleet, is the Soviet Union's only warm-water port in the East.

'When I saw the first foreigner here in 1988,' Sergei told us, 'I was astonished. But we still see very few. Many Russians are shocked that the city has been opened to foreigners but others hope that it will be turned into a free economic zone. Then we might actually see some change. Up to now the city has been controlled by the military and the Communist Party who have resisted change. We're so close to Japan that this area could be thriving but so far the military has prevented this. Even now there are no international flights from here, not even to Japan, which is only one and a half hours away by plane. The military doesn't want the place to be successful economically; for them it's just a good naval base – the bays are perfect natural harbours and the water never freezes in winter. They'd rather there weren't any changes.' In the centre of the city Sergei pointed to the one impressive skyscraper. 'We call it the Pentagon,' he said. 'Communist Party headquarters.'

Sergei's apartment was not only large by Soviet standards but he had recently acquired the apartment above too. As a professional cycle trainer Sergei might have earned 250–300 roubles a month but he wore stylish clothes, foreign dark glasses, Addidas training shoes, had a Sony television and video recorder, and drove a Nissan Laurel that he had told us cost 300,000 roubles. Assuming the most generous estimate of 300 roubles a month, it would have taken eighty-three years' gross salary to afford the Nissan alone. And Sergei was a young man. We wondered how he managed it.

'I am a partner in a clothing cooperative,' he said – but he was not keen to elaborate, saying only that he had a workshop where the clothes were made. Several days later, however, when he'd got the measure of us, he showed us his workshop: it was nothing other than the third room in his apartment, and consisted of three old sewing and two knitting machines. His wife and three friends were the other partners.

'You do this yourself?' I asked him. In reply he sat down at a machine and began sewing a pair of swimming trunks.

'Sometimes I can make thirty a day,' he said.

'And how much do they sell for?'

'In the shop, for fifty roubles each. The shop takes ten and I get forty.' That made 1,200 roubles for a day's work; in three days' work, assuming that they all sold, he could earn the equivalent of his yearly salary. A jean jacket sold for 500 roubles, twice the average national monthly salary, and a sequined blouse for 300.

'Don't you have a problem selling them at these prices?' I asked.

'No. The problem is buying material from the state shops. There just isn't any left, but now cooperatives are starting up to make material too. If we get a free economic zone here in the next two to three years, Vladi will be a boom town.'

The next day Sergei took us to a beach outside Vladivostok for a swim. It was half an hour's drive from the centre, yet we could have been a thousand kilometres back in the Taiga, it was so unspoilt and deserted. With no right or need for people to buy land for business or housing the coast was pristine, with oaks descending the hills to a beach of white sand.

The beauty of the coast had been preserved by inaction and restrictions that prevented private development. Perhaps here, it might be felt, was a Communist virtue: prevention of the commercialisation and exploitation of a magnificent piece of coastline. The truth is that if the coast had had any useful function it would have been exploited by the state long before. As we had seen ourselves and heard from countless Russians the state was unsurpassed in its despoliation and pollution of the land, developing anything of economic value with little regard for ecological or environmental consequences. The construction of the Baikal-Amur railway, where not a single rouble was set aside for environmental purposes, and the destruction of the Aral Sea, which has shrunk by a third and resulted in the salination of huge areas of Uzbekistan and Kazakhstan, are but two cases. What makes such despoliation so common in the USSR is that no bodies exist to check and oppose state decisions. Pressure groups have not been tolerated and can only have limited effect, in any case, where the state has held not only the trump cards but the entire pack. In the West the state keeps private groups such as businesses within the law. But in the USSR there is nothing to keep the state within the law or to call it to account.

Even if the beach we were on had survived by accident, rather than intention, one might be tempted to conclude that at least it had survived for people to enjoy. Again the reality was somewhat different. There was no public transport to this part of the coast and it was accessible only to the small percentage of people privileged enough to own a car.

We had to celebrate the end of our journey in some sort of style, so we bought champagne, *na levo*, from a restaurant kitchen. Bottles priced at three roubles changed hands for thirty; champagne had not been seen in the shops for weeks. Once the initial euphoria was over, however, we realised just how shattered we all were.

'What have we done today?' Howard said at the end of our second day. 'It took us from 9.00 am to 2.00 pm to go to the post office to make two telephone calls and fix the date for our tickets back to Moscow. That's just great! This afternoon we went to a restaurant and managed to negotiate two bottles of champagne for $3. That's just great too! I'm *tired* of negotiating! We've had to negotiate *everything* for the last six months. There are two great restaurants here, great by Soviet standards, but bad where I'm going to be in a week's time. So: I'm not thinking any more.'

We were too spent to have much desire to look round Vladivostok. We looked up Igor, who had been so hospitable to us at Dzhalinda on the Amur, and found him in his student hostel, perched on the very top of an impossibly steep, muddy hill.

He arranged for us to meet in a bar, to which he brought two more bottles of champagne. The bar had two drawbacks: firstly there was no drink, a matter of secondary importance as we, like Igor, had brought our own. Secondly there were no chairs or tables. They had just disappeared. Even Igor seemed a little non-plussed and we left, no one feeling in the mood to sit, cross-legged, in an empty room.

'This is a military bar,' Igor told us as he led the way into another building further down the street. 'They should have chairs here.'

'I always wondered why people joined the armed forces,' Gilles said, as we went in. 'Now I know – to sit down.' Inside there was nothing to reveal why it should have been a 'military bar' other than the precise arrangement of empty plastic chairs and tables. It was quiet and deserted.

'The place is swinging!' Howard said.

Altogether we were eight including Sergei, Igor's girlfriend, Tania, and brother, Andrei, and another girl, Natasha. Andrei was a merchant mariner of massive build, like his brother, but quiet and less jovial than Igor. Early in the evening two small girls, about ten years old, came in to the bar and sat shyly in the corner. Not long after Andrei went up and chatted to them and to the waitress before he came back quietly to the table, his absence having gone largely unnoticed.

'Does Andrei know them?' I asked Igor.

'No. He bought them some ice cream,' Igor said. 'They didn't have any money.'

None of the Russians was keen to go to a restaurant which, for them, was prohibitively expensive, but we had roubles and insisted that they come as our guests. The restaurant was lively and full, and the band, dressed in garish shirts and flared trousers, played the same songs we had heard ever since we set foot in Leningrad. At the next table a man sat slumped in his chair, surrounded by three empty places and half-eaten dishes. His head lolled lower and lower until it touched his soup plate. A little later two attractive women came and sat at his table. They clearly did not know him but they poured his wine into two clean glasses and helped themselves to the untouched dishes. When one of them noticed me watching she shot a quick smile and shrugged her shoulders. At one point the man's head half-rose from his soup plate and he looked at them with clouded eyes. They greeted him amicably but continued to drink his wine until his head sank once again to the table. The waitress looked worried; who was responsible for the bill? When they had finished I asked one of the girls to dance.

'Enjoyed your dinner?' I asked her on the dancefloor.

'We all have to live somehow. You're foreign, aren't you?' she said with a hint of reproof.

'Yes,' I said, 'but being foreign isn't a crime here any more. Vladivostock is an open city.'

'It shouldn't be,' she said.

'Why not?'

'It means there's less for everybody else.'

I remarked that I had not seen a single foreigner in the city.

'No, it's country people from Siberia and the Far East provinces that we object to. Now that they are allowed into the city, they buy everything. There's nothing left in the shops.'

At the end of the evening the police went round the restaurant as usual prodding drunks to get on their way. Our friendly drunk lifted his head from the soup plate and stared blearily at the police. Realising dimly it was time to go, he rose unsteadily to his feet and walked head first into the wall before being escorted downstairs.

As our plane to Moscow left at 5.00 am, we went directly from the restaurant to the airport. Igor and Tania wanted to come with us to see us off, but as the airport was forty kilometres from the town and the plane left at such an unsocial hour we tried to dissuade them. Besides there was no room in the van.

'Then we'll take a bus,' Igor said with a big smile. 'We want to be with you.' And they did, arriving at 1.00 am with a plastic flagon of beer that they had somehow secured on the way. While Howard and Gilles slept, I sat up and talked with Igor and Tania, until overcome totally with sleep. They returned to Vladivostok in the morning on the first bus.

It was characteristic of the official attitude to foreigners that we had been shown to the VIP lounge, of which we were the only occupants; in the morning 280 men, women and children were kept waiting on the tarmac beside the plane until we had been escorted by a stewardess to our seats. But first we handed our bikes up into the hold, marking the end of a journey.

There is surely no better way of appreciating a flight than cycling 12,000 kilometres. Flying for us was almost as curious a sensation as walking in space. Apart from a terrible screeching sound from the engines, the nine-hour flight was uneventful. A stewardess came down the passageway with a trolley on which three items were spread for sale: a single bottle of perfume, thin plastic bags and Bulgarian toothpaste. The inflight meal consisted of a scrawny and eerily grey chicken leg, a hunk of cucumber, a piece of bread, and coffee. There were no alcoholic drinks – nothing other than *kvass*. Still hungry after our lunch we made our way to the steward's cabin where we befriended George, the steward, who handed us entire cucumbers, tinned fish and Armenian cognac. From time to time George took a nip of cognac from an old whisky bottle in his hip pocket.

'I mustn't!' he said, after the seventh swig. 'My wife will kill me if I come home drunk!'

George earned 300 to 350 roubles a month as an Aeroflot steward on internal flights, 'but if I fly to Leipzig I get paid seven American dollars, the equivalent of 140 roubles for a four-hour flight. To make the same money in the USSR I have to make three return flights to Vladivostok from Moscow, a total of fifty-four hours. It doesn't make sense, does it? The last time I flew to Buenos Aires I got paid $28, which I spent on women's clothes. When I got back to Moscow I sold them for 8,000 to 9,000 roubles.'

'So you made three years salary from that single flight!'

'Yes. But you have no idea how hard those flights are to get.'

When I asked George if I could have a look at the pilot's cabin he was very upset.

'I'm sorry. Normally we could have done it for you, but today we only have one pilot. We must let him concentrate.'

'There's no co-pilot on this nine-hour flight?' I asked, astonished.

'Not today.'

'So if the pilot has a heart attack you'll take over, will you, George?'

'Yes,' he replied, with a grin. 'Unless one of passengers happens to be a pilot.' But by now George had finished the whisky bottle. We were back in our seats when we saw him coming up the passageway, pushing a trolley. He dispensed coffee and *kvass* at random, ashen-grey and unsteady on his feet. He was trying his utmost to look professional and sober but as he passed he gave us a sickly grin.

Moscow was grey and grim, rain sheeting down in gusts. Alexei and Sasha met us at the airport, and we drove to Sasha's apartment on the outskirts. Maksim was with us, coming to Moscow to meet Este, his new employer, for the first time. Originally he had planned to stay in Vladivostok and work once we got there, but had changed his plan.

'My mother is not well. She has a problem with her heart due to her difficult life,' Maksim said. 'I need to help her but this journey was my first chance to earn some money. Before I had nothing. But I have finished with my work in Krasnoyarsk. I will never work again for 200 roubles a month!' He spat in disgust. 'Never!'

Maksim, Howard, Gilles and I with four bikes, sixteen panniers, four sleeping bags and tents squeezed into Sasha's apartment which consisted of one bedroom/living room, and a separate kitchen and bathroom. Since we had first met Sasha in Leningrad he had married and Lyena, his new wife, greeted us with great affection. After one night with the six of us, Howard sleeping under and me on top of the kitchen table, Sasha and Lyena moved to her mother's apartment, giving us their entire flat – and they came round to join us in the evening. It was a quintessentially Russian gesture.

18
JOURNEY'S END

BACK IN MOSCOW, none of us was in the mood for sightseeing.
'I want one thing,' Howard said. 'Out!'

After an afternoon being filmed by CNN and interviewed in Red
Square by Moscow Radio, we sorted and packed 800 pounds of gear
and equipment. One thing remained to be done: Alexei told us we were
to have a meeting with SovIntersport before we left. This was curious as
SovIntersport had shown no interest whatsoever in meeting us when we
had arrived in Moscow in May. When Gilles had flown back ill to
Moscow in July he had briefly met Vyshnikov, the deputy director of
SovIntersport, who had told him that he would have to pay for the ten
nights he had spent in the Moscow hotel in US dollars. But as Gilles
knew the bill had been paid in roubles, he had told Vyshnikov that he
would pay for it – but in roubles. We felt sure therefore that the meeting
with SovIntersport was not entirely to congratulate us on the successful
completion of our trip.

After meeting Vyshnikov, who resembled a Western businessman
more than anyone we had seen in six months, we were ushered into the
office of the director, a thin, anaemic man in a black suit with a drawn,
pinched face and sunken eyes. No one could have looked a less likely
candidate to preside over a sports organisation or less interested to meet
us. Once an aide had whispered into his ear, he remembered who we
were and shook our hands feebly.

Seated around a long, polished table he began his speech in a slow
mechanical voice as if he had given it a thousand times before and no
longer even heard his own words. It was hackneyed propaganda; we were
astonished that anyone still spoke in such a stilted, clichéd language, even

though lip service was paid to *glasnost* and *perestroika*. We might as well have been listening to a speech on production targets for sugar beet.

'One person believes in God,' he continued, in a lacklustre voice, 'one believes in the Party, everybody is different . . . It gives me great pleasure to present you with these roses' – a dead-pan expression on his face – 'in recognition of your accomplishment, and these pens and self-adhesive labels. Please advise your friends that we are interested in further cooperation with foreign sportsmen.' We were each then presented with four thorny roses, two self-adhesive labels and a biro with such a flimsy tip that it bent as one tried to write with it.

Howard, Gilles, Maksim and I stared at him. Here was a high-ranking member of the *nomenklatura*, one of the élite whose decisions determined so fatefully the lives of the people we had met on our journey. Everything about him was chilling. His speech over, our meeting with the director of Este and Vyshnikov began.

'We have a few small matters to settle,' Vyshnikov told us ominously, 'and then you will be free to go.' The director of Este, not appearing to relish his role, stood up and began.

'For your flights back to Moscow, for Gilles's flight to Moscow and back to Irkutsk in July, for his stay in the Moscow hotel and for the extra days – by which you overran the expected duration of the trip – we have to invoice you for \$2,305. Of course, you do not have to pay this instant if satisfactory arrangements can be made for it to be paid from abroad.'

This was the limit. We had expected to pay for Gilles's hotel and the flights when illness had compelled him to return to Moscow mid-journey but an invoice for \$2,305 . . . We had specifically and clearly asked SovIntersport to buy aeroplane tickets for us from Vladivostok to Moscow on condition that they could be paid for in roubles.

'It's not possible for foreigners,' Vyshnikov said, 'to buy tickets in roubles, so if you had bought them yourselves you would have had to pay in dollars.' In fact we had bought Gilles's ticket from Krasnoyarsk *ourselves* at the airport – and had paid for it in roubles. This took them by surprise. Moreover, we had the Vladivostok–Moscow tickets – paid for in roubles – in our hands; the price, 134 roubles, was clearly marked. So, we enquired about the extra \$1,260 demanded for having 'overrun the expected duration of [our] trip'.

'Your journey overran by fourteen days. At \$30 per person a day that is \$90 a day for fourteen days, or \$1,260.'

'Overran from what?'

'From 21 September.'

'Where did you get 21 September from?' Howard asked. 'I've never heard that date mentioned before.'

'That's five months from the day you left Leningrad.'

'But why five months? There was never any mention of the trip lasting five months.'

'Este's agreement with SovIntersport was based on your journey taking five months.'

'But I signed an agreement with Vyshnikov, not with you,' Howard told the director of Este. 'And that agreement had no dates.'

'We expected the journey to be finished by 21 September,' Vyshnikov said, lamely.

'We had no set date on the original agreement by which we had to finish,' Howard said. 'Over the eighteen months we negotiated no time period was ever mentioned. Our agreement was Leningrad–Vladivostok, internal expenses covered. Where's the date? Show me the date.' But SovIntersport had no document with a date on and neither did we. In fact neither party had signed a contract, SovIntersport never having come up with one, despite having had a year and a half to do so. To add to the confusion we found that another organisation we had not heard of before, a new cooperative called 'Konkord', was involved.

'The object of SovIntersport is to earn hard currency,' Howard said, at which Vyshnikov winced visibly. Howard was coming into his own. 'If Este, Konkord and SovIntersport made an agreement between themselves, that's fine. But we have only one agreement and that's with SovIntersport. And it was Leningrad–Vladivostok, period. We wouldn't have used the airplane tickets had we known we would have had to pay for them in dollars. We made that very clear, but we were told they were 134 roubles, so we flew rather than take the train. We didn't have any problems buying an airplane ticket in roubles in Krasnoyarsk and maybe we wouldn't have done in Vladivostok either.'

'You spent more money than we anticipated,' Vyshnikov continued, changing tack. 'We have to change the dollars you paid us at the official rate with the Soviet State Bank and that rate is not the same as the tourist rate. The rate at which businesses handling foreign currency are compelled to change is 0.5675 roubles to the dollar. We have no choice in this. It is Soviet law. That is, we received 5,675 roubles for the $10,000.'

'That is all?' Howard said.

'Yes.'

'But you paid the Soviet cyclist who was with us thirty roubles a day, right?'

'Yes,' the director of Este said, uneasily.

'Thirty roubles a day for one month equals 900 a month and we had a cyclist with us for six months – that is, 5,400 roubles, yes?' Howard said, working the figures out on a calculator. 'That leaves just 275 roubles to pay for Gilles's, Simon's and my expenses, *and* profit for Este, Konkord and SovIntersport. It doesn't seem to add up, does it, Mr Vyshnikov?'

SovIntersport and Este were at a loss as to what to say. Without a pocket calculator between them they were forced to make long-hand multiplications on a sheet of paper. One by one they abandoned their demands. The interpreter, a spirited girl, was reduced to a trembling wreck. Half-way through she requested permission to smoke but her hands trembled so much she could not light her cigarette without assistance. Our knowledge of Russian was good enough to understand that she was presenting our case very favourably – an unexpected ally. At the most heated point of the debate, Moscow television arrived to film us and each side withdrew to assess the battlelines. Psychologically, we knew we had won.

'Everyone is allowed to choose their own punishment,' Vyshnikov declared, threateningly. 'This is the first time we have had such problems. There is nothing further to discuss.'

We had defended ourselves on a matter of principle and felt completely justified in resisting what was little better than wholesale extortion.

Throughout the whole of the proceedings Maksim kept his head down and said nothing. For him to witness people arguing heatedly with, and contradicting, high-ranking *nomenklatura* was a new and unsettling experience, as bizarre for him as it would be for us to see someone wrangling publicly with the Pope or the Queen. We paid in roubles, and as we left we thanked the interpreter for her help and courage.

'It's not true that it's the first time there have been problems,' she said, sadly. 'It always happens.'

'For a while I wondered whether our final days in Moscow might not be spent in jail.'

'It would at least make the perfect ending for your book,' Gilles said.

(Three months later, in France, I received a letter from Alexei. 'As regards our slight misunderstanding at the end of our programme,' he wrote, 'I think it's pure nonsense and doesn't matter at all. After some time my colleagues felt regret about it too. Now we see it as just a funny episode – no offence meant. It's just nothing.')

That evening in Moscow, I telephoned the interpreter and arranged to meet her. She had worked for SovIntersport for several years; it gave her an occasional opportunity to travel abroad and she had been once to the United States.

'I loved America,' she said. 'I loved Chicago. The people were so friendly and happy. It was the atmosphere I liked. People had time in their hearts to laugh, to smile – so different from here.'

On our final day in the Soviet Union we gathered with our four Russian cyclists: Vitale, Sasha, Sergei and Maksim, together with Lyena and other friends of Sasha's. Vitale had spent the summer looking after his arthritic mother and his father, who had come out of hospital, and he looked extremely tired.

'I have no plans for the future yet,' he said. 'I cannot plan anything at the moment.' Sergei was unchanged and had recovered from his third-degree burns. His brother had at long last secured an apartment so that by his fortieth birthday Sergei would have a bedroom to himself. Sasha, happily married to Lyena, was optimistic about the future.

'One day,' he said, 'we may even get to visit you in France!'

Howard and Gilles flew home, while I left by rail. Vitale, Sasha, Sergei, Maksim, Lyena, Tatiana, Natasha, Alexei and his wife, Ludmilla, came to see me off with presents of homemade cakes, apples and books, generous to the last.

Six months exactly after we had pulled into the Finland Station in Leningrad and on the day my visa expired, I left from Moscow's Bye-lorussia railway station. Between Minsk and Brest on the Soviet-Polish border we passed long trains pulling Soviet tanks and huge wagons of potatoes back from Poland. Fourteen hours after leaving Moscow we pulled into Brest and border guards knocked at the cabin door. I was asked to step into the corridor while guards checked to see that no one was hiding in the locker under the seat while the wheels were changed to ones appropriate for the width of the European railway gauge. Security was tight: only passengers with tickets and visas to the West were allowed onto the Europe-bound platform, while Soviet border guards patrolled the railway tracks with dogs looking under and between the wagons.

The first impression of Poland was how well-ordered the towns and countryside were. Gone were the dilapidated buildings, the peeling paint, the worn-out areas in front of apartment blocks, the general shambles. Small country roads were asphalted; houses were painted and neatly enclosed by fences. Most striking of all were the new churches, the wayside shrines and crosses made of wood standing in fields or beside the road.

The number of people working in the fields was remarkable; every-where people appeared to be digging, hoeing, weeding and ploughing with horses. Carts, laden high with hay or potatoes, stood in the fields. Men spreading manure onto the fields from the back of a horse-drawn cart was something we had not seen in six months.

Another extraordinary contrast to the USSR was to see houses scattered in the landscape, small, individual, personal houses. They appeared to be well built and well maintained; many were new, neatly painted and had flowerbeds. That people were living independently in their own houses seemed remarkably reassuring.

Looking out over this more intimate, personal landscape, it struck me that it was the collectivisation of Soviet society that most powerfully divided Russia from Europe. Despite the horses ploughing in the fields, Poland immediately felt European in a way that Russia never had. The streets, the churches, the houses, the landscape all breathed a European history and culture, far removed from that of Russia. Harvest was in progress, and potatoes, carrots and cabbages were carefully stacked in wooden crates. In this seemingly insignificant detail there spoke a world of difference. In the Soviet Union, everything would have been thrown straight into a single trailer, and been half crushed and wasted in the process. Instead of vast fields, stretching to the horizon, the land was divided into small, intensively cultivated, strips: first of dry yellow maize, then cabbages, carrots, then a stretch of manured field, a strip of potatoes, clover, yellow rape and then ploughed land and orchards. Although the land was as flat as it had been east of the Polish-Soviet border, it could not have looked more different.

In Germany we stopped briefly in Cologne with just enough time to get to a food shop. Even after only six months in the USSR I was shocked by the quantity, variety and quality of the food for sale. The train shed carriages as it moved through Europe until we arrived at Calais. The only other passengers in the remaining Soviet carriage were two Ukrainian brothers on their way to visit a cousin in Coventry whom they had never met. They were both engineers and although in their fifties they had an innocent, child-like air. It was their first visit abroad and they were at sea, neither speaking a word of English. They had been allowed to change roubles to the tune of £200 for their three-week stay. All they had in the way of luggage were two small suitcases and when Fyodor opened one to give me a painted wooden egg, I saw it contained nothing but presents. Their modest belongings fitted into the second suitcase.

At Dover I steered them towards the non-EEC immigration channel, which they approached like lambs to the slaughter-house, looking around them in amazement at the unfamiliar buildings and incomprehensible signs.

'How long are you visiting?' the immigration officer asked them with a jerk of the head. Oblivious to the fact that they had been asked a question, they continued to gaze around them.

'Get Bill for me, Steve,' the officer said in a tired voice. 'We've got a couple of Russkies here.' The interpreter came over while I listened from a distance.

'How long are you visiting?' the interpreter asked in Russian.

'Three weeks,' Fyodor said.

'And then you're going back?'

'Yes!' he replied, surprised at such a question.

'What are you going to do in Britain? Visit your cousin? He *says* he's going to visit his cousin,' the interpreter told the officer.

'Ask him how long his cousin has been in Britain.' The interpreter put the question.

'How long has your cousin lived in Britain? . . . He says he was *born* in Britain.'

'Are they brothers?' asked the official.

'Are you brothers?' asked the interpreter. They nodded simultaneously. 'You are or you aren't? I can't tell! You are! OK, You're twins? They're twins,' he said to the officer. 'I couldn't tell to start with, they nod so much.'

'Ask them what their work is.'

'What's your work back home?' the interpreter asked. 'They're engineers of some sort, oil engineers.'

'Have they got tickets home?'

'Have you got tickets home?' asked the interpreter.

'Yes,' Fyodor replied, not realising the question meant that he had to produce them.

'Well, let's see them then,' the officer said, impatiently, as if talking to half-wits. 'Yes, they look in order.' At this point the officer sitting at the next podium leant across. 'One of them's got a prison number tattooed on his fingers,' he said maliciously.

'Oh, he has, has he?' the interpreter said, as if the news confirmed his worst suspicions. 'Which hand? Which fingers?' And all three stretched forward, straining to see the prison number, the officer half-raised out of his seat. Fyodor and Alyosha, not knowing what was being discussed, stepped sideways and looked round behind them at the floor to see what was attracting so much interest.

'You sure?' the first officer asked.

'Definite. I saw it. Now he's trying to cover it up,' he said triumphantly. And indeed Fydor was trying to hide his hand, which he had realised at last was the source of the fuss.

'Can I see?' said the interpreter, pointing at his hand. He peered at it and shrugged his shoulders. 'Can't tell!' he said.

The train for London had just departed when we arrived at Dover railway station and the next one would arrive there at 1.00 am. As the train rattled towards Victoria I asked Fyodor about his tattoo.

'It's my initials!' he said, embarrassed. 'I had it done when I did my naval service.'

It seemed unlikely that there would be a train to Coventry at one in the morning, besides which Fyodor and Alyosha could hardly afford it. Knowing that a coach would be cheaper we walked to Victoria coach station which was locked up, the first bus not leaving until 8.00 in the morning. Pushing the trolley we made our way back to the railway station, by which time it was 1.30 am.

'There won't be any trains till the morning now, guv,' a ticket inspector told me. 'Your friends want to lose everything, do they?' he went on. I spun round to find that Fyodor had wandered off like a sleepwalker while Alyosha was gazing into space. The trolley, containing all our earthly possessions, was on its own in the concourse. I ran after it and grabbed Alyosha by the arm.

'You've got to look after our bags!' I told him fiercely. 'You've got to look at them! At them!'

'Fall asleep here for a moment and the lot'll be gone,' the inspector said.

'Is there nowhere cheap to stay near here?' I asked him.

'Cheap? Plenty of cheap hotels, if you call £60 each cheap.'

'But nowhere else?'

'No. But don't let your eye off your bags if you want anything in the morning. These dossers are quick buggers.'

Alyosha had wandered off again. I saw him being approached by an evil-smelling down-and-out, who held out his hand for money. Stretched between Fyodor and the trolley, by the time I had made it over to him, Alyosha was holding out a pocketful of English and Russian change from which the drunk was selecting the £1 coins.

'You mustn't give money to these people,' I said, desperately. 'They're *bad*,' I said, unable to think of the appropriate Russian word. I suddenly felt as if I had two children in my charge, for whom I alone was responsible . . .

It was out of the question for Fyodor and Alyosha to stay in a hotel: £60 would have swallowed up sixty per cent of the funds for their three-week stay in a single night. I had nowhere to put them up; I was hoping to stay with my sister in her tiny flat which could hardly accommodate me, let alone two Ukrainians. Nor could I afford to pay for them to stay in a hotel.

There seemed no option but for them to wait in the station until dawn when they could catch the first bus. If they stayed on their own, however, it was obvious they would lose everything. Both were like utter innocents; they appeared to have no idea that anyone could possibly harbour a desire to harm them. Their only chance of surviving till daylight was if I remained with them, which I resolved to do.

'We have to wait here,' I told them. 'Hotels are too expensive.'

'Can we go to the sleeping hall?' Alyosha asked.

'There aren't any,' I said, irritated less at the question than at the absence of what seemed such an obvious facility to provide. We walked round in vain looking for somewhere to sit down.

'Why are there no benches to sit on?' Fyodor asked, surprised.

'Probably because if there were benches,' I said, thinking about it for the first time and indicating the scattering of drunks and down-and-outs covered with blankets, 'these people would sleep on them all the time.'

'Don't they have a home?' Fyodor asked, looking at the huddled figures.

'Well,' I said. 'No, they probably don't. No, I don't suppose they do.'

We sat down on our bags to weather the cold hours of the early morning and I kept a wary eye on Alyosha every time he wandered off, gazing around him in wonder. On the steps of Lloyds Bank a deranged man ranted and raved, scratching and moaning in a loud voice. From time to time he jumped up and marched around woodenly, shouting and muttering. At one point he bumped into Alyosha who, wandering around, apologised in Ukrainian. Fyodor was particularly intrigued by the black guards and ticket inspectors, never having seen a Negro before.

At dawn I helped them purchase their tickets and saw them onto a coach. But before we left a youth dropped a Coca-Cola can as he passed before us and kicked it vigorously across the concourse. It spun across to the far side of the station.

'Why did he do that?' Alyosha asked, looking at me with a puzzled expression. Why had he done it? I asked myself. I tried to think but my mind remained a blank. I had not the faintest idea. I was half-tempted to run after him and ask him.

I was beaten.

'I don't know,' I said wearily, 'I just don't know!'

EPILOGUE

SIX MONTHS IS a long and a short time to spend in a foreign country – long enough to gain some insight into a different attitude of mind and culture, and short enough to realise that we had but scratched the surface of an unfamiliar world.

Gorbachev's overthrow and the putsch by hardline Communist Party leaders in August 1991 did not come as a complete surprise. During our journey it had felt as if we were passing through a country teetering on the edge of momentous change, being drawn like a ship at sea ever closer to the centre of a maelstrom. A sense of almost inevitable disaster hung in the air and civil war was a prospect that few Russians dismissed out of hand.

What was a surprise was the coup's rapid and dramatic collapse. Few Russians themselves could in 1990 have predicted that Boris Yeltsin would receive support from the Soviet military *and* the KGB in the event of a coup. Over the years Gorbachev had amassed a range of executive powers that exceeded even those held by Stalin and the fear that no constitutional provisions existed to prevent them being used to other ends, should he be overthrown, came close to being realised. Old habits, however, die hard and the Russian tendency to place absolute faith in the capacity of a strong leader to solve the nation's ills is likely to endure.

Yeltsin's popularity and meteoric rise to power are based above all on Gorbachev's persistent failure to achieve economic reform and stem spiralling living standards. Gorbachev's mastery of political compromise, however, held the seeds of his own demise, for by failing to address squarely the drastic measures needed for fundamental economic reform, he squandered the extensive public support he had enjoyed in the initial years of *perestroika*. Yeltsin's rise to prominence also stems from Gorbachev's success, for without the greater political freedom and public discussion of policy generated by *glasnost*, Yeltsin could never have challenged Gorbachev for power. Ironically, in instigating a move towards greater political democracy in the Soviet Union, Gorbachev undermined the very basis of his power.

Glasnost quickly created expectations that its author was unable to satisfy. If there had been evidence that economic reform was even beginning to produce results, his public support would not have eroded away so spectacularly. Gorbachev's political vision rendered it virtually impossible for him to grasp the extent to which transformation of the economy had become inescapable, and support for him faded as his piecemeal attempts at reform began to result in economic dislocation and chaos.

'Half measures just won't work,' a leading Soviet economist commented of Gorbachev's compromise plans. 'You can't be just a little bit pregnant.'

Yeltsin's own criticism of Gorbachev's attempts to fuse incompatible economic programmes, quoting an old Russian proverb, 'You can't mate a hedgehog with a snake', touched a responsive chord with the Russian people.

In 1990, after five years of *glasnost* and *perestroika*, the Soviet Union still had no genuine division of political power between the executive, the legislature and the judiciary; no framework had been established to ensure justice and uphold the law. Innumerable laws had been passed that had never been put into effect; the mechanism for doing so simply did not exist. Yet more than any other figure Gorbachev was responsible for abandoning Marxist-Leninist ideology, once the touchstone of Soviet political faith. Freed of ideological 'doublespeak', it became possible at last for urgent issues confronting the country to be addressed in plain language. Perhaps in retrospect the abandonment of ideology will be seen as Gorbachev's most significant achievement.

In 1990 the Soviet Union seemed neither revolutionary, nor even progressive. Most of the older generation looked back nostalgically to the certainties of the Stalin era while many of the younger despaired of ever seeing real change. For a nation encouraged to believe until 1986 that it led the world in living standards, it came as a shock to be warned that unless there was drastic economic reform their country would cease to be a great power altogether. Coming to terms with the truth about their own country and the outside world is an unsettling experience for many people.

Widespread disillusion, growing economic hardship and old ethnic antagonisms have combined to create a volatile political situation that will prove hard to control. Even with the failure of the coup, the future is far from assured; the possibilities – civil war, famine, plagues – are terrible. In the USSR, however, the hardships of geography and climate, the unconquerable expanses, breed a submission to destiny that is quite unimaginable in the West.

We had hoped to encounter something on our travels of the old Russian way of life but found little more than traces. Russia has had its own 'cultural revolution', not so sudden or visible as in China, but no less devastating. How the Russian people had survived such phenomenal suffering this century to remain so warm, affectionate and generous is something of a mystery.

'The soul is like a rock,' Maksim had said, speaking of the Siberians, 'but the suffering of a human's soul can make it into a diamond.'

In Vitale, Sasha, Sergei and Maksim, I felt we had gained loyal friends who might be unreliable in small matters but on whom, I felt sure, we could depend in great ones. Complete realists, they had few illusions about life and did not expect too much from it.

One thing that surprised us greatly was how singularly incurious they all were about us personally and life in the West. They very rarely asked the kind of questions we expected – about our family, friends and personal lives, our work, or about wider social or political issues. Even at such a momentous time in the history of their country, politics never seemed to loom large. Yet they shared a great sense of humour, often black, and an unfailing ability to laugh at themselves and their own situation.

On my return I suggested to Vitale that he write an account of our journey, as seen from the perspective of a Russian. His reply was characteristically realistic.

'I have no interest to write such a book,' he wrote, 'because life here becomes stranger every day and I'm not sure that anyone here wants to hear about our journey. Everyone here wants to find food, that is all. I think that we were just in time making our journey, for maybe people in the countryside wouldn't give us food now. I don't think there's any future for me here. I don't believe in my country and I don't believe that anything serious is possible here . . . My parents are a little better. My mother, however, can hardly walk, even with crutches, and she cannot go outside as we live on the second floor and our building has no lift. It's almost impossible for her to get downstairs. My father is not so bad and is out of hospital. He's seventy-five and still weak, but from early in the morning until evening he looks for food in shops, waiting in queues, and buys anything he can find. Believe me, it's not too much, because in our shops there is very little. Even less than you saw. Ours is a great life!'

Three months later Vitale wrote from Mexico with unexpected news – he had left Russia for good.

'My parents are sad that I have gone but they are old and there was nothing I could do in Russia to make life easier for them. I have to build a new life.'

Sasha and Sergei wrote to say that life for them continued unchanged. Sergei, at long last, had his own bedroom in his parents' flat; Sasha was enjoying newly married life.

Our journey had profoundly affected Maksim, inspiring him, I believe, to create a better life for himself too. Four months after my return I received a letter from him requesting assistance in securing him South African citizenship. It was, he said, impossible to live better in the USSR and South Africa was one of the few countries to which he had any chance of emigrating. After the coup he wrote to say that its collapse was 'tremendous news for us. Now maybe something will be possible here.'

It was impossible to make such a journey, at such a moment in Russia's history, and not be profoundly affected by the experience. It is not too much to say that it affected our whole outlook on life, our philosophical orientation. Howard married Anya, a Russian girl he met the week he returned to Denver. The wedding was in Moscow in December with snow thick upon the ground. We were all there.

After my return I received two letters from friends in Barnaul and Moscow, from which I quote:

'What shall you describe in your future book?' Anna wrote. 'But don't hurry with your conclusions. I say again that you can't get to know the nature of the Russian people, though many aspects of our life may be clear to you. You have to live with us for some years, to breathe the same air, to work with us, to talk and only after that could you, possibly, understand what we are.'

And from Moscow, Oksana wrote, 'I wonder how work on your book is going. I wish I could read it some day. It must be interesting to read something about our life, written as a sort of stranger's insight into the Soviet way of living which is so very absurd that it sounds unbelievable when you talk about it. But when you see it with your own eyes, you come to realise that this world, turned upside down, still exists, and people learn to live their lives in it and adjust to it, and even learn how to be happy in it, notwithstanding all the crazy laws ruling it. So it's not an easy task to write about Russia and Russian people. Do you realise that? I wish you success and inspiration . . .'

Index

Technical Note

Our journey of 12,000 kilometres was accomplished using Raleigh Chill Technium Mountain bikes with twenty-one speeds and top-quality Shimano DX components. Lightweight Tioga kevlar geodesic discs performed extraordinarily well considering the nature of the terrain. Lone Peak Panniers and Blackburn Racks allowed the team to transport equipment from the Baltic to the Pacific. The expedition's Helly Hansen clothing proved versatile and hard wearing. Sierra Designs tents and Crescent Down sleeping bags kept us alive in Siberian nights and Alpine Aire dried food products enabled us to traverse the swamp. Team members used Fujichrome 50- and 100-colour transparency film with excellent results. A photographic record of the journey is being prepared by Gilles Mingasson and the French photographic agency, Gamma. Lufthansa and Sofi played crucial transportation roles. Without their participation our journey would never have been realised.

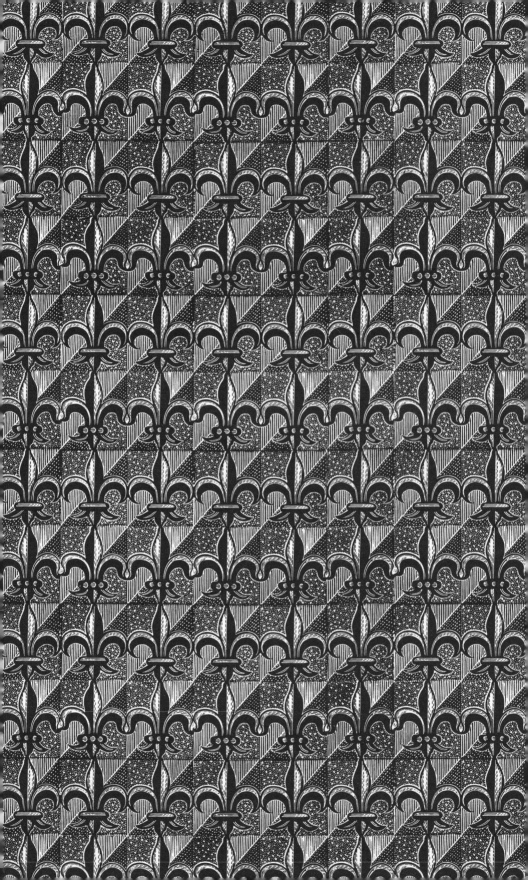